D1376364

Leading the
Lean Enterprise
Transformation

Second Edition

PRAISE FOR THE BESTSELLING FIRST EDITION:

"Any senior executive serious about leading a Lean transformation should start here. Koenigsaecker captures well the essence of sustained Lean success, not just the feel-good kaizen event."
— **Larry Culp**, president and CEO, Danaher Corporation

"Koenigsaecker has spent more time transforming more organizations into Lean enterprises than any other CEO. In this brief volume, he summarizes his 30 years of experimentation by describing Lean, showing how to measure it, explaining the role of value stream analysis and kaizen, and providing a tactical and a strategic action plan for Lean transformation."
— **Jim Womack**, chairman and founder, Lean Enterprise Institute

"This truly worked for us, and continues to make our Air Force better. The message comes with great stories and legendary examples to make *Leading the Lean Enterprise Transformation* readable for all."
— **Michael W. Wynne**, 21st Secretary, United States Air Force

"Koenigsaecker has been one of the most important mentors for me on our Lean journey. His willingness to share his knowledge and experience with the ThedaCare team has been invaluable."
— **John Toussaint,** CEO, ThedaCare Center for Healthcare Value

"Koenigsaecker's long and extensive study and application of Lean at the strategic and tactical levels make him a foremost authority on the topic. He has a unique and valuable grasp of the tools, process and change dynamics at implementing organizational Lean transformation."
— **Stan Askren**, chairman, president, and CEO, HNI Corporation

"Few, if any, American executives can match the variety and depth of experience with Lean transformations of George Koenigsaecker. So it comes as welcome news that George has written a book telling what he has learned and how he learned it. *Leading the Lean Enterprise Transformation* is simple, useful, packed with information, concise, to-the-point, and easily accessible. It will be a great source for companies looking to begin or advance their Lean initiative or managers at any level wishing to deepen their personal learning."
— **John Shook**, founder, The TWI Network

"George Koenigsaecker's story is an inspirational one. In this book, he captures succinctly over 20 years of wisdom about how to lead Lean transformation. This should be compulsory reading for anyone with a genuine interest in the topic."
— **David Fillingham**, chairman and CEO, Royal Bolton Hospital NHS Foundation Trust

"George Koenigsaecker hits a grand slam with *Leading the Lean Enterprise Transformation*, and the operative word is 'leading!' A respected practitioner and sensei in the art and science of Lean, George drives home the point that Lean is as natural in the touchy labor arena as it is in the intellectual labor arena — and leadership is the key to success in both. George further adds value with his focus on Lean in the context of (public and private sector) corporate governance. This is definitely a 'must read!'"
— **A.B. Morrill III**, Major General, USAF, Vice Director, Defense Logistics Agency

"Finally, a hands-on, real-world book written by someone who has actually led several Lean transformations. My only concern is that my competitors get their hands on this book."
— **Peter Desloge**, chairman and CEO, Watlow Corporation

Leading the
Lean Enterprise
Transformation

Second Edition

George
Koenigsaecker

CRC Press
Taylor & Francis Group
Boca Raton   London   New York

CRC Press is an imprint of the
Taylor & Francis Group, an **informa** business

A PRODUCTIVITY PRESS BOOK

MIX
Paper from
responsible sources
FSC® C014174

CRC Press
Taylor & Francis Group
6000 Broken Sound Parkway NW, Suite 300
Boca Raton, FL 33487-2742

© 2013 by George Koenigsaecker
CRC Press is an imprint of Taylor & Francis Group, an Informa business

No claim to original U.S. Government works

Printed in the United States of America on acid-free paper
Version Date: 20120824

International Standard Book Number: 978-1-4398-5987-2 (Hardback)

Visit the Taylor & Francis Web site at
http://www.taylorandfrancis.com

and the CRC Press Web site at
http://www.crcpress.com

Contents

Preface to Second Edition

During the past decade or so, the primary focus of my own Lean learning journey has been to try to really understand what characterizes a true Lean culture and, more importantly, what are the key leadership behaviors that characterized the top leadership of truly successful transformations.

Everything you have just read I would still consider to be true. But I have also been trying to dig deeper and to get to a core that is, perhaps, the few "critical to success" items.

Over this decade I have kept notes every time I heard a senior leader from Toyota talk about leadership, when senior leaders from the few Lean transformation successes talked about their leadership, and every time a true Lean guru would expound on the subject. But I found it to be pretty confusing. Often the same idea was expressed in a way that made it sound like a totally different idea. Often values were mixed with behaviors. Most often I found something that was really important buried in a list of "good" behaviors that are on most Western firms' lists.

Finally, after "collecting" input for years, I decided that I really needed to try to come to a conclusion that was useful to all of us on the journey. As I thought about this, I noticed that any list of good leadership behaviors that I had seen from Toyota was limited to four or fewer things. We all know that "three" is a kind of magic number that folks can keep track of and remember. So I set my goal to come up with three behaviors that were either not on the usual Western list of 15–20 desired leadership behaviors or had to be at a 10× level of energy and commitment. So I am assuming that your organizations already have a list of leadership behaviors that you are working to select and build toward, and I am assuming that those stay in place. What I am trying to find are the "three" that really, really have to be there for true Lean success—either something we often would not have on our list of 20 behaviors, or it's buried on the list but would need 10× the energy and attention to be successful in a Lean transformation.

As part of this year's effort, I have been able to meet with two groups of senior Toyota executives. This was helpful, but I learned that they also consider the short list to be proprietary. However, I think I learned that of the dozen or so on their list, there are really just three or four that are not usually on the Western list, so it helped confirm my focus. I also spent a few days on this subject with the folks at Watlow, trying to build the same thing for them. I also solicited input from folks that I knew who had been involved in key successful Lean transformations about what the leaders did there. The Simpler team includes former senior executives from Danaher, Frendenberg-NOK, HNI/HON, Wiremold, Hillenbrand, etc., and many of them were enlisted to provide input.

As part of a Simpler writing cell on senior leadership training, the "pile" of input began to gradually coalesce into a "big three." I found that when I read the list, it did not seem all that impressive and did not seem it should have taken all this work to figure it out. Nonetheless, a "big three" did emerge. I then tested this on a CEO exchange group (a handful of CEOs who have been on the journey for an average of 15 years and get together each year to look at what is next on their journey and next for Lean in general) and found that with different wording we were pretty close together. One of the group members then ran it by most of the well-known Lean gurus out there, and that input was added to the "pile." As a final test, I ran it by a group of client CEOs of Simpler, all of whom are on the Lean journey, although their length of Lean experience varied widely. This last was in some ways the most interesting of the tests. Before reviewing the "three" that I had settled on, I broke them into three teams and asked them to come up with their lists of only three leadership behaviors—and they should not be the ones on the "standard Western" list, unless it was a 10× level kind of thing. One group came up with the same three, with somewhat different wording. The other two teams came up with two that matched (with somewhat different wording), and their third was "vision," which in my mind should be on any solid Western list of leadership behaviors. Two out of three was a lot closer than I expected.

So, the simple list of three:

1. A DRIVE for continuous improvement.
2. A DRIVE for mentoring and learning.
3. A DRIVE for disciplined execution.

So that seems straightforward and no big deal, right?

The thought on capitalizing the word *DRIVE* is that it is probably 10× the normal or usual level of interest and commitment to this behavior.

The focus on continuous improvement, in both process and results, has characterized all the successful transformational leaders that I have known. It is captured by the Lexus slogan about the "relentless pursuit of perfection." In this case, "relentless" is another way to think about the 10× DRIVE for it. I have also seen this grow into a cultural characteristic of a Lean organization. So don't be too discouraged if this does not seem like the way you behave now; it is the *goal* of the behavior that you want to encourage and develop. I have seen this develop as an organization goes on its own Lean journey, not only among senior executives, but also as a common characteristic of its evolving Lean culture.

The second behavior—a DRIVE for mentoring and learning—can be seen in all successful Lean cultures and is always something that is encouraged from the top. I think we often have mentoring on our Western list of behaviors, but it is an afterthought, as opposed to a Toyota-like emphasis that basically says you cannot really be a manager in the organization if you cannot demonstrate an ability to mentor others and continuously learn yourself.

And the third behavior—a DRIVE for disciplined execution—points to the fact that Lean done well is a lot of hard work, and it takes continuous follow-up to ensure that the Lean practices are both sustained and growing. A phrase that Danaher uses is, "Inspect what you expect." I have seen too many otherwise good Lean efforts fail because senior leadership did not dig deep enough to really learn themselves and then know if their organizations were building the new practices and behaviors.

I still find this list of the "big three" "underwhelming," but it also still seems "right," and if you think about it, it will take a tremendous amount of focus and effort (10×?) to get your organization to practice these every day at every level.

I have considered trading "passion" for DRIVE, and that would probably work, but DRIVE seems to get to the point for me. Many of us who have worked at this think about a Lean culture as a thermodynamic system that takes a constant new input of good energy just to sustain it (because the culture outside tends to pull it backwards) and then even more energy from leaders to move it ahead—in other words, DRIVE.

Good luck on your journey.

Acknowledgments

My journey of Lean learning continues, but it has been built on the work of many others. Starting near the beginning, it is appropriate to recognize the people of Toyota, who have carefully distilled the best practices from around the world, added unique insights of their own, and built a disciplined business system that is the benchmark for how to run an enterprise. The folks who began the work at Toyota, especially Taiichi Ohno, who pulled much of it together, would tell you that the Toyota model is built on a foundation of the teachings of Henry Ford, W. Edwards Deming, those who developed our WWII training methods, and others. And although this is true, the unique insights of Toyota and the company's ability to create a culture that sustains this corporate learning system are truly amazing.

I owe thanks to folks like Frank Petroshus of Rockwell Automotive, who supported the global learning effort that got me started on this path. Also, folks like Steve and Mitch Rales, who bought a company, and then let me experiment with it. And then, my principal *sensei*, three members of Ohno's Autonomous Study Group, who taught me the basics of the tools and principles of the Toyota Business System (TBS): Yoshiki Iwata, Chihiro Nakao, and Akira Takenaka.

Perhaps most important are all the associates at Danaher and HNI/HON, who struggled with my efforts to understand and lead in this new, Lean world. I also want to thank Simpler Consulting LP for providing me with a mechanism for demonstrating that, with a solid foundation in Lean principles, a Lean business system can be applied successfully in any work environment—from health care and other service industries to the military.

I would also like to thank Michael Sinocchi, executive editor at Productivity Press, for his help with the manuscript.

Of course, thanks to my wife, Charlotte, and our children, Danaka, Brooke, and Derek, who suffered through long absences while I was on my journey of learning. None of this would be possible without them.

Introduction

I have been involved with the evolution of Lean thinking for more than thirty years. Over this period of time, there has been, in some regard, great progress, as Lean implementation has moved from high-volume automotive production to medium- and low-volume, nonrepetitive production, to administrative and general support processes, and even to product development and design. Today, Lean is evolving into the public sector, particularly the military, and is now rapidly expanding into the health-care industry.

This book is focused on what I think of as lessons learned from my thirty years of study and application of Lean thinking. I have started eleven corporations on their Lean journeys while serving as either president or group president. Most of the lessons learned from these companies were the result of multiple trial-and-error experiments, where I implemented a variety of leadership practices meant to manage the change and build a new culture. Throughout this book, you will see a number of examples from clients of Simpler Consulting, a company I helped found more than ten years ago. I have chosen to use these examples because Simpler has a deep belief in the Lean principles, enabling sensei to jump into new industries, find new applications for Lean, and demonstrate the effectiveness of Lean principles.

Over the years, I have had the opportunity to benchmark—both in a corporate role and as a Shingo Prize examiner—more than one hundred organizations that have attempted a Lean transformation. Many of the Lean efforts I have observed are what I would consider to be failures; that is, they have not achieved the results that a few benchmark organizations have shown to be possible and, perhaps more important, they have not demonstrated an ability to transform their culture into a new Lean-learning culture that can sustain a high pace of improvement through multiple generations of managers.

That said, the focus in this book is not on Lean tools or Lean principles, which are covered extensively in other books by Productivity Press. Instead, the focus here is almost entirely on the leadership aspects of a Lean transformation. Up until now, there has been no real guideline for leaders to build and sustain a transformational Lean effort in an organization. That is what this book offers.

WHAT YOU'LL FIND IN THIS BOOK

The intention of this book is to provide every reader with a practical guide for effective leadership throughout a Lean transformation in virtually any organization. The chapters are organized in roughly the chronological sequence that a leader embarking on a Lean journey would experience.

> In Chapter 1, I wander through my thirty-year history with the evolution of Lean that resulted in the lessons learned that are presented throughout the rest of the book.
>
> In Chapter 2, I give you several ways of describing Lean to bring us to a common understanding.
>
> In Chapter 3, I describe the simple, yet powerful True North metrics used by Toyota, and how they drive every line item of the income statement and balance sheet in the "good" direction.
>
> In Chapter 4, I explain the use of value stream analysis at the leadership level in a way that drives the True North metrics. This chapter also explains how to structure successful kaizen events that then improve the value stream.
>
> In Chapter 5, I discuss tactical organizational steps that are necessary to achieve double-digit improvements in the True North metrics on an ongoing basis. These include the pace of process improvement activity at which you should progress and the support structure needed to sustain this pace of activity.
>
> In Chapter 6, I examine the development of a corporate assessment-and-review structure that supports the Lean transformation. This chapter also introduces leadership tools such as strategy deployment, transformation value stream analysis, transformation plan of care, and so on.
>
> In Chapter 7, I discuss building a Lean culture, which is the least understood aspect of a Lean transformation.

New to this revised edition are a set of appendices providing further background information and insightful stories on Lean leadership and Lean implementation.

> Appendix A provides a basic Lean tutorial, reviewing the fundamentals of key Lean tools and principles. If you are experienced already, what

you may find are a few "lessons learned" from a management view about how to use and apply the tools. If you are fairly new to the Lean adventure, you should review this appendix to get on the "same page" in terms of these tools, as I have written the book assuming some familiarity with them already.

For this second edition, one of my primary goals was to add a few "other voices" to mine by incorporating appendices on a few "interesting" Lean topics by other Lean leaders. The first of these is

Appendix B, which recounts the Watlow Company's experience building a Lean culture. This appendix is written by Peter Desloge, CEO of the Watlow Company. I have been on the board of Watlow for a decade and have watched and mentored them on their journey. Watlow is an interesting test case—it is multinational with operations in China, Singapore, Mexico, Germany, and several US sites. Although not a really large business, it is quite complex, with products ranging from heaters to sensors to controls. Importantly, it is led by a third-generation family leader who is seriously working to build an organization that will do well through the fourth, fifth, and sixth generations. Peter combines a long-term vision and commitment with an understanding that the future is built on the shoulders of today's performance. After about five years of serious Lean implementation, Peter undertook a journey to define what the future-state culture of Watlow should look like. He worked with Simpler's founder, Ed Constantine, on this. It built on work done by Simpler to define a "Toyota-like" culture for Simpler. It is an excellent review of the Watlow effort to define their cultural future and move to close the gap between today and that future. Very few Lean organizations have gotten far enough to really get serious about the culture they are building, so I think you will find this very interesting.

Appendix C gives an overview of Watlow's Enterprise Visual Management System, or Mission Control, written by Tom LaMantia, president of Watlow. This is a big part of Watlow's management standard work, and the president of Watlow, Tom LaMantia, describes the development of this approach to management in a Lean organization and how it is used at Watlow. This was a development during their seventh/eighth year on the Lean journey, but it is a good practice to start much earlier on your journey. As anyone who has been at this for awhile knows, there is more to do than what you can digest in a year or two, so there are always some things that you work on earlier and some that come later as you digest earlier work and understand remaining opportunities.

Appendix D details Simpler's Transformation Continuum, a system transformation methodology and road map, written by Marc Hafer, Simpler's CEO. As a president of a firm on the journey, one of the things that was always frustrating to me was that I could not clearly articulate what was next for the organization; I could not paint a picture of "what we will look like a year from now." Admittedly, I was still trying to figure it out myself in some cases, but it made it harder for folks to stay on the path. The conversation about "As long as we stay on the path we will be much better a year from now" is a bit ethereal to get most people motivated. As a board member of Simpler, I encouraged the development of this "path." Simpler pulled its most experienced Lean sensei from around the world and set to defining what the path would look like. This is original Lean work, as I have not seen anything like it anywhere else. The basic view that was developed takes you through three major phases of development that occur over time. The rough idea is that if you are aggressive about your journey and stay on the path, then you will make great improvements to process and results each year, but it will still take about a decade to fully explore the potential of Lean. The three phases are then characterized by the dimensions of change in the organization. These include changes in human development at all levels of the organization—changes in organizational structure and culture building, the typical evolution of the Lean tools used, and the kinds of results that evolve as you progress. This whole effort is called the *Transformation Continuum.*

Appendix E provides insight into the Red River Army Depot's journey with leadership immersion in Lean. The Red River Army Depot (RRAD) has been on the Lean journey for about a decade. They have done many things well and have won several Shingo Prizes for their work. One of the complications of military life is that they normally have a new commander about every two years, and given the size of the army, the new commander typically will not have a Lean background. By mid-2010, it was becoming apparent that they were not sustaining and had actually backslid on many of their Lean efforts. A review indicated that a core issue was the lack of deep engagement of the leadership team. Lean was still more of a program than a way of life. This slide back and reassessment is a fairly frequent occurrence for Lean organizations. So under their commander, Colonel Mitchell, they embarked on a restart/recommitment to their Lean journey. One part of this was the selection of Model Value Streams as a focus to obtain significant results traction in a shorter period of time and thus to have areas where the whole depot could "see the future" because it was already in place. But the big part of this was tying the event work at the model lines to an executive Lean immersion plan to build deep commitment of the broad leadership team to the continued evolution of their Lean journey. Given the size of the organization, they were running weeklong improvement events, every week of the month. So a matrix was developed for the top thirty-five leaders in the organization that blocked one week per month for each of them to get full-time Lean-event experience. The thirty-five-person executive team was split into roughly equal fourths, with one-fourth of them to be on teams in the first week of every month, another fourth on teams in the second week of the month, etc., with the plan being to ensure that every senior leader got nine weeklong event experiences during the next nine months. Experience has shown that this is pretty much the minimum experience level needed for a person to really buy into the process. They won't be any kind of Lean expert, but after 9–12 personal weeklong event experiences, they will believe in the process and have an introduction to both the Lean tool set and the issues that teams run into on a regular basis. In this appendix, you will get an overview of RRAD's Lean effort and be able to see a few quotes from leaders about their immersion experience.

Appendix F introduces Simpler's New Product Design System. In the body of this book, I skip over new Lean product development so as to maintain focus. But it is a very important part of the journey. For a manufacturing firm, typically 70 percent of product cost is determined by the design, so all the rest of the Lean work we do is really improving the 30 percent. If we intend to become really Lean, we will need to get at product design. Lean product design is also a relatively unknown area. It is still considered, in my view, to be "proprietary" at Toyota, and most folks who talk about it are really only talking about one or two of the tools and concepts of new Lean product development. New Lean product development can use some of the tools and practices of Lean that most of us have learned, but at an 80/20 level, new Lean product development is a whole new set of tools, principles, and practices that have to be learned. In Appendix F, Rob Westrick of Elekta in the United Kingdom (they design and produce high-tech medical devices) and Chris Cooper of Simpler's European group outline a "Toyota-like" product development system. A key insight is that the "product" of the process is knowledge, and the tools and process they outline are designed to determine what knowledge needs to be gained to achieve a successful design and a path to develop and track experiments to develop that knowledge. In my experience, this is a very different way of thinking about product development.

Appendix G, which tells the story behind the Autoliv Ogden Assembly plant's team-based approach to positive change, was written by Kathy Whitehead and Scott Saxton. Autoliv has done great things in their Lean journey. Under President Mike Ward, they instituted a rigorous problem-solving cycle that was able to achieve double-digit (i.e., 10 or more percent annually) improvements in all four True North metrics. (There is more discussion of True North metrics in the body of the book.) The power of this system is that every single person is involved in root-cause problem solving and improvement. A core metric is that they achieve about 70 problem solutions per person per year; Toyota would target 24 per person. This is a good example of an end-state culture. Autoliv has more than 15 years on their journey, and they have about 5 years just evolving this daily improvement system to its current level.

I hope you find these "other voices" to be as helpful as I have found them to be!

The Author

George Koenigsaecker is a principal investor in several Lean enterprises. He is a board member of the Shingo Prize (the international award for "Lean enterprises"), the Association of Manufacturing Excellence, the ThedaCare Center for Healthcare Value, Baird Capital Partners, Gefinor Venture Partners, Simpler Consulting, and Watlow Electric Corporation.

From 1992 until 1999, Koenigsaecker led the Lean conversion of the HON Company, a $1.5-billion office furniture manufacturer. During this period, his efforts led to a tripling of volume and culminated in HON Industries being named by *IndustryWeek* magazine as one of the "World's Best Managed Companies."

Prior to this time, Koenigsaecker was with the Danaher Corporation, where he was president of the Jacobs Vehicle Equipment Company (whose Lean conversion is featured in the book *Lean Thinking* by Jim Womack and Dan Jones) and group president of the Tool Group, then the largest business unit of Danaher. In addition to leading the Lean conversion of these operations, Koenigsaecker developed and implemented the Danaher Business System, a comprehensive Lean enterprise model.

In addition, Koenigsaecker has held senior management positions in finance, marketing, and operations with Rockwell International and Deere & Company. He is a graduate of the Harvard Business School.

1

My Journey of Lean Learning: Eleven Corporate Transformations

The lessons shared in this book represent my learning over the past thirty years about Lean—or perhaps, more specifically, about the Toyota Business System (TBS). (Note: I prefer the term *Toyota Business System* because it is aimed at the full business. Toyota uses the phrase *Toyota Production System* (TPS) for historic reasons, but those using that term are almost always talking about an approach to running the whole enterprise.)

Over the years, I have seen many companies attempt to apply the wisdom of Toyota to their enterprises, and I have seen most of them fail. For this reason, I am proud that all eleven firms that I started on the Lean journey, as either president or group president (within Danaher Corporation and HNI Corporation), have stayed true to the path and are still practicing Lean learning. Not all eleven are discussed in this chapter; instead, I give you a few relevant examples.

Although I would not consider any of these firms to be perfect in their path to Toyotadom, the first Danaher businesses have stayed the course for twenty years, and the first HNI business, fifteen years. No one can claim to completely understand all the elements of success that have made Toyota the model of a well-run enterprise, but at least the results and cultural foundations that were established at Danaher and HNI were strong enough to have lasted.

DEERE & COMPANY

My business career started with Deere & Company, the farm machinery firm based in Moline, Illinois. By the mid-1970s, after I had been with

Deere for a number of years and worked in a variety of areas, I was given a project to assist in a "strategic alliance" with a Japanese firm called Yanmar Diesel. I went through all of Yanmar's production facilities and visited many Yanmar dealerships in Japan. I also met with Yanmar senior management who, at one point, presented a couple of slides outlining its improvement efforts over the prior three years. I was a student of manufacturing at some level, and I had seen Deere invest 4 percent of sales in capital spending, which generated about 3 percent annual productivity growth. These sorts of numbers were my benchmark, as Deere was the leader in its industry. At Yanmar, however, they noted that they had more than doubled their product range in the prior three years while more than doubling enterprise productivity—and they proved it with major margin gains. At first I thought I did not understand the translation, but upon realizing that it meant what it said, I was astounded. This represented an order of magnitude over our annual productivity gain, but I had not seen signs of significant capital investment in my tours of the Yanmar facilities. A few other Yanmar metrics also were in this same range of an order of magnitude: inventory turns, customer complaint rates, and so on.

It turns out that what I saw was an early application of the TBS. After a lot more conversation, it came to light that Yanmar had three Toyota sensei (master teachers) who visited them on weekends, helping change the way they ran the business. These gains were the results of those long weekends consulting with the Toyota sensei.

Taiichi Ohno was the man who famously pulled together the key concepts to create the TBS. He also generated several aggressive change-management practices that have been forgotten by many since then. Ohno used a Toyota-wide brain trust—the Autonomous Study Group—to design its system. The three sensei at Yanmar were three of the first five members of Ohno's original Autonomous Study Group.

I was blown away by the difference in the rate of improvement on all key performance measures and, to be honest, I was afraid of what I saw. I knew we would need to learn how to practice these approaches if Deere was to maintain its position. After returning to Moline, I arranged for Jim Abegglan, the foremost Western expert on Japanese advanced manufacturing practices at that time, to visit Moline and give a senior leadership review of Just in Time (JIT) manufacturing. But after the reviews, I remember being disappointed: Deere was doing quite well at the time, and the net was something to the effect of, "Gee, George, that was very interesting…thanks for bringing him here, but I don't think we would want to try that Japanese stuff in Moline." In contrast to that lukewarm reception, I was hooked on learning about this different way of running a business and continued to read anything I could find on the subject. Unfortunately, there was not much to read in those days, and much of what there was to read turned out to be incorrect, written by outsiders trying to describe something they did not really understand.

ROCKWELL INTERNATIONAL

A while later, I was recruited to join the automotive operations of Rockwell International. The company was based in Detroit and was a major player in Class 8 (heavy) truck components, including axles, brakes, and drive lines. I took the position, both because it was a promotion and because I thought that, being in Detroit—an automotive town that surely had to be doing things the way Japanese automaker Toyota was—I would be able to learn more about what we now refer to as *Lean*.

As it turned out, Detroit in those days was not much more interested in Japanese automotive practices than Moline was. Nonetheless, I was able to get support from Automotive Group management to lead a small team that would benchmark best practices in manufacturing enterprises on an international basis. We were benchmarking against our own business units: Rockwell had the policy of being either number one or two in the industry. We were in the largest global market; therefore, we were the number one or two global competitor, and we assumed we would be the standard of performance.

The team was principally myself and Bob Pentland, who was considered one of our very best production engineering guys. We started spending about three weeks on the road each quarter, visiting firms and benchmarking their performance.

In those days, Rockwell was building the space shuttle, the B-1 bomber, and similar "interesting stuff," so we had purchasing and sales offices around the world, which meant we were able to get into almost any firm we wanted to visit. We went around the world and quickly found that although European firms often developed a unique process technology and built successful businesses around it, they did not operate in any fundamentally different way from ours. But after the first tour in Japan, we began to see a few firms that were radically different. Over three years, we visited 144 manufacturing enterprises in Japan. Some were the big guys, like Matsushita; some were good midsize manufacturers, like Omron; and others were smaller automotive industry suppliers. We toured all the major Japanese automotive OEMs (original equipment manufacturers) and then started to visit their supply base.

What we saw was that about 15 percent of the firms we visited had radically superior performance metrics. We found firms making essentially the same class of product at four times the enterprise productivity, at 90 percent lower defect and customer complaint rates, and with 90 percent less inventory investment. It was hard to believe. At first we were not sure we really understood what we were seeing, but as we kept finding more firms that operated in this fashion, we realized that this was real performance. We also realized that the firms that had this order-of-magnitude superior performance were all part of the Toyota Group and its extended family of firms. We became believers. Of course, back in Detroit, these findings were just too incredible to be believed, so they were not.

Bob and I were learning about a couple of the basic tools that were used to improve performance—things like better flow and setup reduction that allowed for lower inventories—but we also could tell that we really understood only the tip of the iceberg. We didn't have many ways to learn more, but during our tours in Japan, we had found a "Japanglish" translation of a book by Shigeo Shingo. In it, Shingo described the Toyota approach as he understood it and in his terminology. Between the local translation and Shingo's rather obscure way of explaining things in the first place, it was real drudgery to try to figure out what he was saying. As we rode trains from one Japanese operation to the next, we read a paragraph at a time and tried to decipher what he meant. Since it was the only thing written about the subject, we worked it hard. We also tried to apply the lessons back in the United States and to experiment in our own operations.

JAKE BRAKE (DANAHER)

After a couple of years, I got the chance to run a company in Connecticut called Jacobs Vehicle Manufacturing Company, or Jake Brake. It turned out that Jake Brake had a great product (engine "retarders" or brakes made for heavy diesel engines), and we were shipping to companies like Cummins Engine, Caterpillar Diesel, and Detroit Diesel. We had good quality, but due to patent coverage, we had become arrogant and unresponsive to our customers. We typically were shipping a month late and in monthly batches of products. We also charged a bit too much for the product.

Shortly after joining, however, I found out that the patents had recently run out. Just to make it a bit more interesting, about this same time, a new company called the Danaher Corporation took over the parent of Jake Brake, Chicago Pneumatic Corporation, in a hostile buyout. There were fifteen companies in total that made up Chicago Pneumatic, fourteen of which lost money, so the new owners, Steve and Mitch Rales, had a special interest in how things were going at Jake.

The performance gap we already had between our delivery and our customers' expectations made me think that we had little to lose by trying to radically change Jake Brake with Toyota's practices. I didn't feel as though we knew enough, but we started anyway. Given the magnitude of our crisis, we started very fast. Most of our associates thought that this approach would fail and that we would kill the company in the process, but we started anyway. Over the 1987 Christmas vacation, we moved all the equipment in the plant into a crude cellular flow. When we started up again in January, we began to see gains. We thought about the gains we saw at Rockwell organizations and the Toyota operations we had benchmarked in Japan, and we decided to set a goal of achieving a fourfold enterprise productivity target, which means growing enterprise productivity 2 percent every month for six years. As we put in place our new flow, we naturally ended up with something that looked like product-line value streams (the linked process steps to deliver a product or service to a customer). We also found that we had thousands of problems to solve: set-up reduction issues, quality issues, tool-change issues, material-flow issues, and nearly everything else. So we started to dedicate problem-solving resources to each of these product line "focused factories," as we called them. By midyear, two critical events had occurred:

- The sensei who had worked with Yanmar in Japan retired from Toyota and, with some significant encouragement, I was able to convince them that they should adopt us as their first foreign students.
- Steve and Mitch Rales visited and reviewed what we were doing, why we were doing it, and the initial results.

Steve and Mitch had a real-estate rather than an industrial background, but they had decided to build an industrial firm based on very high debt levels (typical of real-estate investments) and a strong belief that solid, industrial brands (like Jake Brake) would provide stable platforms that would grow the company. In retrospect, this was a good thing. If they had a strong industrial background, they probably would have "known" that this Lean stuff could not work, and we would have been stopped in our tracks. As it turned out, they thought the principles made a lot of sense. They were impressed by talking to our United Automotive Workers (UAW) operators about the changes made so far and encouraged us to continue on.

Over the next two-plus years, we continued to learn from our sensei, who would typically visit and coach us hands-on in the *gemba* (workplace) in *jishukin* events (weeklong kaizen events; see Chapter 3) that not only delivered improvements, but also taught us the principles and tools of the Toyota Business System. We began to build a culture of continuous problem solving and continuous learning. In these two-plus years, we redesigned these focused factories (or value streams) five times, each time taking them to a new level of performance. Overall, we were able to take our lead times down from more than thirty days to one day, with 100 percent on-time delivery. We reduced quality issues by over 80 percent and also reduced total inventory by just over 80 percent. But most of all, we grew enterprise productivity 86 percent, which was right at our 2-percent-per-month target.

While we were doing this, we were continuing to visit Japan to learn. We were taught the application in the production world, but we began to apply the Lean practices to our administrative and product-development process, too. For instance, in product development, we were able to quadruple the total new-product output without increasing the resources and get new products to market in 20 percent of the time it took us to do so in the past.

As we organized our learning and taught it to our organization, we came to call it the Jacobs Business System (JBS), because it was focused on more than just a *production* system. As we gained traction, our group executive, Art Byrne, began to spread the JBS to the other companies in his group, and it became known as the Danaher Business System (DBS).

In 1990, I was promoted to group president for the Tool Group, then the largest group within Danaher, and began to spread DBS to those operations. I also established a DBS office that helped document and spread the new learning. My role was interesting, as I now had five company presidents who reported to me and who saw themselves as the leaders of their companies, which they were. Yet I wanted each of them to go through this very difficult Lean transformation. The change-management issues that come from spreading Lean in this kind of structure were much more challenging than getting a single company on path (like Jake Brake), which had been difficult enough. Aside from the messiness of having five corporations with many locations start on a very new way of doing things, all at the same time, we began to get traction and were able, over the next couple of years, to improve our margins by 4 percentage points, which moved the Tool Group from a small loss to a small profit.

HON COMPANY

At that point, I had parents and in-laws back in Iowa who were at the age where steady health issues were starting to occur. It seemed that it would be good for my family to move back there, if we could, to help out with this. In 1992, I joined HON Industries (now HNI Corporation) and started it on its Lean journey. I became head of the HON Company, the largest business unit of the corporation, and was able to drive Lean practices there. Again, I had my outside sensei coming in regularly to teach my team how to apply the tools, and once again, my role was to manage all the big-time change issues that come up with a transformation of this magnitude. From 1992 to 1999, when I retired from corporate work, the HON Company moved from no. 5 in its industry to no. 2 (growing sales just under 3× through "organic growth"), with momentum toward the leadership position in the industry. Based on the Rockwell benchmarking and the Danaher experience, we set goals for each HON location and each department to:

- Reduce accident rates by 20 percent each year
- Reduce errors and customer complaint rates by 20 percent per year
- Reduce lead times by 50 percent per year until we get to daily production cycles
- Grow enterprise productivity by 15 percent per year

This is a pace of improvement that I would probably not recommend to someone just starting on the Lean journey, as it was challenging, to say the least. But on average, we met these improvement goals each year from 1992 to 1999, and it was this improvement (especially the reduction in our customer lead times) that drove our market-position change. And it paid off, as we were named by *IndustryWeek* magazine as one of the "100 World's Best Managed Companies" in 1999 and 2000.

In retrospect, the thing that is most encouraging about these transformation efforts is that all of these companies stayed on the path and are still on the path today. Danaher has Lean progress that continues in its twentieth year of Lean application, and that resulted in Danaher's twenty-year financial record eclipsing that of Warren Buffet's Berkshire Hathaway as a financial performance benchmark. HON/HNI also continues with its Lean efforts, now in its fifteenth year.

Today I am a private equity investor and am on the boards of several privately owned corporations in which I have investments (Ariens Company, Baird Capital Partners, Gefinor Venture Partners, Simpler Consulting, and Watlow Electric Manufacturing Company). Needless to say, each company is involved in the evolution of Lean practices. The board role has given me another perspective on the issues involved with implementing Lean transformations, because a board member is an adviser with no executive authority. This role sort of fine-tunes my powers of persuasion.

I am also on the boards of three not-for-profit groups dedicated to the spread of Lean knowledge: the Association for Manufacturing Excellence (AME), the Shingo Prize for Operational Excellence, and the ThedaCare Center for Healthcare Improvement.

SUMMARY

The tools and principles that are the foundation of Lean were originally taught in a production setting; the idea to use these same tools and principles enterprise-wide was experimental and evolved over time. The leadership practices discussed in this book are also the result of a variety of real-world experiments. In most cases, for each enterprise-wide practice that I recommend, there were many experiments we tried that did not work very well. Thus, the point of this chapter is to give you an idea of the long learning curve and the basis for the enterprise-wide recommendations and observations coming in the rest of the book.

2

What Is Lean?

What is Lean? There are a lot of ways to answer that question, and many of them are correct—which, perhaps, helps explain some of the confusion around the whole subject of Lean. In this chapter, I describe Lean in a few different ways, to allow you to decide for yourself what works best.

WHAT TOYOTA DOES

The first definition is the one I got to most recently. After benchmarking the operating and management practices of many organizations, it became clear to me that in any dimension of organizational practice, Toyota was at least the coequal of the best in the world. But more importantly, it was coequal in *every* practice area or benchmarking area that I investigated. This consistent first-class performance across all aspects of organizational practice is what truly distinguishes Toyota. That is why my ultimate definition of Lean turns out to be something like "whatever Toyota does."

I have spent a lot of time trying to find organizations that practice a single business area significantly better than Toyota does. Having failed, I have come to the conclusion that I should always seek first to understand Toyota's practice before choosing a direction. This perspective came to me some years ago, at a time when there was not much discussion of Toyota in the business press. Toyota itself encourages this due to its continual modesty about its own achievements. We will talk about this more in Chapter 7, as this modesty is one of the keys to avoiding what the Japanese call *big company disease*—or, more specifically, the arrogance that usually comes with organizational success and is normally the root cause of an organization's eventual failure. Today, the financial markets are *beginning* to appreciate Toyota; its stock market capitalization is now more than the next seven largest car companies in the world combined. Yet, the momentum that Toyota has gained leads me to think that its stock value is an understatement of its true value.

TWO PILLARS

If you ask someone inside Toyota to describe the Toyota Production System—which would be its phrase for Lean—you will typically get several simple and straightforward explanations, each of which is totally correct and each of which provides a substantially different perspective. This lack of a clear written description of Toyota's practice is yet another of the reasons there have not been as many imitators of Toyota's practices as there should be by now.

One such description is that Lean is really about two *pillars*:

- The concept and practice of continuous improvement
- The power of respect for people

Taiichi Ohno would often hearken to the words of Henry Ford, who noted that "our own attitude is that we are chartered with discovering the best way of doing everything, and that we should regard every process employed in the business as purely experimental."[1]

This concept may seem simple, but the hard part is to build a culture that truly lives this concept, every day, in every process. And that culture is purely a people thing. When people at Toyota talk about "respect for people," that phrase encompasses many things, including designing a system that motivates people to want to improve, teaches them the tools of improvement, and motivates them to apply those tools every day. At one level, all that Toyota does is simply this: continuous improvement through people.

IDENTIFYING AND REMOVING WASTE

Another definition of Lean (and of the Toyota Production System) might describe it as "merely" a practice and process of identifying and removing waste. And of course, this would also be a totally correct definition.

Waste is an interesting word, and the folks at Toyota are working to get us to think about it in specific ways. Ohno, as he was building the system, described seven key wastes, as a means to help his people learn to "see waste." His seven key wastes were:

1. Overproduction (making more than what you need or before you need it)
2. Producing defects
3. Movement or transportation (this does not actually make the material or data closer to what a customer of the process would value)
4. Inventory (the storage of overproduction)
5. Overprocessing (the classic inefficiency that we might usually look for)
6. Waiting time
7. Unnecessary motion

I think the key to the seven wastes is not that it is a magical list of waste, but that it provides a beginning point for you to change your view of work and a starting point for you to see waste in existing processes.

The end result of reviewing work is to define each step as either *value-adding work*, or *non-value-adding work* (that is, waste). One way of thinking about this is that value-adding steps *transform* something, either material in a production process or data in an administrative process. Non-value-adding steps, on the other hand, tend to move things around, involve rework, and so on.

Two good questions to ask yourself as you look at each step in your work process are: "If a customer saw me doing this step, would he or she be willing to pay me for it?" and "If I did this step twice, would customers pay twice as much?" When you first document a process, you normally find that more than 95 percent of the time spent *and* 95 percent of the work steps do not add value. But it turns out that you cannot remove all the non-value-added steps in a process. Let's review the example in Figure 2.1, taken from the operations of ThedaCare, a regional hospital group based in Appleton, Wisconsin. In this initial-state map, there are several non-value-adding steps (shown in the darker shaded boxes) that were identified as opportunities to eliminate wasteful activities. During a first look at a given process, it is common not to clearly see every non-value-added step. In fact, in most of these instances, the real issue is more about not being able to see the waste. This is where having a highly experienced sensei can prove invaluable to your organization.

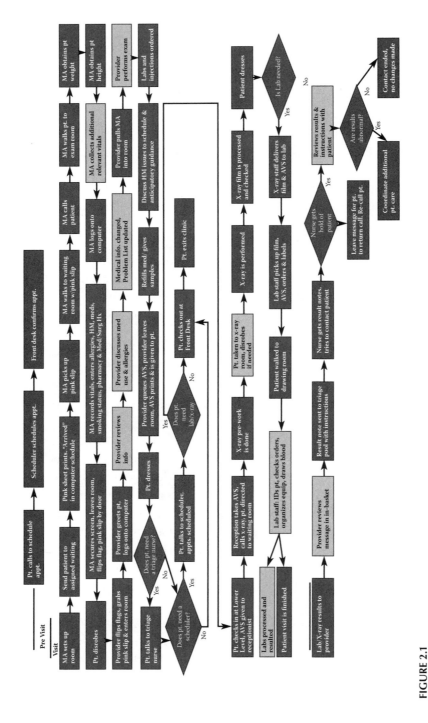

FIGURE 2.1
Identifying non-value-added activities.

If you start to think about waste in this way, you begin to see that the seven wastes are an all-encompassing view of what an excellent organization should be about. You will also find that it is hard to understand this unless you go to the *gemba* (workplace) and struggle with a *gembutsu* (specific process) and the work steps in that process. You have to live and breathe it.

Senior leaders are taught to delegate and not get involved in the details, but the Toyota view is the opposite: Senior leaders should know the work and know it intimately. They get to know the work by getting into the work area. With that in mind, the key first step for a senior leader, one who really wants to lead a Lean transformation, is to be a team member of an improvement team, documenting a process step by step, and separating the value-added from the non-value-added steps. There is really no substitute for the insight that comes from grinding through this detailed process assessment, realizing that 95 percent of the steps are non-value-adding, and realizing that you can remove half of these steps in a week-long kaizen event (see Chapter 3). Ultimately, you will realize that every process in your organization probably looks like this one at the basic work level—and thus the potential for improvement is massive.

Ohno talked about getting leaders to "see waste." I think that what he was looking for was the motivational impact of realizing how much of our hard work, every day, is *not* producing value for our customers and seeing that something significant could be done about it.

Important: Learning to "see waste" is, in my view, the single most important step for any leader to take on a Lean journey, and the one you can't do from your office. You need to get into the workplace.

A PROBLEM-IDENTIFYING AND PROBLEM-SOLVING SYSTEM

Another description of Lean is to think of it as a system, one that is designed to identify problems, and then resolve them at a root-cause level. Given that 99 percent or more of our daily problems are "resolved" at the level of the first symptom, and consequently recur, over and over and over and over, truly resolving them at a root level is a big deal. Within this description, the key to competitive success is to design your

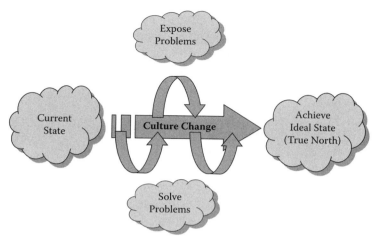

FIGURE 2.2
Continuous improvement: management philosophy spiral.

organization to accelerate this spiral of finding and solving problems at the root cause. The problem-solving spiral shown in Figure 2.2 encompasses this idea.

Of course, this description of Lean is just as correct as the others. And building a root-cause problem-solving culture in the midst of our daily firefighting is incredibly difficult. Let me say this again: Building a root-cause problem-solving culture is *incredibly* difficult!

American management is trained to hide problems, so before solving them, we first need to learn to see them and to admit that they are even there. Toyota sensei talk about learning to see problems as "golden nuggets," because they are the beginning of your next improvement. But is this how you see problems as they crop up every day?

Thus, getting an organization out of the firefighting mode—that is, resolving problems at the true root-cause level instead of putting out the fires that spring up throughout the day—turns out to be very hard to do because it involves changing adult behaviors. (This may be a good time to remind yourself that those tasks that are hard to do are often of significant value. They are also likely to be just as difficult for other organizations, and thus the cultural/organizational learning can create significant barriers to entry from a competitive perspective.)

SIX SIGMA OR LEAN...OR BOTH?

Just to keep things interesting, let's add one more definition of Lean. This is one that dawned on me as I struggled to explain the issues between Six Sigma and Lean advocates. I knew from my study of Toyota that both were part of the total answer, but explaining this to the two schools of thought seemed more difficult than it should be.

The four True North metric areas (covered in Chapter 3) require an organization to use both the tools and practices that we think of as "Lean" as well as those from the "quality" school of improvement. Toyota sees the Toyota Production System as its unique contribution. Therefore, when Toyota people talk about the things Toyota does, they naturally label those things as "Toyota Production System," since this was a set of tools, practices, and philosophies codified at Toyota.

When you look a little deeper into Toyota's internal development, you find that Toyota was a very early adopter of total quality control (TQC). Among other things, they were one of the first recipients of the Deming Prize, in 1961. So all the tools, practices, and philosophies of TQC are deeply embedded in Toyota and are part of their daily practice. But Toyota sees TQC as knowledge adopted from outside, and tends to think of TQC as something that any good organization would practice; it does not even occur to Toyota people to talk about their TQC roots and practices. A number of practices associated with Lean, such as *hoshin kanri* (policy deployment) or the True North metric approach, come right out of TQC.

What we really see when we look at "what Toyota does" is a combination of practices that have been classified in most Western countries as *either* TQC/Six Sigma *or* Lean. The reality is they are all essential elements of "what Toyota does," and in this book it is assumed that the Toyota Business System or the Toyota Way is built on a foundation of both of these schools of improvement. A useful way of envisioning what we are discussing here might be the version of the common Toyota House graphic shown in Figure 2.3. The Toyota Way is built upon the dual pillars of TQC and TPS, which in turn rest on the foundation of human development. This seems to me a much better way of understanding the core of Toyota practice.

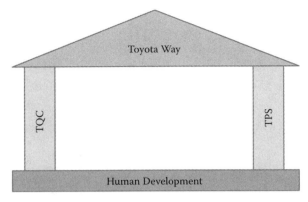

FIGURE 2.3
The "Toyota House," built on the foundation of human development.

SUMMARY

What we are really talking about with Lean is a people-driven improvement system that can improve any work process. This implies that the tools/principles and practices of Lean can improve any kind of work—anywhere in your enterprise—whether you are part of a corporation or not. The ultimate goal of a Lean transformation is to build a learning culture that solves customer problems forever.

The good news is that while your actions are building a new culture, those actions are also "Leaning" all your work processes and reducing waste—reducing defects, speeding response times, reducing manpower requirements, and so on. Done right, this is definitely a pay-as-you-go process. I have yet to see an organization that, by applying Lean practices rigorously, is not able to get a three- to four-month (or less) payback on the full costs of implementation, just from productivity gains.

NOTES

1. Henry Ford and Samuel Crowther, *Today and Tomorrow* (Garden City, NY: Doubleday, Page & Company, 1926, reprinted by Productivity Press, New York, 1988).

3

Measurement Can Be Easy

One of the phenomena that has amazed me throughout my business career is how many areas we measure when running a business. Back in my Rockwell days, we seemed to measure everything. We had at least 100 key measures that we tracked, reported, and reviewed at every monthly meeting. At some point, it became clear that all this measuring had a benefit (we were on guard to so many performance dimensions that we rarely went backward in performance), so if our performance metrics would catch the slightest deterioration, we would dig into them at the monthly review meeting. But what also became apparent over time was that, although we put enormous energy into this measurement effort, we could not improve. There were so many metrics that we were never sure which one might move in a negative direction if we took action. The result was that we had a measurement straitjacket. We could not deteriorate, but we also could not improve.

UNDERSTANDING FINANCIAL
MEASURES: PERSONAL EXAMPLES

It has taken me a long time to understand which financial measures matter, but here's the evolution of my thinking: When I was at Deere in the 1970s, I was mentored by a number of folks, one of whom, Gene Schotanus, was the treasurer. One of the projects he gave me was to develop a cash-flow forecasting model for Deere, the world's largest producer of agricultural equipment. As it turns out, Gene handled this in a very Toyota-like mentoring fashion: I was handed a significant problem, without much guidance on a solution, and the learning came from the struggle to understand, not from direct teaching. In rough terms, this turned out to have a cause chain that was typical of Taiichi Ohno's Five Whys.

So what causes cash flow to increase or decrease for Deere?

- **First why:** Increases or decreases in inventory or receivables are the initial driver of a change in cash flow for Deere. (Deere financed much of its dealer inventory, so accounts-receivable levels were huge—and of course, we had batch-production levels of inventory.)
- **Second why:** Sales changes are the primary driver of changes to inventory or receivables.
- **Third why:** Sales changes are primarily driven by changes in farmers' net incomes.
- **Fourth why:** Farmers' net incomes are primarily driven by changes in crop production (although this is somewhat counterintuitive—reductions in crop production increase net income the most because a small shortage drives prices way up).
- **Fifth why:** Weather is the primary cause of changes in farm production in a given year. Unfortunately, as we tried to get to the next why, we started looking at the impact of sunspots on weather and found that we could not crack the code on long-term forecasting of global weather.

Aside from not being able to create a solid cash-flow model, this effort helped tighten my understanding of the connections in the elements of the income statement, balance sheet, and cash-flow statement.

Another mentor in my Deere days was the head of engineering services, Jim Lardner. He and I often had long talks about how a company could grow productivity, how much was related to economies of scale, and that sort of thing. The idea of productivity as a core financial driver was, therefore, deeply embedded.

TOYOTA'S TRUE NORTH METRICS

As I learned how Toyota measured its business, I became aware of what are often referred to as its True North metrics. These are a select few measures, and if you improve each of them every year, "good things happen." There are four True North metrics: Three of them measure business performance dimensions and the fourth (although it is, perhaps, the first in terms of importance) measures human development. The True North performance metrics are

- Quality improvement (Q)
- Delivery/lead time/flow improvement (D)
- Cost/productivity improvement (C/P)
- Human development (HD)

True North relates to long-term objectives that guide the organization, that is, through generations. The metric for quality as the True North goal is zero defects. But not only is it zero; it is zero defects in everything— every work process, every day, in every country. Toyota realizes that it may never reach this goal, but it will work relentlessly to reduce the gap between its current state and its True North state every year. And it will do so by double-digit percentages: Typically, improvement targets would be 10 to 30 percent per year for each metric area. And improvements must be made in all four metric areas; if you focus on only one improvement dimension, the others that are left behind will eventually bring your overall improvement to a screeching halt.

Toyota fears complacency. In Japan, they call it *big company disease*, the arrogance that comes from success, that leads to complacency, and that ultimately leads to corporate failure. The True North metrics are, among other things, designed to prevent complacency from building. At Toyota, you rarely hear about the celebration of success (they do celebrate, but it's not a major focus), but what you do see is a focus on the remaining gap between where the company is today and its ultimate True North performance. One key result of this approach to metrics is to keep the organization focused on improvement, on closing the gap, and, consequently, on minimizing the focus on "how good we are" and the complacency that comes from this mind-set.

What would be a good True North measure for lead time? Do you recall the discussion in Chapter 1 that a typical process begins with 95 to 99 percent (or more) non-value-adding time and steps? For lead time or flow time, the definition of True North is 100 percent value-adding time. If you have non-value-added time in the process flow, you have a True North gap and a focus for improvement efforts.

Likewise, the True North measure for productivity is 100 percent value-adding steps in the work. Although you might never have a situation in which all waste or non-value-adding steps have been eliminated, you can still focus on improving that process again and again. In fact, I recently saw an interview with a manager from Aisin Seiki, one of the Toyota family of firms. It was interesting to see that after sixty years of Lean improvement, the company was targeting yet another 10 percent productivity gain for the year. Double-digit productivity improvement, year after year, for over sixty years. We have a hard time imagining it, but we need to learn how to achieve it.

What about human development? Toyota understands that to get continuous improvement in the first three True North metrics, it must have an organization in which everyone contributes to improvement. That is where human development comes in. At Toyota, it is not acceptable to only do your work at a very high level of performance; you must also improve your work. To hit double-digit gains in the True North metrics, year after year, Toyota must have everyone in the organization trained in improvement, motivated to improve, and empowered to improve.

The phrase that Toyota uses to describe this is that they must practice *hitozukuri* before *monozukuri*—roughly, "We build people before we build cars." This may seem obvious, but how often have we put the emphasis on building our human resource in order to get the business results we strive for? A Lean measurement practice must include the pursuit of these four True North measures.

HOW HIGH IS HIGH?

As discussed in Chapter 1, when I started at Rockwell, there was growing general interest in benchmarking, so we set up a small team to try to benchmark global manufacturing enterprises and measure the drivers of financial performance—trends in quality, cycle time, and productivity/ cost improvements. Leveraging Rockwell's global presence, we were able to benchmark selected firms around the world. Eventually, we identified about twenty Japanese firms that showed a radical difference in the driver measures of improvement and financial performance. They all turned out to be affiliated with Toyota in some way. We did some pretty solid digging—down to counting cars in parking lots to confirm employment levels—and found some amazing differences for these firms. Figure 3.1 summarizes the differences in core metrics. (Note that, at that time, we did not understand that human development was considered a core metric, which is why it does not appear in Figure 3.1.)

	"Batch" System	"Toyota" System (Lean)	
Inventory Turnover	3x	30x	Cash generation
Customer Complaint Rate	10,000ppm	100ppm	turns company into
Customer Lead Time		−95%	a growth company
Space		−90%	
Productivity	1x	4x	Margin improvement 2 pts/yr for 6 yrs

MOST DON'T REALIZE HOW HIGH "HIGH" REALLY IS

FIGURE 3.1
World-class benchmarking.

There were a number of shocks in the data. We believed that because Rockwell was the global market-share leader, our business units would be benchmarks. Yet, in every case, we found a business making very similar products with radically better core performance. In the area of quality performance, we found benchmark organizations that operated at two-orders-of-magnitude superior quality. That is, if we were at 10,000 defects per million, they would be at 100 defects per million. In the area of flow time, the benchmark firms operated at one-tenth to one-twentieth of our typical flow time, which meant that they received the benefits of much lower inventories and superior customer response.

The greatest surprise turned out to be in the area of productivity. We hoped that this improvement approach might increase manufacturing productivity by 40 percent, and that would have been huge. But what we found were firms operating at 400 percent of our productivity levels—an order of magnitude (ten times) higher than we expected. In fact, we found some businesses that operated at 500 percent of the productivity levels of our global leaders. We were completely amazed that the administrative departments also showed these same general levels of productivity. If a business was the same size as ours, we had 100 people in accounting working on accounts payable compared to their 20 or 25. These numbers held true throughout these true benchmark businesses. We also saw that these Japanese firms focused on improving their core processes in all these staff or administrative areas; in other words, they were applying Lean concepts in administrative areas that were similar to those they were applying in production. One note, however: Most administrative employees are not used to being measured in any of the True North metrics. They may receive feedback on one or more of these metrics, but they are probably not being truly "measured." As a result, they likely will be uncomfortable with that notion, at least at first. See Chapter 7 for more on building a Lean culture.

We learned that we did not need to reduce our defects by 50 percent, but by 99 percent. We did not need to cut our lead times in half, but by 90 or 95 percent. We did not need to target growing our productivity by 40 percent, but rather by 400 percent and across all our work—every job and process in the firm. The task was much greater than we imagined, but so was the payoff. We learned how high "high" really is!

Today, there are few executives who are thinking of making a decade-long journey to grind out improvements of this magnitude. And even fewer really see that this magnitude of improvement has to take place in every aspect of work—from product design to collection of receivables.

Lean is a transformation that builds toward a continuous improvement culture, not a "program" that's designed to make tactical gains. Lean can certainly help as a short-term tactical tool, but the big gains are in the creation of a continuous improvement machine inside your own organization that drives both personal and organizational growth. That could be your legacy to future generations.

At Jake Brake, we knew we should be thinking of a fourfold productivity gain, but we were not sure how long it would take to get there. So we set a target of achieving this goal in six years. The six-year mark was somewhat random, but it gave us an easy monthly target. If we increased productivity at the full enterprise level by 2 percent per month, every month, in six years we would slightly beat our fourfold target. As Figure 3.2 shows, we were irregular month to month, but trended on the 2-percent-per-month rate until well into the second year. Then we hit a recession in the heavy truck industry, and our volume dropped 30 percent. But by the end of the first two-and-a-half years, we were back on track at just under our trend line for 2 percent per month. At that point I became group president of our Automotive Group and undertook the Lean journey with multiple firms in that group.

A few years later, my successor at Jake forwarded to me the productivity trend chart in Figure 3.3. This chart shows a couple of interesting things. If you look at the start date and the starting-point productivity, you can see that after I left, there were about eighteen months with no gain. The

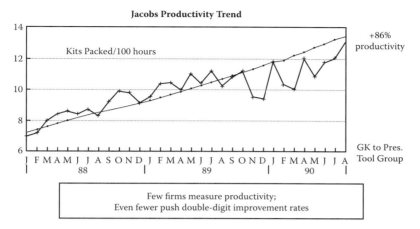

FIGURE 3.2
Lean conversion impact: productivity.

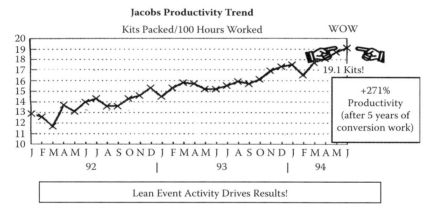

FIGURE 3.3
Lean conversion impact: productivity.

management team was not totally committed to the Lean path—neither to the activity of kaizen events nor to the discipline to drive results. But after a time, the team realized that all the metrics had flattened out, and they restarted their Lean journey by running weeklong kaizen events throughout the enterprise. In the next two-and-a-half years, Jake got back on the same productivity growth curve of 2 percent per month.

At this point, after five years of working the process, productivity was up over 270 percent, and the fourfold goal was looking possible. And by the tenth anniversary of Jake's Lean journey in 1998, the company's productivity was over 470 percent of its starting-point productivity.

In addition, as productivity was growing, lead times and quality were also improving. As we increased our flows and solved the problems that were impeding productivity, we found that our indirect measures of quality—scrap and rework—were going down, as reflected in Figure 3.4. At first, these gains were an indirect benefit of dropping non-value-added steps from the process; by eliminating these steps, we eliminated the possibility of an error. By the end of the second year, however, those indirect benefits slowed down, and we actually had to begin quality problem solving to maintain our trend. Overall, by the end of the first two-and-a-half-year period, we experienced an 80 percent reduction in quality issues.

Lead time was a key focus of our improvement efforts. As we started the Lean journey, we were shipping product in monthly batches, and on average we delivered more than a month late (see Figure 3.5 for a look at the trend). Our customers, firms like Caterpillar and Cummins, were trying to run their engine production lines, and our delivery performance was causing chaos. So we made a first pass through all our production value streams (see Chapter 4) and cut the total lead times about in half.

This took approximately six months of terrific effort. After that, we started through all our value streams again and cut about half the remaining lead times. After that, we started over again, rearranging our equipment and restudying every production process for the third time and taking out roughly half the remaining time. We did this two more times in the first two-and-a-half years, so that we went from one-month batches, to two-week

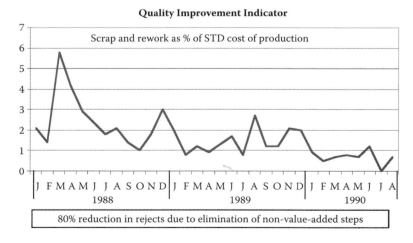

FIGURE 3.4

Lean conversion impact: quality.

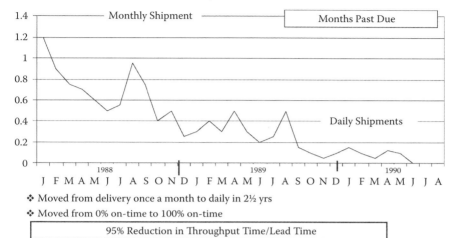

Delivery Performance

❖ Moved from delivery once a month to daily in 2½ yrs
❖ Moved from 0% on-time to 100% on-time

95% Reduction in Throughput Time/Lead Time

FIGURE 3.5
Lean conversion impact: delivery.

batches, to one-week batches, to two-and-a-half-day batches, to single-day batch sizes. Thus, by the end of year two we were on a daily cycle, building every product every day, with one day of production lead time.

It took us six more months to get to 100 percent on time with one-day customer lead time. In other words, Caterpillar could then call a team member in a cell, let him or her know how many brakes were needed the next day, and the brakes would be shipped within 24 hours—100 percent of the time.

If all these numbers seem a little hard to believe, take a look at Danaher Corporation's application of Lean since the first Jake Brake efforts in late 1987. What you see is that the application of the Danaher Business System (DBS) to the core businesses, and then to each new acquisition, has led to compounded sales and earnings growth of roughly 25 percent per year, with a high level of consistency. This is the best track record in corporate America; it is superior to Warren Buffet's Berkshire Hathaway, GE, and so on. *USA Today* reported in 2007 that the Danaher rate of return on a share purchased in the early days at Jake Brake was over 44,000 percent! As always, consistent leadership is critical. Larry Culp, Danaher CEO, was involved with the application of the DBS at Danaher from its early days, and he continues to provide strong leadership for the application of the DBS at Danaher.

THE FOUR TRUE NORTH METRICS IN DETAIL

Now let's dig into each of the True North metrics a little further.

Quality Improvement

Quality improvement is like mom and apple pie. Everyone is in agreement that it is good. But in reality, many companies do not seem driven to improve quality. Because most senior leaders have more of an orientation to the income statement and balance sheet—the pure financial metrics—I find it useful to connect them. One study that had a great impact on my view of quality was the *PIMS Principles* by Buzzell and Gale,[1] who studied a wide range of business strategies and practices in about 300 firms seeking to find strategies that always worked. After an exhaustive study, they found two strategies that always correlated with high return on investment (ROI). One was high market share. This is very well known. It's the principle behind acquiring only the no. 1 or no. 2 firm in an industry if you do acquisitions. Basically, what they found was that higher market share almost always was correlated with higher ROI. But they found something else as well: Higher quality, as perceived by *customers*, always correlated with higher ROI.

As you move from right to left across Figure 3.6, you are going from low market share to medium market share to high market share, and the bars

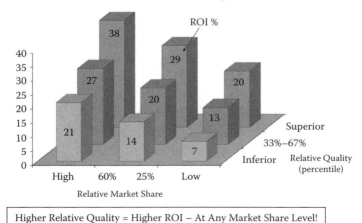

Higher Relative Quality = Higher ROI – At Any Market Share Level!

FIGURE 3.6
Lean conversion impact: ROI.

for ROI level are all increasing. However, as you go from front to back on the chart, you are moving from inferior quality, as perceived by your customers, to median quality to superior quality. And as you go up the quality scale you go up the ROI scale, no matter what the market-share level. If, for instance, you are a low-market-share firm, but you have superior quality, you will generate an ROI of 20 percent, which is a respectable return. And if you are a high-market-share firm with superior quality, your ROI goes up to 38 percent—a great rate of return. So no matter what your industry position today, superior quality will generate the best returns. With that as your frame of reference, you can think about targeting double-digit quality gains—forever—realizing that this is a great business decision.

Another look at quality and how to focus on it comes from the Technical Assistance Research Program (TARP) study. In this study, researchers found that, on average, "of customers who have been disappointed by defects, malfunctions, or other basic quality problems…90 percent go away without saying anything, and do not return" and 85 percent of those also tell "at least 9 other people of their dissatisfaction.… The other 15 percent voice their dissatisfaction to at least 20 other people."[2] I have often found product engineers waiting to accumulate enough customer complaints before they think a problem might be worth looking into. But if you do the math, for every complaint you hear about, you already have something like ten real quality problems and 130 potential customers who have been warned about your quality issues. This is why the Japanese quality gurus used to tell their students to treat each quality issue as a *golden nugget*; it represents an opportunity to improve, and it also represents the tip of the iceberg of the quality issue in question.

On the positive side, well-known management consultant Paul Bender found that "the cost of turning an existing customer into a repeat customer is one-sixth of the cost of acquiring a new customer." So quality improvement is the lowest cost sales and marketing effort you can undertake.

Continuous quality improvement is a growth strategy, and Lean is best thought of as a growth strategy first and a cost-improvement strategy second. Lean is much more powerful when you approach it that way.

Delivery/Lead Time/Flow Improvement

When most executives think about Lean implementation gains, they go right to the reduced inventory levels that can result. Although this concept is true enough and is an appropriate measure to target, inventory—in itself—is just the tip of the flow iceberg. The whole iceberg is really the benefit to customers of having a responsive supplier. Structural improvements to delivery time/lead time/cycle time/response time are usually not seen by executives as being of significant value. In almost every organization I have seen, this increased responsiveness has been of huge value to customers and is a primary driver of top-line growth.

In *Competing against Time*, George Stalk and Thomas Hout[3] reviewed the impact of time-cycle compression (that is, flow) on business growth. As a general rule, they found that reducing lead times to customers by three-fourths resulted in a firm moving to a growth rate that was two to four times the industry growth rate, as represented in Figure 3.7.

So if you are in a 3-percent growth industry, you can usually move to a 6- to 12-percent growth-rate business by shortening your lead times. The financial leverage of this kind of growth—especially when combined with other Lean improvement dimensions—is tremendous. In the 1990s, the HON Company moved from no. 5 in the office furniture industry to no. 2 by applying these lessons of short lead time, increasing their organic growth rate from the 4 percent range to over 12 percent.

At Watlow Electric, which makes semicustom heaters, this concept was applied in one of its business units, a unit that almost always needed to develop a unique design variation for a particular customer application. At the start of its journey, Watlow expected to grow productivity significantly and wanted to focus its Lean efforts as a growth strategy to utilize the human resource it expected to free up. Consequently, instead of just

Company	Business	Lead Time Difference	Growth Average
Atlas Door	Industrial doors	66%	5x
Ralph Wilson Plastics	Decorative laminates	75%	4x
Thomasville	Furniture	70%	2x

Lean can reduce lead time of all customer sensitive processes: Product Development / Application Engineering / Order Entry / Corrective Action

FIGURE 3.7
Reducing lead time by 75 percent: growing at two to four times the industry rate.

working on production lead-time management, Watlow decided to start with its earlier customer-facing processes. What this means is that the industry used about a month to respond to the initial quotation request. If this was accepted, there was typically about a month to prepare engineering drawings that could be reviewed by the customer. At that point, it would generally take about another month to build a prototype that the customer could inspect for final approval. Win rates were typically in the 15 percent range for the whole process.

The initial Lean effort focused on analyzing each of these processes—quotation, application engineering/drawing, and prototype build. The initial target was to study each process three times. It was expected that each complete study of each of these three key processes would reduce the process steps by about 50 percent and reduce the process time by about 50 percent. Then as soon as this was done, they would be restudied to take the next 50 percent out of steps and time. Then they would be restudied a third time to get 50 percent of what was left to ensure that they could always respond with at least 75 percent less time than the competition on each step. So in rough terms, each process went from a monthlong effort to a weeklong one.

Now think about the customer engineer who is trying to get her project done. She has more than she thinks she can do (if it were not this way, we would think we had too many engineers, right?) and is probably behind schedule already. So she sends out a request for quote (RFQ) for the special heater that she needs, and a week later, she has a quote back from Watlow. Since she has not seen any other quotes yet, she tells them to proceed. And then a week later, she has the engineering drawings from Watlow. She has still not seen a quote from anyone else, so she tells Watlow to make a prototype. And a week later, she has a prototype from Watlow, and she still has not seen an initial quote from anyone else. Given that Watlow is a known qualified vendor, it is almost a slam dunk that this engineer's business will be awarded to Watlow. In actual fact, in the first year after putting this in place, this 3-percent growth business went to a growth rate of over 15 percent, and it was time to get cracking at applying Lean in production work to handle the volume.

It is amazing to me that this is not the normal response of an organization. For instance, the fastest growing industry for application of Lean today is health care, and doctors are always surprised to learn that "respondents said they would rather drive further, pay more, and even switch doctors, if it meant faster service."[4] Yet it is always a shock to health-care organizations that speeding up the flow of patients would make a difference.

Also think about the cross impact of flow times on other areas. You have seen that faster flow is something that can grow a business. Now consider the impact of flow on capacity. If the work flows, you need less of almost everything. One example is in the Royal Navy, which has done a complete first pass of Lean to one of its aircraft carriers, HMS *Illustrious*. By studying and redesigning every process—from how it builds up weapons, to how it ties down planes, to how it prepares chips in the galley—the Royal Navy was able to increase the flow of aircraft by two-thirds, which means it was able to sustain about 70 percent more planes in the air compared to its historical performance. In this case, the Lean effort almost gave the Royal Navy a free aircraft carrier—ship, crew, planes, and all—just by getting things flowing. That is over a billion dollars of capacity. Commander Alan Martyn of the British Royal Navy (now retired from the Navy and former Simpler sensei) led the Lean transformation efforts aboard HMS *Illustrious*.

Or take ThedaCare, a leading hospital organization on the Lean journey. It used Lean tools and practices to fundamentally redesign the way the hospital operates at the patient interface. The net of this redesign was that the patient flowed through the procedures needed with fewer disruptions or waiting. This resulted in reducing errors impacting the average patient by approximately 80 percent, time per patient stay by approximately 30 percent, and average cost per patient stay by over 30 percent. So flow not only achieved higher quality and higher patient satisfaction, but also reduced cost by over 30 percent and increased hospital capacity by approximately 30 percent. This theme will recur—the synergy from Lean working together in multiple dimensions of True North performance.

The point is that the True North metric of delivery/lead time/flexibility can be a great driver of growth. Like continuous quality improvement, lead-time improvement is a secret weapon. It shouldn't be, but it is.

Cost/Productivity Improvement

If you look at the income statement of most firms, there are really only two categories of cost that make up over 90 percent of the total. They are (a) outside purchases and (b) costs driven by the number of people it takes to run the business. Most analysts focus on the outside purchases, because that is usually the largest category. However, it can be very difficult to create a competitive advantage in this area, even though outside purchases are the single largest cost area.

Outside Purchases

Much of a firm's outside purchases (things like steel and plastic resin) is driven by global market commodity costs and is thus set for all players. If you have engineered components that are unique to your products (fuel injectors in cars, casters for seating manufacturers), you usually find that these are produced by industry specialists who sell to all your direct competitors. It is very hard to get such a supplier to embrace the challenge of true Lean transformation. In Japan, Toyota usually has an ownership stake in key suppliers and often uses retired Toyota executives to run the suppliers. (As the supplier folks say, the newly retired Toyota executive "descends from heaven" into their chairmanship.) Outside Japan, where it rarely has the stockholding and executive leadership alignment, Toyota has found it very difficult to get supplier leadership to embrace its system. My own rule of thumb is that, at any point in time, only one CEO in twenty is ready to undertake the hard work and risk of a true Lean transformation. You can spend a lot of time trying to get suppliers to get on path and end up being pretty unsuccessful. On top of that, if you are successful, you are likely to see that the improvements used to grow your supplier's business also benefit your direct competitors, thus minimizing the competitive advantage of improving your supply base.

People

If you look at all the line items on your income or cost statement, 90 percent of the ones *other* than outside purchases are determined, over time, by the number of people it takes to run the business. I was not at Rockwell for very long before the car business went through a cyclical meltdown; we lost half of our business and, consequently, had to cut half of all our costs. We struggled to figure out how to reduce the cost of everything—postage, telephones, computers, and so on—and saw that these were all really a function of the number of people in the business. Although it came from an ugly downsizing experience, the lesson was that if we could grow but *not* add people, we not only saved the visible people cost of wages and benefits, but also kept down the costs of office space, more telephones, more computers, the size and number of conference rooms, and so on.

It is hard to find anything that is not driven by the number of people employed in the business. So it dawned on me that the key driver of internal cost is productivity and that productivity determined over 90 percent of our internal costs (our controllable costs; the costs that really determined our added-value and our competitive differentiation).

Although we talk a lot about productivity, few senior managers spend much time trying to understand how to measure it. And very few organizations are serious about setting improvement targets for productivity and driving to meet or exceed them. And yet productivity is the single major controllable cost driver that can determine long-term competitive advantage.

Thus, the value-adding cost of almost all organizations is driven primarily by productivity. Outside purchases do not usually distinguish competitive differentiation; instead, it is what you do with your value-adding costs—your people—in transforming your material or information that determines your value-added effectiveness and competitiveness. *That* is productivity.

Think of it this way: The basic concept behind all productivity measures is output per input. The output is your key value, whether it is brakes produced or patients cured or sustainable sortie rates for an aircraft carrier. The input is human resources—always. You usually do not have to worry about how much each person is paid, but instead just total the hours of human resources that it took to produce one unit of output. For instance, when I worked at Jake Brake, we counted all salaried folks as 40 hours of input per week and all hourly folks at actual clock hours. We felt it was more important to obtain an enterprise measure that included everyone in the organization than it was to count the differences in rates of pay per person. So our productivity measure was hours per engine brake.

As another example, at HON we had product mix to contend with. We were trying to compare business units that made veneer desks with others that made chairs and still others that produced metal files. In that case, we used the dollar value of product as our output and hours as the input. The measure turned out to be X dollars of sales per member hour. Then we maintained a file of the original unit prices, so that price increases or decreases did not look like productivity gains or losses. In the end, it was a unit measure.

As an executive, you will find that you can get buy-in fairly quickly for improvements to both quality and lead times. But you will find significant roadblocks to improving productivity. After all, to get real productivity gains, you have to redesign the day-to-day work of people, and that is big-time change management.

A rule of thumb is that if you spend, say, 30 percent of your time driving your Lean improvement effort, the makeup of that 30 percent may look like this:

- 10 percent of the total to get the organization on path for quality goals
- 10 percent for lead-time goals
- 10 percent for human-development goals
- 70 percent to get on track on productivity

Senior managers typically do not measure productivity and have little experience improving it, so involving them in the process means learning new practices and new behaviors, which is not easy. What's more, most administrative employees have never been measured on productivity—and do not want to be!

Toyota has a manual it prints for the leaders of its key suppliers. In it, Toyota notes, "Productivity: it's a matter of life and death...companies that are more efficient than their competitors in providing customers with high-quality goods and services will thrive. Companies that are less efficient than their competitors will perish." Experience has shown that although quality and lead times can provide growth, productivity is the key to improving margins.

Human Development

Behind all the True North metrics is the concept of people studying their work and improving it on a regular basis. You have to start with the people side. As the expression goes, "The hard stuff is easy, and the soft stuff is hard." Building a culture of continuous improvement to support a Lean transformation is a big job. As Toyota says, "We build people before we build cars." I devote Chapter 7 to the human development/culture side and the key leadership behaviors that support a Lean learning culture, but for now, let's just start at the beginning for an organization undertaking transformation.

First, the organization needs to learn new Lean tools, learn new Lean work practices, and build buy-in for the whole change process. If you had folks who already knew all the Lean stuff, they would be doing it in their work and it would be spreading. But they're not. So, despite much talk about Lean, you should expect very little true knowledge or experience from those in your company.

The key building block of Lean learning, Lean buy-in, and Lean results is personal, full-time participation on an improvement team. Toyota spent a lot of time trying various ways to get "results + learning + attitude change (culture)." In the end, it found that a *jishukin* event—a weeklong focused effort—was the most effective and perhaps the only way to achieve these three kinds of impact: financial results, opportunities to learn, and cultural change. A typical weeklong improvement event involves a team of six to eight people who focus *full-time* for a week on improving one basic portion of a value stream.

The few truly successful Lean transformation efforts you can benchmark are characterized by the use of weeklong improvement efforts. For senior leaders, there is no substitute for actually seeing waste with their own eyes. It is one thing to talk about Lean, but it is a whole different thing to dig into a work process in your own organization and identify all the value-added and non-value-added steps—and see that 95-plus percent of the operation is made up of non-value-added time (in other words, waste). This personal experience—realizing what waste really looks like (and that there is lots of it around)—is the primary motivator for leadership to drive improvement.

Being an event participant also teaches new tools and practices of the Lean world. A few years ago, Toyota in North America did a *hansei* (a deep reflection) to assess its progress on realizing the Toyota Way in its North American businesses. After all, they have been selecting folks to work in that way and training them to do so for more than 25 years. The result of the *hansei* was a realization that there was serious concern about the depth of understanding and commitment to the core of the Toyota Way. The corrective action was a refocus on the use of *jishukin* events. Many Toyota leaders had thought of them as something that generated improvement, but they had lost sight of the power of *jishukin* for learning and building the culture.

For this reason, during a Lean transformation, a key metric in the human development area will be event participation. The goal is to get breadth (for buy-in) and depth (the depth comes from people who participate in more than a hundred events and come to deeply understand and believe—these people are your future sensei, or master teachers). Statistical studies have shown that after two event experiences, there is a high level of buy-in for the overall process of Lean transformation. So an organization should try to get as many people as possible to experience two well-run events, as soon as possible.

There are other metrics in this area; for instance, safety would be a core metric. But the one that will be new to the organization will be the accumulation of learning and culture change experience that comes from the *jishukin* implementation event.

LINKING THE TRUE NORTH METRICS WITH FINANCIAL MEASURES

Let's try to link the four True North metrics with our usual financial measures. First, think through the key line items in an income statement:

- **Sales:** In a Lean transformation, the top line is driven by quality improvements, lead time improvements, and improvements in the new product development process.
- **Cost of sales:** Cost of sales is driven primarily by productivity gains. A doubling in productivity results in halving all people costs. This may take several years, but it will happen. And it will be big.
- **Sales, general, and administrative costs:** The vast majority of this cost is made up of people costs. When you double productivity, you cut those costs in half.
- **Financing costs:** As Lean impacts the balance sheet in favorable ways, you see your debt decline or your marketable securities rise; either way, your financing costs change in a good direction.

Now for a quick look at some of the balance sheet impacts:

- **Working capital:** With increased inventory turns, you find the working capital required to support a given sales level to be lower. If you manage the process, it is also possible to take advantage of some of your lead-time improvements to get faster payment terms from your customers, also decreasing working capital required.
- **Fixed capital:** As you build flow, you find that existing equipment and buildings can produce much higher volume. A typical Lean firm has half the capital intensity of a normal firm in its industry; and advanced Lean firms, which use tools like 3P to reinvent their processes in a Lean format, can run with one-quarter of industry norms for fixed capital requirements. (See Appendix A for more on 3P.)

- **Debt:** Debt is reduced as you free up working capital, but it is also reduced as you increase your net margins and use this to pay down debt. One manufacturing firm with which I have been involved increased productivity by more than 30 percent (enterprise-wide) in its first year of Lean. This turned into 6.9 points of net margin gain, which in turn allowed the firm to pay off its leveraged buyout (LBO) levels of debt in less than three years.

There are two notable concepts here. One is that by driving the four True North metrics, you can impact all these income-statement and balance-sheet line items, together, in the right direction. The other is the synergy of doing all of this at the same time. It is not unusual to see ROI measures go up by multiples as you gain synergy from balance-sheet and income-statement impacts. An example of this synergy can be seen in Figure 3.8, which shows the results of the Heatilator business unit of HON/HNI Corporation. Stan Askren, current CEO of HNI Corporation, was president of the Heatilator business unit during this period of time.

Intense focus on the True North metric areas shows up as a positive financial benefit in each of the categories depicted in this chart. Note that although the True North metrics were all improved by double-digit levels, the financial metrics all improved by triple-digit levels. Every one of these results can be traced directly to the cumulative gains from Lean improvement activities, which have now become quite evident in the overall financial performance of the organization.

❏ Recordable accident rate	−81%
❏ Warranty costs	−69%
❏ Lead time	From 6 weeks to 5 days
➢ Mixed truck load, build-to-dealer order	
❏ Complete and on time	From 84% to 98%
❏ Enterprise productivity	+38%
❏ Inventory turnover	+171%
❏ Sales/square foot	+131%
❏ Operating income percent	+221%
❏ Return on assets	+237%
❏ Cash flow	+519%

HD, Q, D, and C drive all financial metrics

FIGURE 3.8
Manufactured fireplace firm after seven years of Lean.

Keep in mind that simultaneously improving True North measures takes significant change and will be a real challenge. It takes a lot of hard work, especially at the leadership levels. It is not a free lunch, but it can impact your numbers in a way that is hard to imagine—if you can drive the change and build the momentum for your people to truly transform.

I have found that the four True North metrics *do* drive all dimensions of improvement and can be used to focus Lean efforts to achieve both a synergistic impact of all dimensions of improvement and a complete financial impact. However, a Lean transformation works best when there is growth in the organization. In many ways, Lean will free up new capacity: This comes as people capacity (productivity growth) and flow capacity (freed-up floor space, freed-up time on equipment). So when you have good Lean momentum on the four True North metrics, you are also creating capacity in the organization—and this capacity has the greatest financial impact when it is used to achieve higher growth rates. If you are able to use capacity to support growth (which should be increased by better delivery and quality performance as well as accelerated new product development), then you get the gross margin increase flowing through, dollar for dollar to the bottom line—and this is a much larger impact on the bottom line than even the margin gains from productivity increases flowing into margin gains. So a number of Lean firms, among them Danaher, will add *growth* to their True North metric set, thus ending up with Q, D, C/P, HD, and *G*. Although this is mixing the drivers of improvement with one of the results of improvement, for most firms it's a good focus to add, as it provides "leverage" to much of the impact of True North–driven improvement.

SUMMARY

I have yet to meet an executive who comes into a Lean transformation thinking that it will be possible to increase his or her organization's productivity by fourfold, reduce quality errors by 99 percent, or reduce lead time by 95 percent. And yet those are the documented norms for a true enterprise transformation. Those few executives who do conceive that these levels of achievement might be possible must grasp that it will probably take a decade to accomplish.

At the beginning, this timeline may be a discouraging thought. But the odd thing is, after you have made these kinds of annual improvements for a few years, you want to make sure it continues. So if, after the first few years of a Lean transformation, you start to run out of improvement ideas to hit a particular target area, review all the Lean tools (see Appendix A) that principally impact that True North metric. Then, evaluate the breadth and depth of application of each of those tools. It *always* turns out that, by widening the spread of those core tools (and, if necessary, increasing the portion of kaizen events dedicated to that True North metric), additional improvement opportunities exist.

NOTES

1. Robert D. Buzzell and Bradley T. Gale, *The PIMS Principles: Linking Strategy to Performance* (New York: Free Press, 1987).
2. Source unknown.
3. George Stalk and Thomas Hout, *Competing against Time: How Time-Based Competition Is Reshaping Global Markets* (New York: Free Press, 1990).
4. Paul D. Mango and Louis A. Shapiro, "Hospitals Get Serious about Operations," *McKinsey Quarterly*, 2001, no. 2:74–85.

4

Value Stream Analysis Provides the Improvement Plan—And Kaizen Events Make It Happen

A *value stream* is the sequence of work steps that make value flow from customer request to customer fulfillment. In the case of a manufacturing firm, the value streams within a given operation are usually the key product families that are produced. Each family of product normally has somewhat different flows and key processes—and that is its value stream. At the start, crossovers between value streams may disrupt the flow, but these are usually eliminated as the improvement effort progresses.

In a health-care environment, for example, a sequence of services makes up the individual value stream. A patient diagnosed with AMI (acute myocardial infarction, a heart attack) will follow a specific series of work steps for further diagnosis and treatment, through discharge and billing. These steps form the value stream. In the case of the British Royal Navy, an aircraft carrier is a single (although complex) value stream; its output is sustainable sortie rate, that is, the ability to keep more planes in the air that can defend the fleet or attack enemy targets.

So a value stream is the path of work through which a service or product flows to a customer. It is important to get the idea that it does not matter whether the value stream produces a product or a service, because the concepts still apply in roughly the same manner. To take the health-care example, ThedaCare initially looked at the value stream within one of its main operations. The initial-state value stream analysis (VSA) is shown in Figure 4.1.

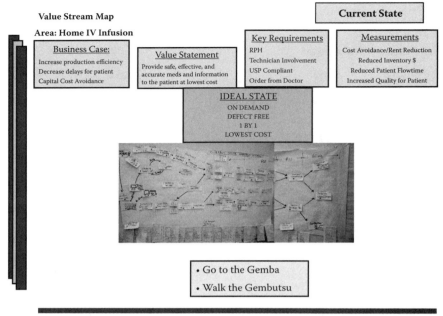

FIGURE 4.1
ThedaCare: initial-state value stream map.

TAKING A WALK TO CREATE AN INITIAL-STATE VSA

The creation of the initial-state value stream is done, quite literally, by walking the value stream step by step. It is critically important to determine the actual work practices that are being followed day to day. This walk through the world of actual work is always eye-opening. It is never as the paper or computer says it is. There will be tasks you thought people were doing that they are not doing. And just as often, they will be doing daily work tasks that you had no idea they were doing.

What you find is that no one in the entire organization can tell you all the steps in the current value stream. The individuals doing the work do not know what work others in the value stream are doing, so there is a lot of rework designed into today's processes. You may find that workers have been trained by talking to the outgoing worker or by his or her boss for a short period. The result is that they walk away with a list of work steps to do, without knowing why they should do them. This approach leads to a set of knowledge that is not even sufficient to provide a basis for improving the process.

Furthermore, in the case of administrative processes, we tend to swoop in when there is a problem, redesign a few steps, almost always adding some extra inspection or rework, and then depart (after all, there are other fires to fight, so we could not spend the time to actually understand this process from end to end). The net effect is that the typical administrative process has a negative productivity growth rate of 1 to 2 percent per year from the firefighting approach to improvement.

Initial-State VSA and the True North Metrics

The initial-state VSA does a couple of things. First, the analysis provides the base level for the process. A good initial-state analysis should, at a minimum, document the value stream's performance against the four True North metrics. This means that there should be some human-development measures taken during the analysis—things like accident rates, turnover rates, and so on. Quality data should also be gathered, and the data should show where the key issues are (providing the raw material for a quality Pareto chart). The initial-state analysis should also show where delays occur and where the flow is blocked. And, of course, the analysis should show where human resources are consumed.

Most materials on value stream analysis have missed the True North metrics aspect. Instead, they typically focus on people/productivity measures and time/delivery measures, but miss the quality and human-development metrics. A baseline is needed for all four True North measures.

Helping You See the Waste

An initial-state VSA is usually the first step in learning to see waste. For this reason, I strongly recommend that the leadership team of the business unit should be the team to conduct the first value stream analysis in the startup of a Lean transformation and determine the status of each work step: Is it value-added or non-value-added? That is, if customers saw us doing this step, would they want to pay for it? This will be the first time the leadership gets a personal picture of what waste actually looks like in a value stream that they own.

Seeing this waste does two things:

1. It puts the leadership on a path to learning what waste looks like.
2. It begins to provide leadership with the motivation to improve.

When you document real work, it is pretty hard to come away thinking that what you've just seen is a fine-tuned value stream that cannot be improved. In the early stages of Lean, getting the senior leadership to learn to see waste is by far the most important impact of a good value stream analysis.

In the diagram itself, each key waste is usually noted with a waste opportunity *burst* (callout). This little graphic notes an area of the value stream where improvement is needed and the type of improvement needed. These bursts inform the next steps, in which you apply the various Lean improvement tools.

Without getting into a detailed discussion of each of the tools in the Lean tool kit, there are Lean principles and tools that address key issues with each True North metric area (see Figure 4.2). If there is flow blockage and time being consumed, you may, for instance, use setup reduction to reduce batch sizes. You may set up a kanban system to minimize flow disruption around a monument process (a single process that constricts the flow of multiple value streams through a single-process step). You may establish a one-piece flow to keep the process moving, and so on.

Improvement Dimension

Human Development	Quality	Delivery / Flow	Cost / Productivity
Team Participation 6S Safe Workplace Design Ergonomic Kaizen Teian Suggestion System	Zero Defects 5 Whys Andon Poka –Yoke Self / Successive Checks 7 Statistical Tools CEDAC FMEA Taguchi Methods	Takt Time One Piece Flow Pull Load Load S.M.E.D. Kanban T.P.M. 3P Supply Chain Development Heijunka	N.V.A. /V.A. Standard Work Shojinka
TVSA **TPOC** **Strategy Deployment** **Lean Practices**			

FIGURE 4.2
The four True North metrics.

BRAINSTORMING TO CREATE AN
IDEAL-STATE VALUE STREAM

After documenting the initial state of the value stream, the team then brainstorms about the ideal value stream. The idea is to try to envision what this value stream could look like if all the non-value-added steps could be removed. It will not actually be possible to remove all the non-value-added steps in the first improvement pass through the value stream, but by taking a look at this "perfect process," you set the improvement bar high. Normally, when you work on improving an area, you think about improving it by some meaningful (but small) amount, say, a 5 percent improvement. You would see this result as a significant step ahead.

One key aspect of determining the ideal state is to see what a flow process could really look like. A flow process will typically have something like 95 percent fewer steps than the current process. If you start with this "ideal" value stream as your point of reference and think in terms of adding back as few steps as possible, the ideal provides you with a different paradigm for your improvement, as shown in Figure 4.3. This paradigm

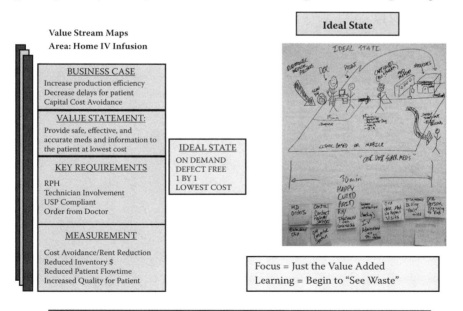

Profitable Lean Conversions Through Involvement

FIGURE 4.3
ThedaCare: ideal-state map.

will typically involve removing about half of the total steps in the value stream. Your new view of the value stream will lead you to set improvement goals for removing half the steps, instead of only 5 percent of them—an order-of-magnitude improvement from the usual practice.

CREATING A FUTURE-STATE VALUE STREAM

The next step is to create a future-state value stream that represents the improvement you actually plan to do in this value stream over the next six to eighteen months (see Figure 4.4).

In this step, you identify the key waste opportunity bursts and set up a work plan to address each of them. This work plan is usually made up of three kinds of effort. Some of the improvements will be *just-do-its*, quick-hit fixes that become obvious as you conduct the value stream analysis and can be assigned to an individual to implement immediately. Other (very few) improvements will involve a traditional project-type effort. An

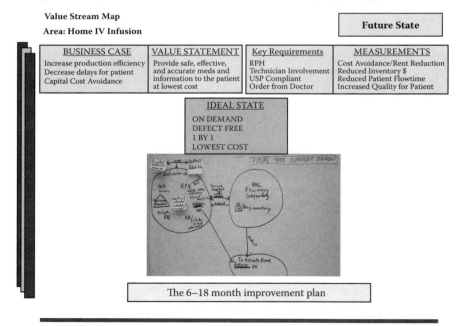

FIGURE 4.4
ThedaCare: future-state value stream map.

example might be a change in software to fit with the new work practices. But the major improvement impact will come from kaizen events focused on making substantial and fast improvements within the value stream in just one week.

Improvement Goals

One of the key deliverables during a future-state value stream mapping event is to be sure that you have a solid, achievable action plan for implementation (see Figure 4.5). In order to establish an effective action plan, you will also need to set future-state improvement goals for each True North metric (see Figure 4.6).

At the beginning, you will not know how high you should set your improvement goals. If you were able to see lots and lots of value streams done in many kinds of organizations, what you would find is that, as a rough average, you should think in terms of *halving.* You should target cutting out half of the total work steps in the process by the time you implement all the events, projects, and do-its. So if you cut the work steps in half, it is reasonable to think that you can reduce human resources in this value stream by half, reduce errors/defects by half, and expect to reduce flow times/lead times by half. If this were the first time you were to do a value stream analysis, you would probably balk at setting improvement targets this high. Yet if you do not set high goals, you certainly will not achieve high levels of performance. This halving, then, is a good place to start, because it is significant, yet it is fairly normal in terms of Lean results. If you still find these high levels of improvement difficult to embrace, you may need a sensei who has lived through this kind of improvement to push you and your organization to set goals that are appropriate for a solid value stream improvement effort. My Toyota sensei normally summarized good targets for a value stream improvement plan with the phrase "halve the bad and double the good."

Work Plan and Responsibilities

The future-state work plan should set out dates and responsibilities for each do-it, each project, and each kaizen event. Doing a value stream analysis without developing an improvement work plan or implementing actual improvement is *muda*—or waste in itself! You will occasionally

Action Plan

ThedaCare at Home: IV Infusion VSA

Impact Key: $ = Reduced Cost Q = Increased Quality CS = Increased Customer Satisfaction EOC = Increased Employer of Choice

Event	Project	Do It	Description	Deliverables				
				Who	Plan Impact	Plan Date*	Comments	Status
X			Infusion Intake & Clinical Evaluation Process (17, 46, 3, 15, 24)		$ Q CS EOC			
X			Centralized Compounding Standard Work @ AMC (36, 24, 22, 11)		$		Improvements at AMC Pharm to prepare for move from Fox Point	
X			Centralized Compounding 6S Event @ AMC (10, 2, 34)		$		Improvements at AMC Pharm to prepare for move from Fox Point	
X			Create Outpatient Infusion Cell @ AMC (21, 28, 44)		$ Q CS EOC			
X			Inventory Consolidation / Kanban (19, 38)		$ EOC			
	X		Standardize clinical role of outpatient infusion for RNs (13, 9, 35, 43, 18)		Q EOC			
	X		Improve process for delivery to home		$			
	X		Computer System Integration (30, 8, 14)		$ Q CS EOC			
		X	Transfer of Services to DME (5)		$			
		X	Insurance Database (36)		$ CS			

Profitable Lean Conversions through Involvement

FIGURE 4.5
ThedaCare: action plan.

R.I. EVENT REPORT

Location: ThedaCare   Date: 1/18/05

RESULTS:

1:

Team Topic	Measurements of Results	Before	Future Potential	% Change	Comments
Home IV Infusion VSA	Patient Flowtime (hrs)	4.0	2.5	-38%	
	Sum Manual Touch Times	6.7	4.5	-33%	
	Inventory $ @ THAC	$75,657	$25,000	-67%	
	Inventory Turns @ THAC	13.9	24.0	-73%	Duplicate Inventory
	Miles Driven Fox Point to AMC / Yr	15,600	5,200	-67%	
	Handoffs Outpatient	6.0	3.0	-50%	
	Handoffs Home Care	9.0	4.0	-56%	
	Annual Rent Required	$ 56,000	$ -	-100%	Required to maintain 2 Pharm Labs
	Required Capital to Renovate Pharm Lab @ Fox Point	$ 200,000	$ -	-100%	Will consolidate into AMC

Surveys

1 (overall satisfaction): 4.1	5 (initial presentation): 4.0	9 (prep. and team): 4.0
2 (consultant perf.): 4.6	6 (participate in future): 4.4	10 (reason for topics): 4.6
3 (results impact): 4.3	7 (leaders' meetings):	Overall Avg. (Q1 to Q10): 4.3
4 (learning experience): 4.4	8 (prod'n sys. principles): 4.1	Comments +: 9 -: 3
Key Manager Survey Score/10: 8.9	Comments: Rick Berry: TCAH Manager . . . GREAT JOB!	

Profitable Lean Conversions through Involvement

FIGURE 4.6
ThedaCare: results.

find organizations that have documented lots of value streams, but never actually gotten around to improving anything—that's muda.

A final caution on constructing value streams: Computerizing your value streams seems to be a common disease that has spread throughout most organizations. You should vaccinate your organization against this disease. A computerized map is stored on—well, a computer—which makes it pretty inaccessible and difficult to be seen in a simultaneous mode by a team of people. It is far better to display your value stream map in a very visual manner in a very public area near the *gemba* (workplace). This forces a deeper level of learning and creates a visual and team-based approach. In addition, only someone with strong computer skills will be able to draw a computerized value stream, and you want anyone to be able to draw one.

When a value stream is depicted using sticky notes, everyone can participate in the construction and modification of the value stream. If the people who do the work and who supervise the work aren't involved in the development of and modifications to the value stream map, the whole change-management effort may stall.

THE RULE OF 5×

Many senior managers use an interesting paradigm when approaching improvements: Do it perfectly the first time *and* get the full result of the approach. This is sort of a big-bang view of improvement. With Lean, however, there is an understanding that you cannot see all the waste when you first look at a value stream. After you have conducted your first complete cycle of value stream improvement—say, after eighteen months of hard work, studying every work step in your value stream, and making the key improvements outlined in the initial work plan—then it is time to start again.

What you will find is that the first pass of value stream improvement did, in fact, result in significant improvement. But something else very interesting happened. Those improvements also made the next level of waste visible. So, if you start all over and redocument your newly improved value stream step by step, you will be able to come up with a second pass. A new value stream improvement plan will typically take out half of the remaining steps—and defects—and time in the value stream.

Becoming Lean is all about doing this many times, not once. A good rule of thumb is to think in terms of planning to study every value stream and every work process at least five times (5×) before you think you are becoming Lean. If you realize that you need to plan to do this level of process study, you will think very differently about how you organize to support your Lean transformation.

Every restudy takes you to a new level of performance and is profitable by itself. After you have gone through every value stream five times, you will typically have removed about 90 percent of the waste that you started with, and you will have reduced errors and defects by 90 percent, reduced time to provide the product or service by 90 percent, reduced the needed labor by 80 percent (yes, 80 percent!), and reduced accident rates and member turnover rates by 90 percent. These numbers are hard to believe, but those few organizations that have actually gone through value streams five or more times have achieved these levels of improvement. The most important achievement is that your organization will have taught itself to believe in *continuous* improvement. Very few organizations manage to get this idea. I think that very few people really comprehend the phrase "continuous improvement." People may hear the words, but what they think is "step improvement"; in other words, "I am going to do this thing, get this gain, and then be done."

Organizations that have done five passes (5×) of improvement through their value streams do not need to push improvement. By that time, everyone in the organization knows that, as Henry Ford said, "Our own attitude is that we are chartered with discovering the best way of doing everything, and that we must regard every process employed in the business today as purely experimental."[1]

As an example, the HMMWV (Humvee) value stream at the US Army's Red River Army Depot (RRAD) had problems accelerating the up-armoring of HMMWVs to protect soldiers from improvised explosive devices (IEDs). If you initially saw this issue in the news, you may also recall that it disappeared from the news about a year later. The reason was the accelerated rate of Lean implementation in the remanufacturing and up-armoring process within the US Army Materiel Command.

Figure 4.7 shows the expansion of output at the Red River Army Depot over a fourteen-month period, within the same floor space, with a threefold increase in productivity. The team at Red River was able to achieve over a two-hundred-fold increase in output per week. Of course, this did not happen with one easy pass through the value stream. As Figure 4.7 shows, the first-pass HMMWV value stream analysis and implementation took only about four months but achieved a twenty-fold improvement in output. Much more was needed. So the folks at Red River started all over again.

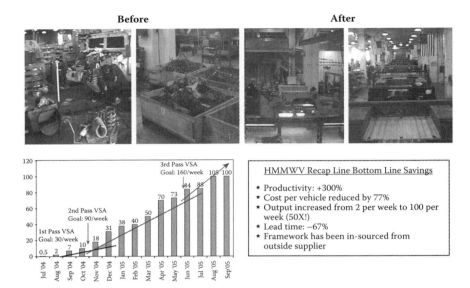

FIGURE 4.7
Red River Army Depot: HMMWV Lean transformation.

They redid their value stream analysis based on the new and improved value stream that came from a detailed gemba walk. They came up with many more waste-opportunity bursts and proceeded to attack these with kaizen events, do-its, and projects. After about eight months, they achieved roughly a 140-fold improvement, but still more was needed. So they again walked the newly improved value stream looking for opportunities for improvement, and then started implementing a new value stream improvement plan. This third pass took them to just over a two-hundred-fold improvement in output per week. Within a few months, they achieved their required output rate. Thus, with three consecutive passes through this value stream, they were able to achieve a dramatic increase in output and productivity, and also provide dramatically increased protection for US troops in Iraq.

As another example of multiple passes through a value stream, recall our review of Watlow's use of this idea to improve its customer-facing processes in its custom-heater business (see Chapter 3). In very round numbers, the industry norm was to take about three months (three one-month customer processes consisting of quoting, engineering, and prototype building) to complete the bidding process, at which point they earn about 15 percent of the bids as orders. Watlow's business was growing at about 3 percent per year. We knew that when we started Lean in the production areas that we would free up production resources at something like a 20 percent per year

❏ **Watlow**
  ➢ Manufacturer/designer of heaters and controls
  ➢ Focus: Prototype engineering - quote, design, and prototype build
  ➢ Baseline data:
    • Lead time: 20.6 days of engineering time
    • Productivity: 62 engineering man-hours/unique prototype
      (not previously measured)
    • Process first pass yield: 2.6%
    • 51 hand-offs in the engineering only cycle
    • No standardized process; many stops in the flow
    • Metrics either not tracked or not visible
  ➢ Approach
    • 4.5-day rapid improvement event
    • Created an engineering prototype development cell
    • Balanced work flow to the typical labor hours required
    • Provided standard work documents for cell management
    • Flow charted the process; created spaghetti diagrams to reveal wastes
  ➢ Results: First Pass
    • Lead time target of 15.5 days well within reach
    • First pass yield improved to 42.4%, a 1531% improvement
    • Productivity improved to 49 man-hrs/prototype – a 20% improvement –
      redeployed 1 to 5 engineers
    • Number of hand-offs reduced to 32, a 37% improvement
    • Established visual metrics tracking within the cell
      ... What does this mean for you ....

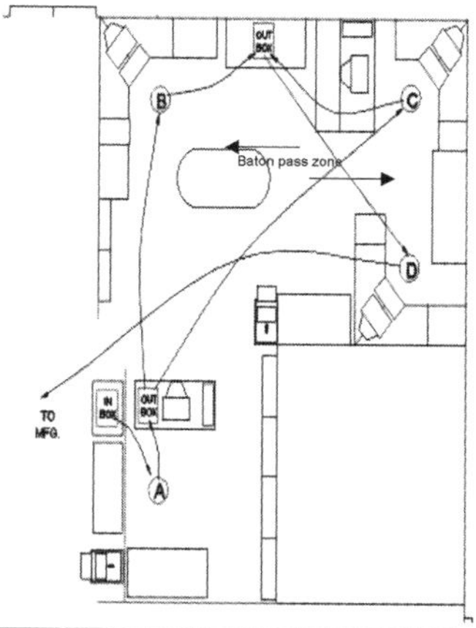

Goal = Implement three passes of this value stream = Provide quotes, designs, and prototypes
in one-quarter the time = Grow 2 to 4 times the industry standard

FIGURE 4.8
Engineering: quote design and prototype.

rate. So, instead of starting the Lean work in production, we decided to start with the three one-month customer processes (see Figure 4.8).

The impact was almost immediate. By the time Watlow was in the midst of the second pass through each of these value streams, its growth rate had surpassed the fourfold expectation—and now it really was time to get going in production areas!

An interesting sidelight of this work was the administrative productivity aspect. What you find is that working the four True North metric areas creates a synergistic effect on total results. So in addition to the productivity growth that came from dropping non-value-added steps in the quote–engineer–prototype–build processes, the faster cycles and response times led to a more than fourfold increase in win rates, amounting to a greater than fourfold productivity gain.

One other corporate example of making multiple passes on the same value stream comes from one of the Shingo Prize–winning operations: the Freudenberg-NOK GP (FNOK) business in Ligonier, Indiana. Ligonier produces a variety of vibration-control products used in all kinds of automotive applications.

What you see in Figure 4.9 is the impact of multiple passes through the same value stream. This is the "relentless pursuit of perfection," as the phrase goes. The starting productivity was 55 pieces per associate per hour. In its first weeklong kaizen event in the work area, team members

Repeat Kaizens on the Same Part Number

FNGP Ligonier, Indiana, Factory, 1992–1994

	FEB 1992	APRIL 1992	MAY 1992	NOV 1992	JAN 1993	JAN 1994	AUG 1995
Number of associates	21	18	15	12	6	3	3
Pieces made per associate	55	86	112	140	225	450	600
Spaces utilized (sq. ft.)	2,300	2,000	1,850	1,662	1,360	1,200	1,200

•At least six complete reviews of each process are necessary to achieve full lean results
•Given good preparation and follow up, more Kaizen event = more results

Baseline performance before start of lean initiative on this three-shift operation with seven associates per shift.
During this period, OSHA-reportable accidents and workers' compensation costs both declined by more than 92%. Total
capital spending over this period was less than $1,000 for a right-sized, in-line painting system permitting single-piece
flow.   Source: *Lean Thinking*, Womack & Jones

FIGURE 4.9
Reversal of law of diminishing returns.

increased the output to 86 pieces per hour. This was about a 50 percent productivity increase. Many organizations would have thought, "Wow, we have increased productivity 50 percent—I guess we must have gotten all the improvement we can," and then have left the area for good!

FNOK went back to the same area the next month, restudied it, and got an additional 30 percent productivity gain. It then went back six months later and did it again; this time it got a 20-plus percent gain. Given the law of diminishing returns, if you had the fortitude to stick with this for three passes, you would begin to think that the gains were getting smaller and it was probably time to go improve someplace else. However, the FNOK team stuck to it and went back again two months later and got a 60 percent productivity gain. Again, not satisfied, they came back a year later and were able to get a 100 percent productivity gain, to 450 pieces per hour. And then eight months later FNOK hit it again, with a 30 percent productivity gain. The end result at that point was that its output per person was more than ten times the starting point (proving that it is possible to reduce work content by 90 percent if you are willing to aggressively restudy an area several times). Realistically, most of us would have stopped at the first 50 percent—and that is the difference between most of us and those few who actually relentlessly pursue perfection.

At the time of the Ligonier Shingo Prize Award, FNOK had been, as a corporation, on the Lean journey for six years. In that time, the company had conducted more than 8,000 weeklong kaizen improvement events, resulting in a corporate-wide quality improvement from more than 2,000 ppm to less than 50 ppm and reduction of work-in-process inventory of more than 80 percent, all while generating a corporate-wide productivity gain of over 175 percent.[2] That's the power of Lean, applied *continuously*.

A MODEL VALUE STREAM

ThedaCare's first several years of improving hospital value streams led it to go back and take it from scratch in the fourth year of its Lean journey. ThedaCare decided to attempt to create the model for the future of health care. This is what Toyota would refer to as a *model line*. The purpose of the model line is to create an example that is so advanced in its overall performance that anyone observing it can easily see that this is a successful approach exhibiting a breakthrough level of performance. A model line is both a highly developed example and a key change-management tool.

The model line is normally the first area that goes through the multiple passes of improvement. The multiple passes create breakthrough results, but the area also begins to operate in new ways and begins to develop Lean management practices. The model line both demonstrates the power of Lean and begins to build a new learning culture that will sustain the improvements for the long term. It is the model for the future of the rest of the organization—in results, in developing people, and in building a new culture of continuous improvement. To create its model line, ThedaCare CEO John Toussaint (John is now CEO of the ThedaCare Center for Healthcare Value—an institution aiming to improve value in the whole health-care system) looked at the core health-care delivery value streams in ThedaCare's flagship hospital by using value stream analysis and set up a major new work plan for the next level of improvement (see Figure 4.10).

In this redesign of its core value streams, ThedaCare redesigned the work processes of physicians, pharmacists, and nurses, and also redesigned the physical structure of the hospital floors to fit a new model of flow and collaborative care. In the collaborative-care model line, the patient is cared for by a team made up of the nurse, physician, and pharmacist. The team is there at the start to set up the plan of care for that patient in a team-based approach, using the combined knowledge and experience of all three disciplines.

Reinvention of a Core Healthcare Value Stream

❑ A vision of hospital care with nursing at its center
❑ A new model of inpatient care delivery based on:
  ➤ Change in team roles and responsibilities (<u>people</u>)
  ➤ Innovation (<u>processes</u>)
  ➤ Principles of poka-yoke, pull production, and visual management
❑ Provided in an environment designed specifically for the model, to reduce waste, to ensure safety, and to promote healing.
❑ Enabled by T.I.S.
  ➤ Three vertical value streams
  ➤ Twenty-eight RIEs/projects

FIGURE 4.10
ThedaCare: collaborative care.

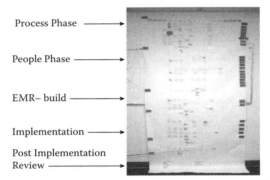

Process Phase
People Phase
EMR– build
Implementation
Post Implementation Review

THEDA♀CARE

FIGURE 4.11
Planning: vertical value stream map.

The process of creating this model value stream actually was based on the development of three vertical value streams and twenty-eight kaizen events. (*Note:* The vertical value stream map is a tool developed by Simpler Consulting for Lean project management, as shown in Figure 4.11.)

ThedaCare's model line demonstrates the application of a number of key Lean concepts, including *poka-yoke* (mistake proofing) and *jidoka* (stopping the process to fix errors). In addition, ThedaCare incorporated the true voice of the customer by inviting its patients to be members of the improvement team. Figure 4.12 shows where toll gates were built into the process flow to ensure quality of patient care.

Overall, the ThedaCare model line reduced error rates by more than 80 percent at an organization that was already a national benchmark for

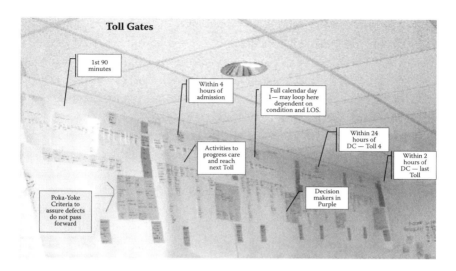

FIGURE 4.12
Value stream toll gates.

patient quality performance. In addition, by flowing care to patients, the average length of stay was reduced by 28 percent, despite a slight increase in severity rates. The financial impact was a cost reduction in per-patient stay of more than 30 percent. This was truly a breakthrough level of health-care performance.

THE POWER OF WEEKLONG KAIZEN EVENTS

The dramatic improvement examples noted at ThedaCare, the Red River Army Depot, FNOK, and the British Royal Navy were all built with the use of weeklong kaizen events. Toyota has used the weeklong kaizen event since its early days. In Toyota-speak, it is called a *jishukin* (voluntary study) event. In daily use, it was often referred to as a "five day and one night" event because of the intensity of the work effort expected of the team members—the concept being that you worked so hard on improvement in that week that you only got the equivalent of one night's sleep. This idea reminds me of Marine Corps boot camp practice; part of the initial approach of weeklong kaizen events was for the same reason that the Marine Corp does it—to push you so hard they break you down and then rebuild you in the new model.

There were many experiments in the Ohno days about the ideal structure for these kaizen events. In the end, the weeklong structure proved to be best. It was long enough that you could take a significant chunk of a value stream and both redesign it and *implement* the new process during the same week. It was also short enough that you could not take a long time discussing whether you were going to do it or not if you were going to finish by week's end. Much of the early kaizen event design was based on principles of change management—the realization that to drive improvement, you would first need to get folks to go to the gemba (the workplace) and actually make changes to the work and not just study the work.

So there was an intensity that you rarely see today. When my Japanese sensei first started teaching me, we were close to the original model. Although this was very exciting, over time, we decided that we could achieve the needed impact with a bit less stress and a bit more sleep!

Kaizen events are the primary mechanism for instituting improvement to value streams. One reason is that we are typically organized around the model of firefighting in the way we run our daily businesses. In this model, the adrenaline rush of the firefighting *always* pushes out the steady focus needed for root-cause improvement. Although daily improvement is the long-term objective, it is more of a long-term end state than a way to get there. If you focus on daily improvement in a firefighting organization, the firefighting will always win, and you will find that you are not spending any time on root-cause process improvement. So one benefit of kaizen events is that, as a business leader, you know that you have a half dozen of your team members focused on improving things for at least that week. If you run your kaizen events well and follow up thoroughly (which for most firms is *not* the case in the first year or so), your rate of improvement is roughly proportional to the pace of kaizen events. Again, a key assumption is that you run the events well and follow up diligently in the areas studied. (Of course, the fact that this is normally not the case is a side effect of the firefighting style we usually start with.)

Another aspect of weeklong kaizen events is that they are learning experiences for the team members. As a *Fortune* magazine article on Toyota noted, "Toyota has long maintained that the Toyota Way can only be grasped through constant practice in the workplace under the tutelage of a deeply experienced master."[3] Kaizen teams are ideally coached by someone with deep experience in the application of Lean tools, practices, principles, and leadership behaviors.

From my personal observations at Danaher and HON/HNI, it became apparent that you could count the number of weeklong kaizen event experiences as you would college-degree credit hours. In terms of getting a college-degree level of Lean knowledge, you can count each event week that you *personally* participate in full time as a credit hour. Typically, about a dozen weeks of this intense application experience is roughly like graduating from kindergarten. You know that it works, but are pretty unsure about what to do to replicate your success in another area. If you stay on the learning curve and keep accumulating kaizen event experiences, you find another threshold at about thirty-six to forty events. At this point, you are familiar with most of the Lean tools that are being used inside your business and are competent as a team member to use them. The interesting thing is that, although you know how to use the tools, you typically do not yet believe in the core Lean principles you are supposed to apply when using them, and consequently you will often go awry in tool application. You can often get off track because the principles will feel wrong for a very long time. Although the core Lean principles are easy to understand, they are the exact opposite of how we have been taught to organize work, so they are very hard to apply. It turns out that if you follow your sensei's lead and continue to build event experiences, somewhere around sixty events, you begin to believe the principles, and you are now able to lead kaizen efforts effectively because you not only know the tools, but also can implement them in a way that is consistent with the principles of Lean.

Somewhere around 100 event experiences, individuals undergo a personal transformation—the word *conversion* also comes to mind. These folks have seen that applying the tools and following the principles have always led to significant improvement, regardless of the kind of work being studied, and they now know what is possible. This makes them frustrated with the current state of waste, and, very importantly, self-motivated to drive improvement—forever! At this point, individuals will drive forward with Lean improvement regardless of the support they get. In fact, they will change organizations, if necessary, to keep working in an environment where improvement is the norm. These individuals are now ready to be sensei in their own right.

When you have developed a cadre of people who have significant personal experience, you are on the road to self-sustaining continuous improvement. The key is not that they know everything there is to know about Lean, but that they are now absolutely sure that they know how to create improvement and that they will never stop.

Weeklong kaizen events are how you get Lean results, but they are also how you learn, and, further on, they are also how you become motivated to improve forever. So they have a cultural impact. The right way to think about kaizen events is that they provide three kinds of results: improved business results, basic learning in tools/principles and practices, and a cultural change that builds a true learning organization that will drive improvement forever. It becomes a bit like the mountain climber's explanation for why he climbs a mountain: "Because it is there." The Lean leader's attitude toward waste is the same: "I work to remove waste because it is there."

For an organization, kaizen events can be used as a measure of culture change or attitude change. The bottom line is that participating in weeklong Lean kaizen events creates new attitudes and behaviors. When I joined HON, I required every general manager to get a dozen kaizen events under his or her belt during the first year—they all had to graduate from kindergarten. One of these business unit general managers, Dave Melhus, went on to become the executive vice president for Vermeer manufacturing. He started the Lean effort there. He had gone through the kindergarten training program and knew that it had an impact. So Dave, along with Mary Andringa, CEO of Vermeer, did an analysis after about two years of Lean effort at Vermeer. They compared the scores on its member survey to the number of Lean events that each individual had been on (see Figure 4.13).

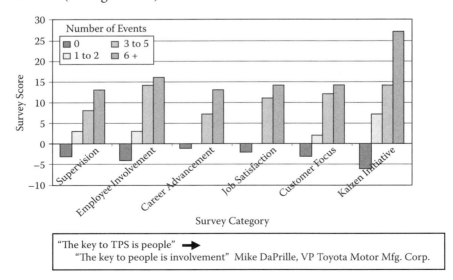

FIGURE 4.13
Survey scores compared to event participation.

The numbers in Figure 4.13 are the variation from the company's average score for that particular member survey question (the typical score was in the 50s). So, for instance, if you had not been on any kaizen events, your attitude toward your supervisor was slightly negative compared to the company-wide average, a rating of –3. If you had been on one or two kaizen events, you moved to slightly positive in terms of your attitude toward your supervisor, a +3. If you had been on three to five kaizen events, you moved to a +8 score on attitude toward your supervisor, and if you had been on six or more events, you moved to a +13. With typical average scores for most of these questions, a +13 was a really big difference.

Going through the key questions in the member survey, it was evident that the more kaizen event experience you had, the better you felt about the company: You liked your supervisor; you felt good about employee involvement and career advancement opportunities; you had higher job satisfaction; and you became more customer focused. Altogether, you had fundamentally improved your outlook on your workplace. This is a measure of the culture-building impact of the weeklong Lean event experience.

A similar study at ThedaCare of the impact on attitudes/culture change of event participation is shown in Figure 4.14. In this particular instance, seven of the ten areas surveyed showed that the satisfaction scores moved in a positive direction. Of those who participated in two or more events, the overall satisfaction level was higher, and the key emphasis category identified was, "I would recommend this organization to a friend as a good place to work." The other major finding of this study was that the positive increase in attitudes toward the organization increased rapidly and significantly from the second event through the eighth event. After eight events, the survey scores began to level off at an exceptionally high level of personal commitment to the organization.

SUMMARY

Value stream analysis is a way to provide a plan and a way to begin to learn how to see waste. The more times you go through a given value stream, the better it becomes. So one of your early objectives should be to select one value stream that you will go back to multiple times to prove to your organization that you really can improve continuously. In addition, kaizen

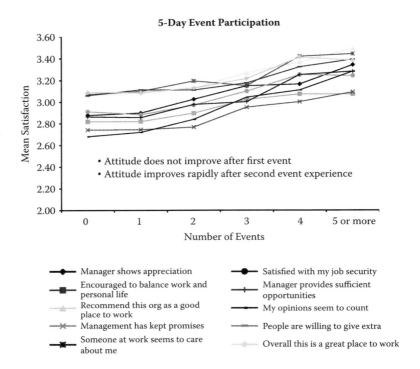

FIGURE 4.14
RIE (event) participation survey.

events not only generate the Lean gains you seek, but also provide the path for organizations to learn the tools, come to believe the principles, and begin to transform their cultures.

NOTES

1. Henry Ford and Samuel Crowther, *Today and Tomorrow* (Garden City, NY: Doubleday, Page & Company, 1926, reprinted by Productivity Press, New York, 1988).
2. Joe Day, CEO FNOK, Shingo Prize Conference keynote presentation, 2002.
3. Clay Chandler, "Full Speed Ahead," *Fortune*, February 7, 2005.

5

Tactical Organizational Practices

In this chapter, I give an overview of a number of the day-to-day implementation practices of a Lean transformation. I call these "tactical organizational practices" (as opposed to the higher-level, strategic organizational practices discussed in Chapter 6), which include the link between double-digit annual improvement rates in the True North metrics and the pace of process study/improvement. I cover some guidelines surrounding the level and type of support resources that make this pace something that can be sustained for the long term. I also look at guidelines that are specific to supporting continuous improvement in administrative areas, as well as redeployment guidelines and practices. This chapter gives you key Lean practices that are essential to achieving Lean results while building organizational buy-in and morale. I tried several approaches before settling on the guidelines I discuss here. These may not be optimal practices, but they are workable ones that have succeeded consistently.

THE *N*/10 RULE

Your pace of overall improvement is roughly proportional to the pace of successful process study and change—in other words, to the pace with which you implement events in support of your value stream improvement plans. In fact, you can, very roughly, tie kaizen event pace to achievement of double-digit improvement gains in the four True North metrics (see Chapter 3). At the very least, there is a normal pace of events/process improvement required to deliver a given level of improvement results.

From experience at both Danaher and HON/HNI, a good long-term event pace of roughly *n*/10 seems to work well. The *n* is the number of people in the value stream being worked on (or in the total site under transformation or in the total company, if an enterprise-wide transformation is under way). Dividing the population by 10 (*n*/10 rule) gives you the approximate number of annual events required (that is, weeklong teams of six to eight people, studying and improving a process within a value stream). So in a site of 1,000 people, a long-term sustainable rate of process improvement would be about 100 kaizen events per year. This is a pace that should deliver double-digit gains in the four True North metrics, something in the range of 10 to 30 percent annual improvement in quality (external customer complaint rates, internal defect rates, etc.), lead time (customer lead times, inventory levels, etc.), cost (productivity at the enterprise level), and human-development metrics (event participation rates, accident rates, turnover rates, etc.).

At the HON Company's seventeen business units, we targeted and met improvement rates that included:

- 20 percent annual accident rate reduction
- 20 percent annual reduction in both customer complaints and defect rates
- 50 percent annual reduction in lead times until we got to a single-day cycle (This was a principal strategic objective because improving customer responsiveness is a means of generating growth through Lean practices and then absorbing resources—especially people resources—freed up by the Lean effort.)
- 15 percent enterprise productivity growth (typically as a result of about 15 percent sales growth with the same employment levels each year)

These improvement rates are aggressive, but they have been exceeded during other Lean transformations I have witnessed. They take a lot of discipline, but a key point here is that you cannot expect these rates of improvement without doing the hard work of studying and improving processes—the *n*/10 rule part. Improving these four True North metrics at double-digit rates each year will drive every line item on the income statement and the balance sheet in the good direction. At HON, we basically grew 15 percent per year without adding new human resource (some normal attrition allowed for some new blood every year), without adding floor space (increased flow provided almost all the needed floor space), without adding much working capital (faster flow means less inventory per dollar of sales), and with reduced fixed capital per revenue dollar due to better utilization of capital assets.

To give you another example of how this works, take a look at the progress at Freudenburg-NOK (FNOK) during its Lean transformation, as outlined by its CEO, Joe Day, during a Shingo Prize Annual Convention. Figure 5.1 shows FNOK's annual event pace and annual net financial savings.

FNOK was roughly a 5,000-person organization, and it targeted a more aggressive event pace of around $n/5$. At the $n/5$ pace, this resulted in a target of 1,000 events per year. As FNOK started its journey, company leaders ramped up their effort over the first three years. The first year was 1992, which was a partial year due to midyear startup, and employees conducted 200 events in various business units that year, generating $2 million dollars of net savings. In 1993 (the first full year), they ran 600 events and had net savings of $4 million. In 1994, they hit their target event pace of 1,000 events per year, which they then held for the next seven years. The interesting thing is that the annual savings ran $7 million per year in 1994, 1995, and 1996. By 1997, as their skills matured and as they began to have true sensei grow internally, FNOK's net savings grew to $16 million. With additional maturity in the following year, 1998, FNOK saved $19 million. In 1999, savings grew to $21 million, then grew again in 2000 to $30 million, and again in 2001 (the year prior to the Shingo talk) to $31 million. This is one of those counterintuitive aspects of Lean; normally we would expect diminishing returns over time with continued application of the same tool kit. But with Lean, we see it time and time again: Organizations that stay on the path are able to demonstrate that their gains grow as their

Freudenburg NOK (FNOK) Corporate-Wide

	1992	1993	1994	1995	1996	1997	1998	1999	2000	2001
# of Events	200	600	1000	1000	1000	1000	1000	1000	1000	1000
$ Savings in millions	2	4	7	7	7	16	19	21	30	31

> **IF YOU CONTINUE APPLYING THE TOOLS, YOU CONTINUE TO GENERATE SAVINGS**

FIGURE 5.1
Reversal of law of diminishing returns.

human development progresses through more and more experience with Lean tools, practices, principles, and leadership behaviors.

So, there are two lessons in the FNOK example: (a) the impact of the $n/10$ kaizen event pace and (b) the fact that you begin to get really good at this stuff only in the fifth or sixth year of a Lean initiative; the gains will then accelerate through the tenth year or so.

Another aspect of the FNOK transformation effort that is typical of larger, multi-site organizations is the way FNOK ramped up its pace of Lean process study and improvement. They took about three years to achieve their targeted long-term pace of improvement. This type of ramp-up is often done by choosing an initial model value stream at each site to begin the effort. Improvement work starts at the $n/10$ pace based on the total employment level in the model value stream. Typically, at the time the organization is completing the "first pass" of the expected 5× passes through the model value stream, they will ramp up a second value stream at the same site, while sustaining their $n/10$ improvement pace in the first (model) value stream. And as the second value stream approaches the completion of its "first pass," they will start up a third value stream at the site and sustain the $n/10$ pace in the original two value streams. In this manner the pace builds in a regular fashion, which helps with the acceptance of so much change and new learning in the organization.

DESIGNING IMPROVEMENT TEAMS

Over the years, the organizations in which I worked tried a wide variety of theories about who should be on a weeklong improvement team. The best practice turned out to be a team of six to nine people that included as required members:

- A supervisor from the area being studied: He or she will provide detailed knowledge of the current process, and will then own the new process after the event week.
- Two to three members from the area: They know the way the work is done today; they will be helping the rest of their team buy into the new methods after the event; and their personal kaizen event experience is also part of the long-term cultural change process. These first-level members will not only gain new problem-solving skills,

but they will also come to appreciate and support improvement in their work areas. It turns out that the most motivating way in which people can be involved with their workplace is the improvement of their own work processes. In fact, the lack of improvement in work areas and processes is usually a very large source of personal frustration every day at work.

- One or two team members who have significant prior kaizen team experience: They add efficiency to the team, both in terms of knowledge and also in terms of already believing that this Lean stuff will work. These are the folks who will be getting a lot of event experience and who will become your own future sensei as they get their 60 to 100 event experiences over the years.
- One or two optional team members: They may not add much value to the event itself, but they will be there for their personal learning. Keep in mind, however, that too many optional team members can be distracting, due to their inexperience, so you want to limit their numbers on each team. There should be no more optional members than there are experienced Lean team members.

A typical event team has a team leader and an assistant team leader. The best practice in this area is for the team leader to be a budding sensei—someone with significant Lean experience in your firm—and for the assistant team leader to be the supervisor of the area. If the area supervisor becomes the team leader, he or she will tend to try to minimize the change rather than maximize the improvement. Still, the supervisor should be close to the action during the event week, so serving as the assistant team leader works well.

In the optional team-member category, consider including management and other executive staff, who can use the event to get personal experience learning to see and remove waste. The most successful Lean organizations require all executive staff members to experience a minimum number of events in their first year in the firm. Part of your overall transformation plan of care (covered in Chapter 6) should be a detailed plan of how you will use each kaizen event to enable another senior executive to learn.

Senior executives should be team members—not team leaders—when they are on a team. Senior leaders usually don't have strong enough Lean skills; they usually don't know the work area very well. The best learning experience for them is to be participating, full-time team members. The more senior the executive, the more he or she will feel it is okay to be on the team only part time. This destroys the executive's personal learning experience, and it is also disrespectful of the rest of the team. The best practice for executives who are scheduled to participate on a team is for them to be treated as if they were on vacation. Senior executives somehow manage to get in a few vacation weeks every year, and the organization runs just fine anyway. The event-week participation needs to be treated the same way.

One other optional team member you may want to place on a team is a vendor, especially if the vendor's firm supplies material or services to the value stream you're studying. Likewise, from the other end of the value chain, you may want to ask a customer to serve on your team. Occasionally, firms will also allow individuals from other organizations interested in Lean to get kaizen event experience as team members. This is not essential to your success, but it is a good way to share your learning.

KEY EVENT FAILURE MODE

Some companies hold a weeklong kaizen event, make process changes, and then do not expect to follow up in the weeks after the event, so all the required improvements do not get made. This is the most common event failure mode, at least until companies get tired of the waste inherent in the practice.

Typically, team members produce a *kaizen newspaper,* which is a list of items remaining to be completed at the end of the event week. Of the changes, 95 percent will already have been made, but another 5 percent call for some purchased material, a bit more toolroom time, and so on. It is not unusual for these items to be neglected, which is why they need to be highlighted. Although these items may seem, to management, like a small list of relatively unimportant items, to the people in the work area they are critical to success. They are also indicative of management's true support for the change—or lack thereof. And for those who really do not want to make any changes, this nagging list of items left undone is sufficient reason for them *not* to stick to the new improved method.

But there is also a more basic Lean concept at work in the immediate time after a formal improvement event. Ohno talked about how removing a layer of waste makes the next layer more visible. Much of the system design behind the Lean approach is aimed at this goal; in fact, in the typical system design, waste becomes visible by bringing work to a stop when there is an unresolved problem. What you do during an event removes waste (things like excess inventory, excess people, and so on). After the event, in which you made significant improvement and moved the system much closer to true one-piece flow, you will find that the system is designed so that smaller problems that used to be hidden under excess people and inventory will now surface, typically by stopping the line or the flow of value creation. In fact, the process comes to a halt for successively smaller and smaller problems. Lean is about root-cause problem solving, and the system is trying to show you the next layer of previously unidentified problems, so that you can go solve them at a root-cause level and create the next level of improvement.

Of course, when you are a normal firefighting organization, each time the system comes to a halt, it appears as though the new system does not work—but it is working to expose additional waste. This means that, for several weeks after an event, you need to keep a significant portion of your dedicated kaizen resource in the work area solving all the small problems that the system is pushing to the surface as it makes the next layer of waste visible. The good news is that this will also provide the next level of improvement. The bad news is that if you do not solve these new problems, the system will tend to come to a stop, and you will most likely go backward.

THE 3 PERCENT GUIDELINE

Another rule of thumb that results from experimenting with various levels of Lean support is the *3 percent guideline.* In order to prepare for an $n/10$ pace of events, conduct the events, and then do quality follow-up and problem solving afterward, you need some dedicated resources to support the Lean journey.

Personal experience has shown me that firefighting organizations are incapable of having people work part time on improvement. At various times, I have hired new members meant to be dedicated to improvement projects, but I found that they inevitably got sucked into the firefighting, and my carefully created improvement resource disappeared. So I learned that if I wanted to ensure that some of my total organizational resource was truly dedicated to fundamental improvement, I had to have full-time folks who were not allowed to firefight. Instead, their mission was making sure that our work practices and processes would be better tomorrow than they were today.

Full-time Lean resources are critical when taking an organization to the next level of performance. To make sure the company does not slide back to the old practices after each improvement event, I have found that the appropriate support organization is about 3 percent of the value stream, work site, or business unit total employment. These "3 percent" individuals do much of the preparation work before events, are usually team members during events (and because they will get the most event experience, they are your only real source of future sensei), and support the area supervisor for follow-up problem solving after an event.

In fact, about half the work of the 3 percent full-time Lean staff is event follow-up. After an event, the system will be pushing long-hidden problems to the surface. The area supervisor may have limited experience with Lean philosophy and problem solving, and probably has a firefighting mentality. To balance this, the 3 percent provides a surge of Lean problem-solving resources to respond to hidden problems that are coming to the surface. If these skilled problem-solving resources are not in the work area in the weeks immediately after an event, the team in the area will be overwhelmed and will see the whole effort as unsuccessful. (Trust me, this no-follow-up approach yields almost a 100 percent failure mode in the first couple of years of most organizations' Lean efforts.)

Many executives look upon building up this 3 percent group as a resource drain. My view was always the opposite, because I wanted to build up a resource that I knew was going to make us better every day. Throughout my career, I have found these dedicated improvement resources to be the prime source of financial improvement and, thus, one of our most important assets. Even executives who agree, however, have trouble figuring out how to build up this kind of resource, given day-to-day budget constraints. The answer turns out to be straightforward, albeit demanding. You use the resources you gain through productivity improvements to flesh out your dedicated Lean team.

Typically, an event week might have four kaizen event teams focused on four of the key issues identified in the value stream analysis. One or two of those teams will likely focus on improving productivity in some area of the value stream. For example, at HON, in a two-year period, 49 percent of our teams (491 kaizen event teams in total) focused primarily on the use of the standard work tool. And of the 491 total improvement teams, the average productivity gain was 45 percent. Given this, we could pretty well establish the number of people we could free up before the event even took place. Knowing that we would free up people resources with each kaizen event, we set a standard that for every five people we freed up through the Lean effort, we would add one full-time person to the dedicated improvement team.

This basically said two things: (a) We are going to fund our improvement resource through our improvement efforts, and (b) we are going to reinvest 20 percent of our productivity savings into resources that accelerate our pace of improvement. We were able to fully fund our 3 percent dedicated team by the end of the first year of Lean—without hiring anyone and without shortchanging the resources from an existing work area.

Selecting People for the Full-Time Improvement Team

We selected the best person in the organization to join the full-time improvement team, not the actual person we had freed up that week. Instead, we used the freed-up human resource, through our redeployment process, to "pay" for dedicating the resource that we needed. You will be investing a huge amount of time and effort in each dedicated team member's personal learning, so you want to make sure that each is your best and brightest. In the Lean world, the definition of the best and the brightest is somewhat different from everyday practice. The basic selection criteria parallel those that Toyota uses for hiring. You want to select people who:

- Can learn new things
- Can identify and solve problems
- Work well in teams
- Can communicate well

Like many things at Toyota, this list may look simple, but it is the result of incredibly careful thought and trial. For example, take the selection of people who can identify and solve problems. Toyota's experience is that those are two separate skills. In its selection process, Toyota uses simulation and other methods to find folks who can identify problems; many people do not seem to be aware of problems even when they are all around. Obviously, having the ability to solve problems is of no value if you cannot identify problems to solve.

In addition, in a manufacturing organization, you may find it useful to look for associates who are tech-heavy; it really helps to have a few toolmakers, a couple of maintenance folks, and a few manufacturing or industrial engineers on the full-time Lean team. In fact, you want about three-quarters of your typical team to be "techie" in this sense, because many of the problems they must solve will involve process knowledge, tool design, and so on.

One other way to consider the ideal makeup of the 3 percent full-time Lean team would be to think about it in thirds:

- Roughly one-third of the team should be individuals who are targeted as future general managers and value stream managers. This part of the team constitutes your management-development training program and the source of your future senior leadership. They would ideally spend two to three years on the full-time team. This is long enough for them to become competent at using the tools and come to believe that they really work!
- Roughly one-third of the team should be individuals who are targeted for a career job as your future sensei. Your goal for them would be that they spend a minimum of five to six years on the full-time team so that they not only understand the tools, but also come to believe the underlying principles. These are the folks who should get to 100 personal event experiences. They are the ones who will ensure that your organization can stay on the path and really build the long-term learning culture that Lean is all about.
- Roughly one-third of the team should be individuals who are, or are soon to become, supervisors and middle managers. They would spend one to two years on the full-time team. They would not become experts in this short time, and they also would not really believe in all the principles. But they would be supportive and generally knowledgeable and help build the everyday Lean organizational practice.

Selecting the Leader for the Dedicated Lean Team

Another key question on the 3 percent guideline is who should lead this dedicated team. The answer will probably surprise you. It should be the heir apparent for the site or business unit. A fairly common failure in Lean is when a general manager "gets it" and starts to build a Lean learning organization. Then, five years later, this person gets promoted, and the heir apparent takes over—except that he or she has been doing another key job in the business and has not been directly involved in the Lean transformation. The heir apparent will talk the talk but is not really committed to the Lean transformation. The solution is to make that heir apparent the leader of the dedicated Lean team, where he or she will become deeply knowledgeable about the Lean transformation. Taking this approach also has great communication value at the start of your journey. Everyone usually knows who the heir apparent is anyway (or, at least, they know the couple of folks in the running for this role), and if this person is put in charge of the full-time transformation effort, you've sent a clear message that the Lean transformation is very important—and that we all had better pay attention.

Most organizations do the opposite and look around for someone who is simply available to put in charge of the Lean effort. Well, the reality is that if someone is available, there is usually a good reason for his or her being "available," and everyone in the organization is also aware of that. If you want to kill your effort before you get going, go find an "available person" to lead your dedicated team! If you want to succeed, on the other hand, commit your strongest manager to your full-time Lean efforts.

Keep in mind that when you are starting the journey, you don't have the experience to believe deeply in its success, so deciding to commit your strongest managers to lead this effort full time will be a leap of faith. But it is a very necessary one. Even if it doesn't feel "right" to put such a person in charge, it is a decision that will pay off for years to come.

Also remember that the dedicated Lean team you build will be the only people to get significant kaizen event experience, which means that they will become your own internal sensei. These are people with enough Lean experience to ensure continuity of your improvement effort—forever.

The Watlow 3 Percent Experience

I have been on the board of directors of Watlow for a number of years. Board members are advisors to management, but they do not make operating decisions; management does that. My experience on various boards has challenged my ability to influence (as opposed to command).

About six years ago, Watlow began the Lean transformation journey. At the beginning, we had conversations about the $n/10$ event pace and the need for 3 percent full-time support to make it work well. Of course, there is a lot to take in when you start the Lean journey. But this is one of the more common things for management of any organization to "not take in"—for quite a while—and Watlow lived up to that norm. As my Toyota sensei used to tell me, "Easy to say…hard to do!" At least Watlow did measure and keep track of the support level. Recently, after six years of encouragement and organizational learning, Watlow achieved the 3 percent full-time support target on a company-wide basis. I asked Steve Desloge, Watlow CFO (and also the Lean team champion) what Watlow had learned about building up to the 3 percent full-time support level, and Steve provided this chronological overview (see sidebar):

> **2005: 1.4 percent of total employment dedicated to full-time Lean team.** We didn't have high-level visibility and focus on full-time support until late 2006. We just did not understand its importance to maintaining the pace of change and sustaining the improvements.
>
> **2006: 1.7 percent of total employment dedicated to full-time Lean team.**
>
> **2007: 2.3 percent of total employment dedicated to full-time Lean team.** In 2007 we began to see the bigger picture. We began to think more holistically (by working to define the "Watlow Way" culture, for instance), and we started to see faint glimmers of the linkage to human development.
>
> **2008: 2.7 percent of total employment dedicated to full-time Lean team.** We finally brought high-level visibility and focus to the target of building the 3 percent full-time Lean team. We made it a True North metric at each site and at the full enterprise level. We integrated the target into our mission-control-room operating system and held people accountable for getting to the target level. We began to see a very clear link between having sufficient full-time improvement team resources in each site and realizing our targeted pace of overall improvement. Those sites that had only 1 or 2 percent dedicated resources fell behind on the *n*/10 pace and improvement on the True North metrics. Those sites with 3 percent or more started to see real movement in performance. Site leadership began to believe this and executed on their commitment to 3 percent full-time support.
>
> **2009: 3.1 percent of total employment dedicated to full-time Lean team.** We finally hit the 3 percent target in May of 2009. We actually added full-time resources during the recession. Meanwhile, we started to see turnover in our full-time Lean team members as they began to be promoted to positions of higher responsibility in the organization. As we increase our efforts to engage *all* of our team members (for example in problem solving, daily improvement, etc.), we are experiencing a much heavier pull on our COI resources for support and teaching. We plan to maintain at least the 3 percent level to continue our desired pace of improvement.

Steve's review gives a great overview of why the 3 percent level is such an important part of your transformation effort and how essential it is to hitting your improvement goals—in terms of both business results and human development. An easier (and faster) way to learn this lesson is to follow the recommendation of starting each new value stream with 3 percent full-time Lean support and then sustaining that as you start on the next value stream.

ADMINISTRATIVE TEAMS

Teams focused on improving administrative processes are much like any other improvement team—and also different. They are similar in that they use the same tools and principles that are used to drive Lean improvement in other areas. But they are different because the people doing the work think about their jobs differently.

The first thing to give some thought to is how we have organized administrative work everywhere. We decry batch manufacturing procedures that operate through "process villages," which combine all similar machine types in separate departments, because this requires us to move parts between those departments to complete the assembly. In some cases, a warehouse operation also had to be added between each value-adding process step. Most of the world knows that this is a poor way to organize work and that it creates great waste. Generally, if you move a batch operation to a Toyota flow-style operation (with five passes through each value stream to get deep Lean improvement), you will get astonishing results: 90 percent less flow time and inventory, 90 percent fewer defects, 90 percent lower accident rates, and 80 percent less work.

In the same way, most companies have organized administrative work in a similarly dysfunctional batch style. Functional departments are akin to process villages, where the work of that functional specialty is done. But when you actually want to complete a process—to get an administrative value stream to flow—you find that you have to confront your process villages and the fact that the data you are trying to turn into information travels in boxes from department to department. Think, for example, about the flow of data you use to pay a vendor. It starts with a purchase order; then you get a purchase receipt at your dock; then you get a trip to the inspection function to approve the receipt; then you travel to accounting to tie all the pieces of paper together; then you usually do a rework step or two; then eventually you get approval to pay (often from another department); and then you pay the bill. And almost all of these work steps go through the mail system, adding more non-value-added work.

Lean folks have kaizened processes such as this, and one of the more thorough approaches has been to have a robust supply chain, where you can pay the vendor automatically upon ordering because you know all of the other required actions will happen. In any case, the end result is that every administrative process is organized on batch concepts and has batch levels of *muda* (waste), meaning there is great opportunity.

Despite all this opportunity, you almost never find True North metrics in administrative areas—In fact, you almost never find *any* performance metrics at all in administrative areas. What you find instead is great resistance to the idea of being measured. In operations, folks are used to the idea of their work being measured in some fashion, but as you run Lean events in administrative areas, you often have trouble getting the team members to admit to their gains. They will usually be okay telling you about their quality gains, or even their throughput gains, but they almost never volunteer that they have made a productivity gain. In other words, if you drop half the steps in a process, which then leads to a halving of lead time and a halving of errors, it probably stands to reason that you will also halve the work content. But the gains tend to be hidden by the admin folks themselves. These productivity gains are there (and may even be easier to put into place than in a production area), but the concept of incorporating productivity gains into an admin area is foreign, so you have to manage the improvement process more closely than in other areas.

One idea I put into place in my companies is to have the administrative Lean teams report to the controller's office. Controllers know that they are not responsible for generating an outcome, but they are responsible for describing it accurately in numbers. This characteristic makes it hard for teams to report to them with inconsistent or incomplete results. For this reason, having the admin team report to the financial or accounting area is likely to get real measurements in place and real results achieved.

One other suggestion is to set up dedicated administrative Lean teams instead of mixing Lean teams in admin and operations. In my experience, whenever I found a good team leader from operations who knew how to apply the Lean tools and asked him or her to lead an admin team, they were always successful. The problem is that these folks do not like working in admin areas where people are not used to measuring their own performance, so they would keep drifting back to operations. Instead, I started setting up dedicated admin Lean teams that did nothing but Lean events in administrative areas. These poor teams could not run away from admin! And they got better and better at it. Another benefit of Lean teams that worked only on admin areas is that the mix of skills on admin teams needed to be different from production. Where the tech skills for production involved toolmaking and similar skills, the tech skills that were helpful on admin teams involved folks with real knowledge of the information technology (IT) system, how to change software, how the financial system really worked, and so on. They were still tech oriented, but it was "office tech."

I recently came across an e-mail from my controller at HON, Bob Hayes. This was an e-mail from 1998 about an administrative improvement event he had led that week:

> We did an improvement event this week on mainframe reports. Through Pareto analysis, we identified the highest users as Sales (including several Marketing reports) and Accounting. By reviewing every report with its user list and asking "why" five times, we were able to reduce the number of annual reports generated by these two groups from 1,920 to 1,236 (a 36 percent reduction) and the annual pages printed from 1,305,860 to 864,000 (a 34 percent reduction). A very productive part of this was that Tom Sorenson (one of our key IT guys) was available to eliminate reports as we went!

In most manufacturing firms, at least half of the members are not in production—and usually are paid more than production workers—so you normally find that two-thirds of your employment cost and potential for productivity gains lies in the administrative processes. The net result: You cannot become a Lean enterprise without getting deep into administrative Lean work—period!

When we checked the results of our administrative teams at HON/HNI, we found that they averaged a 33 percent reduction in cycle time for the process/value stream, a 46 percent reduction in the number of steps, and an 85 percent increase in productivity. Powerful stuff!

REDEPLOYMENT

Redeployment is an interesting Lean practice area. Typical of many Toyota-like things, the right approach is just the opposite of what you might normally do. Think about how companies usually handle redeployment of personnel. Let's say you have just bought a new IT system or a new super-wonderful machine, and now you can run the area with one less person. How do you select the person to redeploy? Most managers have been taught to optimize that team, and that means that if you can now run the team with one less person, you would naturally select the worst performer and move him or her out of the area. (In fact, some managers go so far as to give a great review to a poor performer, hoping that some other area will hire that person away.)

Even though team members know that this person is the low performer on their team, they still have worked together for a number of years (perhaps even met some of their family) and don't want to see them "get hurt." Likewise, the low performer has an equally traumatic experience; this person knows that he or she is the low performer on the team and is afraid of getting fired. So morale suffers, everywhere.

The Toyota practice is simple. Instead of moving out the low performer, you move out your best performer. Toyota's logic goes something like this: We have kaizened the work process in the area, allowing us to free up a member for redeployment. In doing this, we have solved some quality problems, made the work more repeatable, and made it easier to do. We do not really need the same level of skills that we needed before the improvement. So let's take the best member of the team and redeploy him or her. This person is likely to see a move to a new area as an interesting, perhaps challenging, change. And everyone knows management is not going to be firing the best person on the team, so morale holds up well. And, of course, other areas of the company are happy to accept this new person onto their team, so this person is easy to redeploy. If you don't have a job opening today, this person will make a valuable contribution as a temporary member of the full-time kaizen team. When a job opens up that fits, the employee will have increased his or her Lean skills and become even more excited about being part of your organization's team. Although this seems sensible, keep in mind that it is the exact opposite of the standard practice that all of your people have been trained in. This is another example of the sort of thing my Toyota sensei was talking about when he said, "Easy to say…hard to do!"

Redeployment is like productivity in general. Our organizations do not really know how to measure productivity, nor how to increase it on a regular basis. Measuring and growing productivity are almost always new skills for the organization to learn as a key part of their Lean transformation. As with productivity measurement and growth, no one really knows how to implement redeployment. Most people have just not been in situations where they have worked in an area for a week and, at the end of it, freed up three or four people.

A good general practice for redeployment is to work the process while the improvement team is in action. By the middle of the week, the improvement teams will have a pretty good idea of how many people they will free up. On Wednesday afternoon of the improvement week, the Human Resources Department (HR) should get together with the various team leaders and find out what they expect in terms of freed-up individuals. At the same time, they should review who the best performers are in the work area. This is somewhat easier to do midweek, when the supervisor is not yet really sure that folks will be freed up; you will find that they have a *really* hard time giving up their best members. HR will need to make this a vigorous review to ensure that those identified really are the best. Then, on Thursday, HR can review the backgrounds of these "best" members and see if there are immediate job fits for them, either in positions that are currently open or in jobs where other members will be retiring soon. If there is a "fit," then the redeployed member can be notified on Friday. If there is not an immediate fit, then HR can start them on training for a job that is open or soon to be open, or they can be added to the full-time improvement team as a "temporary" member until an appropriate job opens up. If they are one of the best members and they are on the improvement team for a period of time, they will not only make good contributions to the improvement efforts, but also grow their personal skills, making them even more desirable to potential hiring managers.

If you leave excess personnel in an area after an event, you almost ensure that the work team will go back to the old inefficient work method. After all, they have the people to do it the old way and they *know* the old way, since they have been doing it that way for years! That's why a solid redeployment process is essential to your Lean success.

OTHER LEAN TRAINING

You have seen the primacy of the *jishukin* (event format) as a method of achieving results (see Chapter 4), developing Lean learning and building a stronger culture. There is, however, a role for a limited amount of the traditional types of training for Lean. There are three principal target groups:

- **All employees:** This group should get an introduction to Lean principles and concepts. This may be as little as one day's worth of training, perhaps spread over several weeks/months. This may be classroom-style training (taught by members of the dedicated Lean team), or it may be simulation exercises (there are a number of good ones that help in teaching the basic idea of flow versus batch), or you might create learning maps. At HON/HNI, we designed (with the help of Root Learning Inc.) learning maps to cover the basic principles of Lean, basic financial literacy, and so on. A *learning map* is a custom-designed game board that turns the learning experience into a game. The topic of the learning map can vary. At HON/HNI, we developed learning maps that taught basic principles of Lean, basic financial literacy, and industry dynamics to support the need for change.

- **The dedicated Lean team:** This group needs an introduction to its new role and what work it will be doing. This training often comes from an outside sensei group that might be teaching your organization the new Lean knowledge.

- **Senior leadership:** This group needs a deeper understanding of Lean. There are a number of approaches. One that has worked involves reviews of key Lean books, where a chapter is reviewed and discussed at each monthly or weekly executive team meeting. Another is conducting Lean leadership workshops with outside sensei. But just keep in mind that the greatest deep learning will come from personal experience on an event team—that is, learning to see waste and remove it.

SUMMARY

Experience has shown that if you want to sustain significant improvement gains over the long term, you will need to do the following:

- Establish a regular pace of process improvement activity at a level that seems high to the folks who are not yet part of an improvement culture.

- Build a dedicated support group of your best folks, who will help sustain this high level of improvement activity and also be your future sensei.

- Be thoughtful about the makeup of each improvement team and its goals.

- Give special focus as to how you organize your administrative Lean efforts.

- Develop a robust redeployment process that provides the human resources to support your Lean efforts and the productivity gains to improve business results.

6

Strategic Organizational Practices

Governance is *the* key issue with Lean. Although individual Lean concepts and tools are easy to understand, to be truly successful in the application of these concepts and tools, the majority of the organization must change the way it looks at work. And this is hard to do, because we have spent our careers building an image of how work should be organized and done. This fundamental change in the way you see work—and how you think it should be organized—is the most basic change needed to be successful at Lean. And so far, the vast majority of organizations that start on the Lean transformation journey are not successful at making this transition.

UNDERSTANDING GOVERNANCE

Governance is about the governors—the leaders of the organization and what they do. The track record so far shows that normal corporate governance practices are insufficient for the challenges of a Lean transformation. Even Toyota, which today is managed by the fourth generation of leaders who have practiced the business system they have built, does not provide a particularly helpful benchmark. Toyota represents the end state that you can aspire to, but simply mimicking what it does today will not get your organization moving in the direction of successful transformation. The current generation of Toyota leadership is long-removed from the change-management practices needed to start a successful transformation. Toyota is doing an amazing job of sustaining its culture, but the company cannot show many recent examples of outside firms that it has been able to get on a similar path to building a sustainable Lean-learning culture.

If you look outside Toyota for models of successful transformation— organizations whose financial metrics have demonstrated that their Lean practices generate additional customer value on a continuing basis—the list is pretty small. Many organizations have made incremental gains, but few have shown that they can get continuous gains, and fewer still have demonstrated that they can do this on a regular basis with new companies they acquire or create. In this regard, Danaher is perhaps closest to the mark. Danaher has had compounded increases in earnings in the mid-20 percent range since starting its Lean efforts in 1987. And every year, the company acquires new, non-Lean organizations that it gets onto this path. Danaher is still learning and building its culture, but some of its practices are worth thinking about.

IMMERSION

Lean learning is hands-on learning that comes from the personal struggle of applying new concepts and tools to your own workplace. Successful organizations have developed an approach to bringing their leaders new knowledge that changes the way they view work. It is not necessary for senior leaders to get to the point where they are experts at the application of a certain Lean tool or deeply knowledgeable in the full range of Lean tools. The real key for senior leaders is to get just enough personal experience to allow them to begin to see waste in the work that surrounds them every day. Once they begin to see the seven wastes in the daily work that is all around them, they have the incentive and motivation to attack this waste and reduce it. For leaders, learning to see waste is the key.

At HON/HNI, new managers, whether internal promotions or external hires, get four weeklong kaizen event experiences in their first year on the job. Leaders first participate in a standard work event in a production area, because it is typically easier to see waste in a production process than in other processes. The shock value of how much waste is in the area studied combined with the fact that half of that waste can be removed within the same week will often make the first up-close event experience an eye-opener.

In the second weeklong event, leaders participate in a value stream–analysis event, in which they begin to see waste in terms of quality, time consumption, and productivity at a high level—sort of a 20,000-foot view of waste. This is then followed by a weeklong administrative standard work event, which will open their eyes to what waste looks like in purely administrative processes. A fourth weeklong event is required with the 3P tool (production preparation process, see Appendix A), which is used to invent new product and process designs, and also to align process and product development with Lean practices. So HON/HNI requires four weeks of kaizen-event-based immersion as the starting point.

With this as the foundation, HON/HNI requires every manager to get an additional three full weeks of event experiences every year thereafter. It "encourages" this by making achievement of three additional weeks of event experience a condition for eligibility in that year's bonus program.

At Danaher, the immersion process for new leaders is a formal thirteen-week process. In the process, about two-thirds of the time is spent on kaizen event teams operating in a variety of different Danaher businesses. About one-third of the time is spent on Lean governance, benchmarking good Lean operations and management practice at various locations, joining strategy deployment sessions, and going to a week of formal Danaher Business System (DBS) Leadership Training. The immersion is conducted under the guidance of a personal mentor (a senior Danaher manager who is deeply knowledgeable and committed to DBS) who constructs the specific plan for the new manager and coaches him or her through the thirteen weeks of immersion.

The point is that it will not be sufficient to think you can transform leaders with a single week's time commitment or only in classrooms. Instead, the first critical step in governance is to develop a plan for how you will immerse senior leaders in a Lean approach to organizing your work. This is the key to success, and you will need to put more effort into it than you think. (See Appendix E for the Red River Army Depot's journey with leadership immersion.)

GUIDING COALITION

John Kotter, who writes about change management, talks about establishing a guiding coalition to help a CEO guide the Lean change. A *guiding coalition* is the senior management group that will guide the transformation process for the whole enterprise. The thought behind this involves several key issues:

- A change in culture will need more than one senior person who is working to embed the new culture in the organization.
- The Lean path is not perfectly clear, so the input of multiple senior leaders will help with midcourse corrections.
- Any key player who is on the outside looking in will tend to fight the process.

Thus, a good initial task for the guiding coalition is to develop the immersion experience that will be used for their own education, as well as for other leaders, as the Lean process expands.

This is the point at which organizations often implement their transformation value stream analysis (TVSA; see Appendix A). The goal of TVSA is to take a look at the basic business strategy of the organization, see how the organization's key value streams (at the highest level) fulfill key stakeholder needs and enable the strategy, assess the potential of Lean to accelerate and deepen the strategic impact, and then begin to build the transformation plan. Part of a TVSA is also to determine how to track and measure the True North metrics and how these metrics will tie to financial performance.

After that, the initial improvement focus needs to be selected. This should be an area (a value stream) that is significant to the company, ideally one that has potential to grow with improved lead times, quality, and so on. But most important is that it is an area where the local leaders really are leaders—individuals who will commit the extra personal effort needed to experiment with new Lean ways and bring their team along on the often-confusing and difficult Lean journey. I suggest that the most important criterion for the first targeted value stream focus area is the quality of leadership in that value stream. A good leader can make even a poor plan succeed, and a poor leader can kill the best of plans.

There are a few things to keep in mind as you start. You select a key value stream based on the quality of its leadership and its importance or impact. Then you need to ensure basic improvement resources. Three key steps should be taken:

- You need a sensei to teach your organization Lean tools/concepts and to coach your team on the leadership issues.
- In the value stream you select, you need to dedicate 3 percent of the total head count to ongoing support for improvement of this value stream (see Chapter 5). By initiating the 3 percent rule only for a single value stream, the number of people dedicated to improvement

starts low and grows as each new value stream starts up. But after the first value stream is operating, it will be generating a flow of improvement results that will cover the cost of starting up the next value stream, so you really only invest in folks to start the initial value stream—that is, future resources are paid for by productivity gains and redeployment from initial value streams.

- You start improvement events at a pace that will build sufficient gains to have impact, will build experience (Lean learning) fast enough to grow your own future sensei, and will show the long-term potential to build a new culture as all members get personal experience with learning to see and remove waste.

Experience has shown that this pace is related to population, which makes the *n*/10 rule (see Chapter 5) about right. Typically, it is important to have a regular rhythm of at least one event-week per month. A less frequent event pace will lead to too much lost momentum between events and insufficient impact on results in performance, learning, and culture building.

Also keep in mind the rule of 5× (see Chapter 4). Once you get through the first pass of improvement in the initial value stream, keep your 3 percent dedicated resources there and start the next pass of improvement, at the same time using some of the savings/freed-up resources to fund the establishment of an improvement organization for another value stream. You will, of course, need to prove to yourself and your company that the five passes of improvement are not only real, but also that the results are often greatest in the fourth or fifth passes. These types of results are just too far away from everyday experience to believe until you prove them to your own organization with your own work. But focusing on multiple passes of Lean improvement will build this value stream into the *model value stream*—the area where the results are compelling to all who see them and where the culture becomes so established that it will sustain the improvement through generations.

Too many firms set up dedicated full-time Lean staff to support their Lean transformations, but then allow these folks to just get wrapped up in administration and never get any real learning from personal event experience. This approach never works. The full-time resources for improvement must be required to get monthly event experience so they grow their own learning of what waste is and how to remove it. The vast majority of the dedicated Lean resources should be at the level of the individual value streams, focused on continually hitting True North improvement metrics for their value stream.

You may want to establish a transformation mission control room, where the guiding coalition will normally meet. (See Appendix C for more information on Watlow's mission control room.) The room should also feature a hard copy of the TVSA, the Total Plan of Care (an outline of key steps in the transformation journey), the personal immersion/development plans for key leaders, the strategy deployment plan, the initial value stream analysis and plan, charts of True North metric performance, and so on. And all this material should be visually displayed on the walls of the mission control room.

COMMUNICATION

You really cannot overcommunicate when undertaking any large change in your organization. One way to think about communication is to review some of the data from a study of sales presentations, which noted that three days after a presentation, you can recall only about 11 percent of the information presented. So if you think your message is important, think about repeating it about ten times. We tend to think, "I told them that already!" when we probably should be thinking, "They remembered only 11 percent of what I told them, so how will I get the other 89 percent across?"

It is good to repackage the message several times and use different mediums. Make full use of company newsletters, company video messages, and every other possible avenue of communicating the basics. And the basics are:

- Why do we need to change (what are the key competitive or customer drivers)?
- Why have we chosen this path?
- How will this path work?
- What will each person's role be in this transformation?

You may also want to try some new forms of communication, as discussed in the two following sections.

Lean Simulation

About 99 percent of Lean education will come from hands-on experience (see Figure 6.1). However, the 1 percent that comes from traditional

FIGURE 6.1
Team doing a Lean simulation.

educational approaches is still important. The whole organization needs to get some basic idea of what Lean is all about. A basic introduction to Lean is a solid step. Another good step is to take groups of members through a *Lean simulation,* which is a mock-up of a work area that demonstrates basic batch practices and then shows the evolution to flow.

A Lean simulation usually takes about four hours to conduct. When done well, it introduces the key principles of Lean—flow, pull, value streams, and so on—and it usually does so in a way that words cannot do. Well-done simulations give participants a mental picture of the waste in your current batch approach and show the potential for improvement in quality, lead time, and productivity. It is really great to see someone "get it" after participating in a simulation.

Strategy Deployment

One Lean strategic organizational process is *hoshin kanri,* which is also called *hoshin* planning, management by policy, and policy deployment. (Simpler Consulting uses the term *strategy deployment*, as discussed in Appendix A.) The basic idea of strategy deployment is to review key strategic efforts for the next year, identify how Lean improvement can accelerate and enable these efforts, set True North goals to support the strategic direction, establish the pace and pattern of improvement effort for the year to achieve these goals, and then establish a monthly review process.

Most monthly review meetings or monthly operations meetings are focused on financial metrics and have a budgetary outlook. Strategy deployment will do a similar thing, but with a focus on improvement—the process to ensure that our performance tomorrow is better than our performance today, forever.

With strategy deployment, an annual effort is undertaken to set improvement goals for the organization that will enable the chosen strategic initiatives, and then to break these improvement goals down to each lower level of the organization, and, at the value-adding level, develop the improvement work plan to meet these goals. Typical questions include:

- What value streams will we have to improve to meet this year's goals?
- How many improvement events will likely be needed to achieve this?
- What will the focus of those events be?
- Who will support those events?

This annual planning effort will not detail exactly what improvement work you will be doing six months from now, but it will give the folks who need to drive the value stream improvement efforts a good idea of the pace of improvement work they will need to sustain to hit the overall goals.

After the annual improvement plan is set, monthly follow-up meetings are used to assess progress and share learning. Typically, each value stream team reviews the results of the prior month, taking a fast look at the *rate* of improvement—in other words, did the team hit the improvement for human development, quality, lead time, and productivity? Reviewing this information takes up about 10 percent of the meeting time. Instead of spending time talking about the result numbers, this meeting spends time talking about what *drives* the numbers.

So after the short review of "Did we hit our improvement targets this past month?" the value stream team reviews the key improvement events implemented in the past month and the key lessons learned from these. If a goal hasn't been met, the value stream team identifies additional Lean-event efforts to catch up to that goal. Next, the value stream team reviews the key events planned for the upcoming month and estimates whether this will be sufficient to meet the month's improvement goals.

This dialogue provides great learning for the whole organization. The lessons learned can be shared from one team to another, and management can help identify possible corrective action steps to get back on track when an improvement target has been missed. The purpose of the meeting is to spend time learning about what is working and talking about corrective action, as opposed to spending time reviewing the numbers. Stay focused on the here and now: Did we make it last month? If not, what are we doing about it? What have we learned? Will we make it this month? If so, how? If not, do other folks on the team have ideas on how to accelerate the improvement pace?

At some of the initial meetings, you may need to use a timer, allowing a set time for each value stream review. World class is five minutes per review, but my best was about fifteen minutes per review. People have a strong tendency to ramble and not focus on key issues, so a timer, combined with the knowledge that there is a very strict time limit and that certain topics must be covered within that time limit, can change this rambling to a tight focus. You will also find that the meetings become more efficient each year, such that you will have a much better process after three or four years.

When you first start strategy deployment, it can seem kind of clunky. But one of the first things you see is that in the week before the monthly meeting, there is a huge flurry of improvement work going on, which means that even if you're still in a firefighting culture, at least the team is focused on improvement for some of their time. This flurry of improvement focus is worth the effort of the strategy deployment process, in and of itself.

The important things to keep in mind revolve around use of the True North measurements to drive improvements directly related to strategic plan targets, and the use of the strategy deployment meetings as 80-plus percent learning experience through the exchange of improvement ideas… and less than 20 percent about the numbers themselves.

It might be useful to see a strategy deployment review. This one is 20 years old, so it's no longer revealing anything about the current business strategy, but more importantly, it shows how such a review can be simple and unpolished and still be a part of efforts to achieve improvement at order-of-magnitude rates. Figure 6.2 is the strategy deployment overview chart used at Jake Brake in 1990. It communicated to the overall membership how various elements fit together to answer company-wide questions about why we were in business, what we intended to do to be successful, and how we would do those things. Figure 6.3 is another internal communication document that was used to explain how the overall improvement objectives for 1990 would be cascaded down to the value-adding level of work in the organization, and how these value stream–level improvement plans would be reviewed each month by the president and his staff.

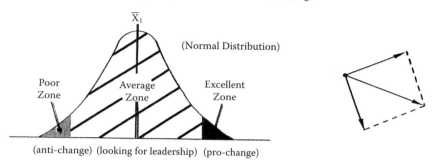

Toyota also likens the organization to a classic bell curve regarding individuals' attitudes to change

$\overline{X}_1$

(Normal Distribution)

Poor Zone

Average Zone

Excellent Zone

(anti-change) (looking for leadership) (pro-change)

If you only support change agents, the antibodies will get more active and will multiply, completely offsetting the impact of your change agents

FIGURE 6.2
Strategy deployment overview chart.

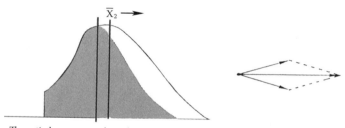

$\overline{X}_2 \rightarrow$

The anti-change group always becomes a fifth column that resists the lean conversion. The anti-change group is removed from the organization.
Ninety percent of the organization that is looking for leadership now shifts toward the new direction.

By addressing a few antibodies, a few change agents will pull the total organization into the future

FIGURE 6.3
Internal communication document showing improvement objectives for 1990.

ANTIBODIES

Taiichi Ohno, the Lean guru at Toyota, used to note that every organization had antibodies inside it, just as the human body does. When a change or infection tries to enter the body, the *antibodies* do two things: They get really active fighting off this new thing, and they also multiply. They add converts to their effort. This is normal. In fact, the stronger the corporate culture, the stronger the antibodies; the antibodies are there to protect the existing corporate culture.

You have undoubtedly noticed that there is often not a clear description of the corporate culture when you first join an organization, but that, over time, you learn the "rules." Well, the folks that teach the corporate culture are the antibodies. They are usually respected and long-term members of the organization.

The problem, of course, comes about when the organization needs to change. During times of significant change, the antibodies—who, again, tend to be some of your most respected and experienced members— become the folks who try to prevent improvement and change. When these antibodies emerge, leadership needs to address them.

Antibodies exist in every organization and will automatically resist anything as radical as a Lean transformation. And they will do so with the best of intentions. From their perspective, the historic success of the organization was based on doing things a certain way, so changing how things are done risks everything. The more successful the organization, the stronger the antibodies are and the harder the task to get any new direction moving.

Toyota has occasionally depicted the presence of antibodies as a normal distribution curve, with the tails on each side representing either the antibodies (poor zone) or the *change agents* (excellent zone), who are those few key leaders who are attempting to move the organization in the new direction. You absolutely need to support the change agents, but this is only half the answer. If you support the change agents and start moving in new directions, a few interesting phenomena will happen.

First, the antibodies will get more active (informally at coffee breaks, for example) in resisting the new direction. They will also talk more members, those who are close to their views, into becoming new antibodies. The end result is that if you only support the change agents, you end up with turmoil as the mass of members in the middle hears two opposite messages about where the organization should be going—both messages coming from respected members of the organization. This is where leaders have to lead. The best thing to do is to make it clear that (a) the organization is going to go on this journey, (b) the role of every member is to work to support this change, and (c) those who will not or cannot change need to think about finding another organization where they would be more comfortable.

The faster you identify each true antibody and address him or her, the fewer antibodies you will have to address in the end. Over time, as folks gain personal experience with the process, most of the significant anti-bodies will most likely buy in, but you must address the first few early so they don't multiply. If they do multiply, you will never be able to stay on track long enough to convert them, so early action is key.

One caution: When you start on this journey, it is new to everyone, which means that any thinking person will initially question the direction. This may make everyone appear to be an antibody. The difference is that real antibodies never accept the answers to any of their questions and don't want to participate in the process. It does not take long to see the true antibodies, as opposed to those who have genuine questions about the company's new direction.

LEAN YEAR BY YEAR

A well-planned and aggressively led Lean transformation will follow a regular cultural transformation pace over the first four years or so.

Year One

When you start the Lean journey, the idea is totally new to your whole organization, so the concepts take time to sink in. However, at the end of the first year of your Lean transformation effort, you will be impressed by the improvements made in specific events and in some targeted value streams. You will see individual results that look promising, but you may not see that the enterprise financial metrics have moved as much as you had expected. Overall progress will likely be slower than you hoped for.

You will see a lot of "two steps forward, and one step back" experiences in that first year. This is a by-product of the nature of hands-on learning, because your improvement teams are totally new to both the ideas of Lean and the Lean tools, so they make mistakes trying to interpret how to apply ideas like one-piece flow. In addition, the poor follow-up practices that exist in the firefighting culture at most companies keep you from maintaining and sustaining all the improvement. The end result is that by the end of the first successful year of a Lean transformation, most of your members will still be confused by the new approach or upset by the pace and magnitude of change. Unlike most corporate initiatives in which, by year's end, you expect to be able to declare victory, you will not see that with a Lean transformation.

It is also worth noting that, by the end of the first year, less than 20 percent of your organization will have actually experienced Lean work in their areas. So most of the organization will still be on the outside looking in, and this group is usually not very supportive.

Year Two

The second year is usually the year of major resistance. The antibodies that see the Lean effort continue into a second year (when most programs in the past have ended) get reenergized to kill it off before it can really hurt the organization. Yet your change agents will still be inexperienced, and every time they make a mistake in trying to apply the new principles, your remaining antibodies will highlight the mistake.

By the end of the second year, you will be making an impact on value streams that represent 30 to 40 percent of the organization, which means the majority of your organization still will not have direct learning experience about Lean. A member survey given at the end of the second year of a successful Lean journey will probably say something like, "The jury is still out on this Lean thing."

Year Three

The third year is a year of consolidation. Managers and full-time Lean resources are gaining experience with the process. Individual events have more "two steps forward and *no* falling back" impacts. By the end of the third year, the compounding of results in quality, lead times, and productivity/cost will be large enough to demonstrate that the process is truly successful. Also, by the end of the third year, your member survey might say something like, "We are making great progress—but I wonder when we will be done."

Year Four

The fourth year is characterized by "change" having gradually become the new norm. The processes of continuous improvement and continuous change are becoming institutionalized by the end of the fourth year. You can feel and see tremendous positive momentum building in the organization.

You may still not have touched 20 percent or so of the organization with Lean efforts, but you can see that you are creating a new culture—a true learning organization that can improve forever. Your end-of-year four-member survey would change again; instead of members wondering when the process will be done, they start to hope that it can go on forever.

Most leaders think that they can get to the year-four state in one year. I have never seen anyone be able to do that, even in the best-led Lean efforts. So it is good to realize that there will be tough sledding for much more than a year. If you are on track, you will be seeing positive results, accumulating new skills within the organization, and building new cultural norms all along the way. But it will take about four full years for the best-led Lean effort to begin to be established as the new way of doing things. After all, you can't expect to build a new culture in just a couple of years!

SUMMARY

All of this comes together as a new way of running your enterprise—in other words, you establish a new management system, like the Toyota Production System or the Danaher Business System. Although you can look at models from other companies, you have to build the system yourself. And this takes time and energy.

Most corporate leaders have been trained to manage. We were taught the virtues of delegation. We have degrees called *masters of business administration*, which focus on *administration*. Most of us were not taught how to lead, that is, how to take an organization in new directions. This means that our model of how to manage is not particularly useful when we actually want to successfully transform an organization. The model we need instead for this is true leadership—a willingness to demonstrate that we do not have all the answers, a willingness to go to the *gemba* (workplace) and learn how it actually works, a willingness to admit that we have to gather new knowledge and hone new skills to succeed. Most senior leaders feel that others expect them to know the answers, but with Lean, the key to success is to know the questions and be willing to pursue the answers diligently.

7

Building a Lean Culture

Now for the hard part: Lean culture. Over my thirty years as a student of Lean transformation, my path of learning has progressed in the way that it does for most people. For years, I was focused on learning about the *tools* of Lean. How do you reduce setup time? How do you use standard work? How do you analyze a value stream? There was a lot to learn, and it seemed like every time I thought I had something down, I learned some new aspect of it or discovered an entirely new tool that I hadn't known existed. So I lived in the world of Lean tools for a long time.

As I struggled to get results from these Lean tools, I started to add knowledge, and with that knowledge, I began to develop approaches to getting results—what you might think of as good Lean *practices*. The learning of Lean practices has, for me, been both haphazard and slow, mostly through trial and error, with multiple trials and many errors before I found practices that worked well and consistently.

Along with learning about Lean tools and the learning or invention of Lean practices, there was also a point at which I began to *believe* in the core principles of Lean—flow, pull, focus on value, and so on. These concepts are all remarkably easy to talk about, but they are incredibly difficult to practice. My own belief in the core principles of Lean came gradually. At various times, I could look back and recognize the point at which I started to believe in any one of the core principles of Lean.

It gradually dawned on me that this Lean stuff was valuable only if it was a long-term organizational practice—that is, if it became the new way of running the enterprise, if it became the new company *culture*. Being an operating manager, the idea of thinking about culture did not come to me right away. But, over time, it became obvious that all the rest of my learning was *muda* (waste) if it just disappeared when the personal push or energy behind the effort went away. Eventually, the focus of my learning was to study the culture that sustains Lean transformations, and this has been my focus for the past dozen years.

DEFINING CULTURE

Perhaps it is good to go over this word *culture*. An organizational culture is defined by the behaviors or habits of its leaders; in other words, the culture is formed by what these leaders *do*. "What they do" is essential to the company's success. When you add lots of these "what they dos" together, you see the fabric of a new culture.

My learning in this area started by observing individual leadership practices that were different from typical Western practice. Originally, I did not see that these were part of some larger fabric of overall practice, which they are.

One example is selection processes. I've worked at companies where we used to joke that our "selection process" was that we held a mirror up to a person's mouth: If his or her breath fogged the mirror, we would hire them! It was meant as a joke, but like most jokes, it was based on a strong element of truth; we weren't looking for a whole lot more than a living, breathing human being.

So as part of my benchmarking, I decided to review the Toyota selection process, which includes about a dozen key steps that take a full week of time on the part of the applicant. The Toyota process includes not only the normal hiring stuff, but also groups of applicants doing simulations of problems in the workplace, doing simulations of the actual work to be done, being interviewed and rated by a team of assessors, and so on. So the process looked pretty complex and was about 100 times as demanding as our normal practice. And what did this rigorous process select for? Just four things. The whole process worked to identify individuals who:

- Like to learn new things
- Can identify and solve problems (recall that these are two separate skills)
- Work well in teams
- Communicate well

The contrast between the simplicity and focus of the selection goals and the exhaustive process to assess these characteristics was surprising to me.

It was a classic of many things "Toyota." It was the opposite of traditional leadership behavior, where we draw up a long list of desired traits without having any process to figure out whether we got them. Most company managers look for people who have done the kind of work for which they are hiring, which is the easy way to be sure they can do the work. But Toyota has a preference for people who have not had prior experience with the work (because then they do not have to unlearn bad habits before they can start learning good ones). Toyota is not looking for the strongest people, the fastest people, or the smartest people but for people who can work together as a team to make improvement. I'm paraphrasing here, but I heard someone at Toyota say something like this that brings their human-development system into perspective: "Most companies produce average results by hiring the smartest people, but allowing them to work with broken processes. We produce excellent results from average people who are focused on continually improving our processes." Which system do you think will win most often?

As I tried to build organizational buy-in for a new, exhaustive selection process, what seemed to help folks understand the huge time investment was to contrast it with our typical capital purchase process. In most organizations, if you make a million-dollar investment in new capital equipment, you have a study done by some technical group; then this study is reviewed by management; then the study is analyzed by financial folks, until the proposal starts to go up the approval ladder, with reviews and signatures at each management level and on to the group president or CEO level. We had hundreds of hours of evaluation for a million-dollar capital investment. Yet, when we hire someone, it is with the expectation that he or she will spend a full career with us—and we certainly will spend well over a million dollars in total compensation over the time of that one person's career—yet we typically spend almost no time working to improve the quality of this decision.

See how this way of thinking is a fundamentally different culture (Figure 7.1)?

THE BUILDING BLOCKS OF LEAN/TOYOTA CULTURE

I have found it hard to learn about Toyota culture. Partly, this is because I have not actually worked inside Toyota. But I have also found that the

FIGURE 7.1
Learning about leadership and culture.

way people get introduced to the culture inside Toyota is so subtle that most people who worked at another culture before joining Toyota did not contrast the new way people interacted.

It is usually only the folks who worked in a US firm, worked for Toyota for at least a decade, and then chose to leave, who have come to understand the contrast between working at Toyota and working almost anywhere else. From talking with these folks and studying everything available to outsiders about Toyota behavior/culture, I have built up a list of observations. I know the list is incomplete because every once in a while I discover a new behavior, habit, or leadership practice that is built into the way things are done at Toyota and *not* built into the way we usually do things. But here is the list, as of today, of Lean's core values and leadership behaviors.

Serve the Customer

Most firms say they serve the customer. Most do not practice it, at least not consistently. At Toyota, this mantra is the starting point. All actions are first evaluated in terms of their impact on the customer. Of course, Toyota has profit goals, but it recognizes that the key to success is satisfied customers. The goal is to maximize customer satisfaction while minimizing the cost or waste to satisfy those customers. Profit is what is left after serving customers in the least wasteful way. All kaizen is customer-focused. Seems simple, but keeping this goal in front of everyone, every day, on every decision is a massive task that requires enormous leadership focus and commitment.

Seek What's Right, Regardless

At Toyota, there is a premium on integrity. There is a basic understanding that if you cannot trust the information used in the organization, you cannot possibly provide the best value to the customer. And there is a premium on true courage. At HON/HNI we used to call it *active honesty*. The idea was that true integrity was not only "not lying," but it was also speaking out with the truth, even when the truth would have negative consequences. Another way to think of this is *courageous integrity*. One example of this is the Toyota practice of "bad news first," where the opportunity to improve is focused on before accolades are given.

Decide Carefully, Implement Quickly

There is an interesting contrast here. Non-Lean companies are usually rushing to a solution—without spending time getting to a root cause—so the solution turns out to be a Band-Aid˚, and the company faces the same issue over and over and over again.

At Toyota, there is a deep respect for understanding the problem before seeking the solution. One way of thinking about this is the practice of using the work group to address any problem in the workplace by asking "why" five times in a row to find the underlying cause for the problem. Solving this underlying problem will keep the surface problem from ever recurring. This is the kind of thinking that allows "average people to build great processes that achieve superior results." Another example of this "decide carefully, implement quickly" approach is the use of A3 problem solving. This visual approach to problem solving typically involves using one sheet of paper that includes nine boxes or steps. Its aim is to make sure you have asked the right question to truly understand the problem *before* you jump to implementation.

And walking through the logic of the A3—what Toyota folks call *A3 Thinking*—will build a solid approach to developing solutions that you can implement quickly and only once. This is typical Toyota style: Focus on spending a lot more time than you think you have time to spend at the front end of the process/project, and reap huge rewards by eliminating the rework that you get from trying to implement surface solutions or half-thought-through solutions.

Candidly Admit Imperfections

This one is huge. From my observation, it is, in fact, the cultural cornerstone. The basic idea is that all improvement starts with humility. Right away, this is another opposite from non-Lean cultures. When you ask senior managers of non-Lean businesses about the value of being humble, they really tend to think you may have lost your mind. We need to be proud! We can't be humble about who we are and what our organization does!

But how does any improvement start? It starts with recognition that something could be better. The foundation of this is the idea of humility. If you are humble about your success, you are open to seeing ways that it can be improved. The opposite of humility is arrogance, which can almost always be traced back to the beginning of the downfall of any organization. With a humble outlook, you are open to *hansei,* a deep reflection on both your current approach and the approach others have to a similar situation. From hansei, you move to a challenge to improve to the highest level. And from the challenge comes the breakthrough level of improvement. So there is a causal link from humility to hansei to challenge to improvement. This attitude can be seen in comments from everyone at Toyota. For example, David Absher, a maintenance supervisor at TMMC (Georgetown, Kentucky), commented, "We are nowhere near excellent, but we are on that journey." You can see the attitude of humility, the sense that there has been hansei, the view that a challenge has been set, and the assurance that the improvement process is under way.

A few years ago, Fujio Cho, chairman of Toyota, was speaking at an annual meeting of the global automotive industry in Traverse City, Michigan. The CEOs of the major global automotive firms were each giving a talk, saying what you would expect: They noted the progress their firm was making, how good their products were becoming, and so on. You have heard the talk a hundred times. Then Cho started to speak, and his comments went something like this: "We see things differently at Toyota. The sense of crisis that we feel stems from our fear that we have not kept up." I cannot imagine a non-Lean CEO making those comments, because they feel they need to be beating their chests in public, that their teams would be discouraged if we talked about shortcomings. But Cho talks to the world, and especially his own team, about the need to accelerate improvement and the concern about losing momentum, while his firm's stock market capitalization is roughly equivalent to that of the whole rest of the global automotive industry combined.

Speak Honestly and with Deep Respect

One key part of Lean culture is the value of speaking with integrity, even if it hurts. Deep respect is equally important. The point is that, as a supervisor, you have to build the personal skill to be able to honestly assess the strengths and weaknesses of your team members, and then, most difficult of all, review shortcomings in a way that shows deep respect for the individual and helps each accept a review of shortcomings as something positive. Sounds simple, but it's really hard.

Go, See, and Listen to Learn (*Genchi Gembutsu*)

Toyota has a strong bias to always go to where the work is occurring and observe what is happening there. The idea is to truly understand the problem. There is a belief at Toyota that reports and meetings that occur away from the actual site of the work being discussed will lead to incorrect assumptions and conclusions. The Japanese phrase *genchi gembutsu* means roughly "the real thing, in the real place."

There are stories of new hotshot university graduates being hired at Toyota, and then spending their first full day in "the Ohno circle." This is a chalk circle a couple of feet in diameter drawn on the workplace floor, where the newly minted graduate would spend his or her first full day—with no instructions. The new grad, however, would eventually start to observe the work that was going on around him or her and, if he or she was good, would eventually notice some aspect of the work that did not seem to make sense or did not look efficient. At the end of the day, Ohno would ask for the grad's observations and test his or her ability to observe real work, in the actual workplace, and see possibilities for improvement. This was the first step for future leaders—personally building the skill to see waste in the work that surrounds them. This was boot camp for future Lean practitioners.

This attitude can be seen in how Absher describes Toyota's Georgetown, Kentucky, operation, where there are about 7,000 total members. "It is like we have 7,000 industrial engineers working here. They see waste, and they know how to remove it." That is the culture you want to build—where your human resource really is your resource.

Another example of understanding the real workplace can be seen in product development practices. As Yugi Yokaya, chief engineer for the Sienna minivan, noted, "I must drive through all fifty states, all Canadian provinces, and Mexico, seeing firsthand how people use minivans." The real thing, in the real place.

Deliver on Meaningful Challenges

There is a strong fundamental belief at Toyota that people are at their highest state and create their best results when they are responding to a significant challenge. You will find this reference to "challenge" throughout Toyota's management practice. The idea is that a significant challenge will energize a team and will be the source of motivation to achieve a breakthrough result. It has to be a goal that can be achievable, but also one that will not be *easily* achievable. As Teriyuki Minoura, president of TMMNA (Toyota Motor Manufacturing North America), noted, "It is a basic characteristic of human beings that they develop wisdom from being put under pressure." Or as Absher describes it, "We set really high targets, and then try like crazy to get there. If we don't reach a target, we try to figure out why we fell short. Is there anything we can do to take another step?"

Does your maintenance supervisor think like this? Does *everyone* in your organization think like this? Keep in mind that you create diamonds (in this case, great leaders) from coal (average material) by thoughtfully putting it under great heat and pressure.

Another example comes from a challenge that former CEO Katsuaki Watanabe has given to the whole of Toyota (which I've paraphrased): "We must design a car that can cross the whole world with a single tank of gas, that will clean the air as it operates, and that will never harm either a passenger or a pedestrian." This is a challenge that will stretch the creativity of the whole of the global Toyota organization. By stretching their creativity, Toyota expects to achieve a breakthrough in automotive design. They probably will not meet this exact goal, but the challenge of working at it will create solutions that no one can envision today—Toyota has set True North for car design—and will work diligently to close the gap every year. Senior business leaders often shy away from setting this kind of challenge, but thoughtful challenges provide the most inspiring work for human beings.

Be a Mentor and a Role Model

The following Toyota expression is perhaps the most fundamental expression of its culture: "We build people before we build cars." Toyota takes this seriously. The first role of anyone in any level of supervision is to "build people." And the key to building people is careful mentoring. Because the building of people is job one at Toyota, the skill of mentoring is taken very seriously. One interesting aspect is the way mentoring is assessed. Non-Lean managers usually spend a lot of time trying to impress their bosses—carefully preparing presentations to demonstrate how smart they are and how they did a really great job. Of course, this is all *muda* (waste)! A basic approach at Toyota is that mentoring is a given; in fact, you cannot be promoted until you have demonstrated that you are a solid mentor. And the *only* way you can demonstrate this skill is with a result—that is, the personal growth of the people on your team, those you have mentored. You do not demonstrate this by *talking* about how good you are at mentoring. In fact you have to be silent and let your students speak for you, by demonstrating how much they have learned, by showing the challenges they have met, and presenting the improvements they have made.

To get consideration for promotion, you have to have the people on your team demonstrate how they have grown. Think about this for a minute. Just how powerful and transformational would it be to have a culture where the only way you could look good was through the success of those you mentored? It is hard to imagine the cultural impact of this one leadership behavior alone.

THE ACTION PLAN

One of the complications for non-Toyota companies trying to institute a Lean vision is that we have to start where we are, with the cultures that we have. And it turns out that some of the behaviors that are part of the where-we-are may make it difficult to actually get there.

When you go back in history, you find that in the early days of building a Lean culture and Lean business system, it was generally not possible to just talk folks into doing it—they had to be "strongly encouraged" to start the journey. Ohno noted at one point that only strong management leadership will get the organization on the new path when he said, "I utilized my authority to the fullest extent."[1] From hearing various stories about Ohno, you begin to realize that if he said he used his authority to "the fullest extent," he allowed no alternative but to comply with the new approach. This is a dilemma for most leaders starting the journey, because we want to build consensus and use a teamwork approach. The problem is that most teams will not accept Lean principles by just talking about them. Of your organization, 99 percent will not start this journey based on talking about it; team members will have to get some personal experience in order to begin their own journey of Lean learning. They have to experience the principles, and they may have to be "strongly encouraged" to get the personal experience that will lead them to a new view of how organizations can work effectively. No one on the team believes the core Lean principles at the start. It will take about five years of deep experience before they will truly believe the core principles and practice them in their daily management.

Chances are, you will also have *antibodies,* people who are actively trying to derail your effort to change the culture (see Chapter 6).

Giving Your Leadership Team Personal Experience

You will find it necessary to *require* certain types and levels of engagement in order for individuals to begin their own journey of new learning. And you do this by giving them personal experience with learning to see waste and remove it. The place to start is with your leadership team.

When I started the Lean transformation effort at HON/HNI, I required every business unit general manager to get at least twelve weeks of personal, full-time Lean-event experiences in his or her first year as a condition of continuing in that role. When we started, most of them thought this was crazy. But now Danaher's executive immersion program requires thirteen weeks of full-time experience and learning about the Danaher Business System (DBS) for every business unit president and all of his or her direct reports. This level of experience for senior leadership is the only proven model for aligning senior leadership.

Today at HON/HNI, a similar leadership immersion process is in place. Those new to HON/HNI management roles (whether an outside recruit or an internal promotion) are required to attend a structured set of four weeklong kaizen events in their first year. After that, they're required to have two more weeklong kaizen event experiences each year as a condition for remaining in the bonus program.

Something happens to a person as he or she accumulates these early kaizen-event experiences. One study found that associates' attitudes toward an organization improved significantly with each additional kaizen experience, continuing until it began to level off at a very high level after eight event experiences. Experience has shown that the impact of learning to see waste—personally—and then realizing how much waste can be removed in a week is transformational. Personal kaizen experience is the most significant building block for a successful Lean transformation. At the same time, it is very hard to get senior management to realize that it is essential.

After you have an effort under way for senior leadership, look to build the breadth and depth of your foundation. The breadth will come from event experiences over a number of years for every member of your organization. This is how to get to the point that Toyota's Absher spoke of, where everyone in the organization acts like an industrial engineer.

It generally takes two events for team members to begin to believe that this "Lean stuff" might be a good idea, three to seven events for a personal commitment to the Lean philosophy to develop, and eight or more events to get the belief to a very high level. To take everyone up this curve may require ten years, so the important thing to keep in mind is that this commitment and growth in problem-solving ability is steadily growing as each member accumulates events throughout the organization.

Daily Improvement

Another fundamental approach to inculcating the Lean culture is called *daily improvement* (the practice of daily problem solving, at the root cause, by everyone in the organization). I do not like to discuss this up front, because when most CEOs hear about it, they immediately jump to the conclusion that this can be a shortcut to achieving Lean results. The idea that some CEOs get when hearing about daily improvement is that all they really need to do is a little problem-solving training across the organization, and then simply ask everyone to improve every day. With any luck, by this point you realize that something this significant would not be that easy. In fact, achievement of daily improvement is the result of transformation and not an initial step.

Typically, it is best to initiate a serious focus on daily improvement after you have spent about two years spreading basic Lean training and experience through kaizen events. However, daily improvement, like many Toyota practices, has more than one purpose and result. Daily improvement is an approach to pushing ahead on your True North metrics, but it is also a successful approach for accelerating broad buy-in (culture building) of Lean across the organization.

For example, at ThedaCare, after several years of a steady kaizen event pace, management observed good improvement results and a number of people who were excited about where they were going. But not all the people—and perhaps not even a majority of the people—felt this way. Although ThedaCare had a fairly broad cadre of people who had built up significant problem-solving skills from their cumulative event experiences, it needed to get everyone involved in improvement somehow. The solution was to add a focused effort on daily improvement that would involve 100 percent of the organization.

The approach included four key building blocks:

- A one-day Lean education program for 100 percent of the organization
- The establishment of visual management boards that highlight abnormalities in every area throughout the organization
- The implementation of 5S in every area throughout the organization
- The institutionalization of a daily improvement process based on problems that were highlighted in the visual management system, and use of the basic problem-solving skills from the one-day training to address these problems

Similarly, at HON/HNI we instituted a Teian-style improvement system (see Appendix A), built around standard Toyota practice, in the fourth year of our Lean journey. This had the impact of broadening the buy-in while building broadly based, daily problem solving and daily improvement. (See also Appendix D for information on the evolution of daily improvement at the Autoliv Ogden Assembly plant.)

Challenging Your Team to Build Knowledge

Depth of knowledge is at least as important as breadth of knowledge, and you can get to some depth faster than you can achieve breadth. Those who build deep experiential knowledge can usually accumulate about an event a month and will build their improvement skills to a high level in about three years, leading others in the process. In five to six years at this monthly pace of learning, those individuals will not only refine their knowledge of the tools and practices, but also be at a point where they believe the principles and practice them every day.

As this learning is taking place, you need to apply the ideas of challenge and discipline. You need to challenge your organization, and especially your leaders, to achieve double-digit annual rates of improvement in the four True North metric areas, while double-checking that these four core drivers are flowing through to the financial statements and aligning with strategic objectives. Properly applied, the challenge of significant True North metric gains and the discipline to achieve results through the process will drive the Lean improvement activity. Keep in mind that there is synergy between substantial expectations for improvement and the activity of improvement. Success requires both activity and expectations for results and achievements. And you will find that meeting these challenges builds your people. Think about the overall culture and the habits and values you want to build into your people.

As an example, one of the boards on which I participate is a privately owned firm called Watlow. After struggling with the initial issues in getting started on a Lean path, Watlow undertook an effort to formalize the Watlow Way, its version of the Toyota Way, in conjunction with its sensei from Simpler Consulting. Watlow worked in a visual format, Toyota style. Now Watlow is working to align all associates' habits and behaviors with those it has identified as ideal in the Watlow Way. Watlow is also designing a selection system modeled after Toyota practice. The goal of this selection system is to ensure that newly hired Watlow members already have a high degree of alignment with the future-state culture that Watlow has defined in its Watlow Way. Figure 7.2 shows the ninth box of Watlow's cultural A3; as the "insight" box, it explains the culture they aspire to, the cultural "end state."

For this revised edition, I asked Peter Desloge, the CEO of Watlow, to provide an overview of the approaches used to define their future culture, communicate it to the full organization, work with each current member to identify and close gaps in their own personal performance against the desired behaviors, and develop a selection system to increase alignment of new members with their desired culture/behaviors. This is included as Appendix B.

This is a journey that we all need to start—but that will really never end.

A couple of years ago, Toyota conducted a *hansei* (deep reflection) on where it was in its journey to build the Toyota Way within the North

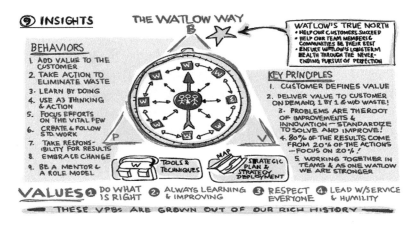

FIGURE 7.2
The Watlow Way.

American business units of Toyota and its affiliates. Although there were many interesting lessons that came from this hansei, two stand out:

- It used the primacy of hands-on learning, the Socratic approach to teaching/mentoring (teaching through thoughtful questioning), and the structure of the weeklong *jishukin* event as a learning and implementation model.
- When summarizing the results of the hansei, Toyota asked the question, "What is the most common roadblock to the Toyota Way in North America?" The answer: lack of personal involvement.

SUMMARY

Building a long-term learning culture is the most difficult part of any Lean journey, but it is also both the most powerful and the most personally rewarding part. As Kosuke Ikebuchi of Toyota has noted, "Westerners put too much emphasis on tools and technology, and not enough on philosophy and leadership behaviors." Building this Lean-learning culture can be—and should be—your legacy in your organization.

As a parting thought on culture, I have seen a couple of descriptions of a leader at Toyota. As usual, they are keenly focused descriptions that at first appear to be simple, but on further reflection reveal depth. Here is my favorite version:

A leader at Toyota should:

1. Possess a desire to lead, as true leadership is hard work.
2. Possess leadership ability, which is defined as the ability to get results through others.
3. Have a demonstrated desire and ability to mentor.
4. Possess a personal drive to pursue perfection [kaizen], through the Toyota Production System.

A FINAL THOUGHT

One of the things I have noticed over the years is that it is often hard to really understand a Toyota presentation, talk, or coaching moment because there is usually no special emphasis on the few key things that are so different from our normal practice and that we will really need to focus on. As I reflect on this revised edition, I believe that I may be accused of the same shortcoming. The title of this book is **Leading** the Lean Enterprise Transformation. I have reflected on the importance of leadership and leadership issues, but I think I may not have actually hit it hard enough to really make the point.

The few organizations that are truly successful with Lean—that have created outsized performance over multiple generations of management—have a common emphasis on leadership. I think of Lean as exceptionally powerful, but also exceptionally *leadership-intensive.*

Within Toyota, most managers at each level of the organization would be thought of as administrators; they run the system and ensure that things are moving along in a steady fashion. But Toyota would also identify a small proportion of management at each level of the organization as warriors or warrior types. The analogy is the samurai warrior, but the more specific core attributes of these managers are a fearlessness about pushing the system ahead, an intensity of commitment to improvement that is truly uncommon—a willingness to go the extra mile to make the organization progress. This group represents only about 5 percent of the total management team, but it is an increasing proportion of the management team as you go up the hierarchy. And, they are the key to moving the system and the culture to the next level of accomplishment. They have a commitment, an intensity, and a sense of mission around Lean improvement that is very rare, and very powerful. Warrior types are identified early on and are nurtured—and tested throughout their careers.

At Danaher they speak of "DBS zealots." The idea is the same. That is, only a small proportion of their management team will truly drive the system ahead and create the organizational energy to achieve uncommon results. As with Toyota, Danaher makes a special effort to identify, nurture, reward, *and test* these individuals as their careers evolve.

This small set of truly exceptional leaders is the key to making breakthrough impact. The first opportunity to identify these folks is during their 13-week immersion process, in which they are not only learning but also being tested and assessed by their mentor as they move through an intensive Lean experience. You will be able to identify most of your future warriors during their initial immersion experience.

AUTHOR'S NOTE

At this point I need to thank the team at Simpler Consulting, who worked with me to take our combined experience and observations and build the cultural attributes noted in this chapter. The outcome for Simpler is what it calls its tree, which is a model of the culture that it aspires to. See Figure 7.3.

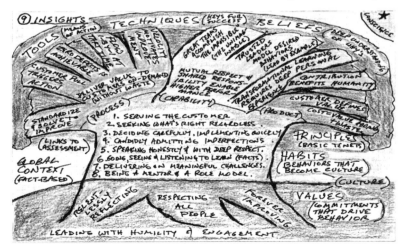

FIGURE 7.3
Simpler Consulting tree.

For this revised edition, I asked Simpler to provide their overall perspective on a complete Transformation Continuum (see Appendix D, written by Marc Hafer, Simpler's CEO). Simpler has well over 100 Lean sensei who have transformation experience at the most accomplished Lean organizations in the world, including Toyota (US and UK), Danaher, HON/HNI, FNOK, etc. A couple of years ago, a large group was pulled together to take our combined knowledge and define the complete journey of Lean transformation. This Transformation Continuum outlines the major phases that organizations go through on their journey, and it captures the evolution of various key attributes, such as human development and redesign of structure and culture, as an organization progresses through the phases of development. It is a living document, but in its current state it gives a good perspective of the breadth and depth of a total Lean transformation.

I also asked Chris Cooper, vice president of Simpler Europe, to provide an overview of what a Lean product development system looks like. In a manner similar to the one used to compile the Transformation Continuum, a group of Simpler sensei with Lean product development experience worked together to design an integrated Lean product development system. Most of what I have seen in other discussions of Lean product development has been just components or aspects of an overall system rather than an integrated flow of work to create successful new products through a Lean process. Although it was my intention with this book to focus on the leadership aspects of a Lean transformation, I feel that many organizations would also want a better understanding of the path to Lean product development. Chris's overview of what Simpler calls the Simpler Development System is available in Appendix F.

NOTE

1. Taiichi Ohno, "Evolution of the Toyota Production System" (unpublished manuscript).

Appendix A: A Lean Tutorial

This appendix does not attempt to show how to use every Lean tool; you can find that in many other books. My intent is to provide you with a basic tutorial on Lean. Even if you're familiar with the Lean toolbox, you may want to review this section because it offers you a summary of the tools that are used over the course of a Lean transformation. You also get a valuable perspective on how each tool is used, when it should be used, what it can accomplish, and how it drives the True North metrics.

I organize these tools into a few general categories: top-level tools for executive leadership; tools that principally improve quality; tools that principally build flow; tools that principally improve cost and productivity; tools that support human development; and tools that are specifically used in the area of product or service development. Almost all of these tools have a positive impact on the four True North metrics, so I group them under the True North metrics that they tend to impact most directly. As noted, setting True North improvement goals in the double-digit area (10 percent or more per year) will have a positive impact on each line item of an income statement and balance sheet.

TOP-LEVEL TOOLS FOR EXECUTIVE LEADERSHIP

A few tools are oriented toward the enterprise-level perspective of the transformation process.

Transformation Value Stream Analysis

I discuss in Chapter 3 how value stream analysis can help an organization learn to see waste in its work, and how such analysis can help build an improvement plan. In addition to value stream analysis, there is a tool called *transformation value stream analysis* (TVSA) that takes a top-level view of a corporation (see Figure A.1).

TVSA identifies key value streams at the top level of the enterprise, assesses their performance as seen by the multiple stakeholders in the

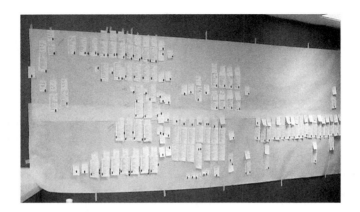

FIGURE A.1
TVSA example.

organization, and integrates this with the strategic plan of the organization. TVSA takes the insight developed in your strategic plan and builds top-level value stream objectives around the strategic needs and direction of the enterprise. TVSA also helps the executive team understand the potential kinds of improvement and pace of improvement that Lean can bring to bear on each value stream and how these improvements fit with the enterprise strategic plan.

You will be able to choose a couple of key value streams in which to begin your Lean transformation. These will be value streams that are important to the strategic direction of the firm and will demonstrate the power of Lean improvement to all stakeholders in the enterprise.

Strategy Deployment

The strategic deployment tool has a couple of other names (policy deployment and *hoshin kanri*), but the tool is essentially the same in each version (see Chapter 6 for details). It is a methodology that takes the enterprise improvement targets and deploys them down through the enterprise, all the way down to the first-level workforce where you find most of the value-added steps. The basic concept is a cascading of goals from one level of leadership down to the next level, where the goals are turned into value stream improvement plans. This part is called *catchball* by the Japanese. It is meant to be an exchange of views and knowledge about the improvement effort between two levels of leadership.

You'll begin to ask the following questions:

- What value streams will we need to work on to achieve the enter-prise-level improvement goals?
- What pace of activity do we plan to achieve these goals?
- How will we organize to achieve that pace of activity?
- Do we think these goals might be achievable?

Early on, catchball is difficult because the top leadership typically does not have the Lean experience to know what results are truly possible. For that reason, this tool is often not implemented until the second year of a Lean effort, after some experience about what is possible has been built up in the enterprise.

The process cycles downward through each level of leadership. Ultimately, at the first level of the organization, there is a work plan for improvement activity for each value stream that is targeted for improve-ment during that year. And then this process cycles back upward until it confirms the corporate improvement goals and demonstrates that the plan will achieve those goals.

The planning phase is typically done once per year and is a learning experience by itself. Then there is a monthly strategy deployment meet-ing to review progress made (see Figure A.2), issues that have come up,

FIGURE A.2
Strategy deployment in action.

and opportunities for shared learning. Most companies tend to have a monthly performance review meeting that is financially driven. Although the meeting tunes the company's direction, it is fundamentally focused on variance to a financial plan. What strategy deployment does instead is create a process that focuses the enterprise on fundamental improvement and on learning from the ongoing improvement experience. Just having the monthly strategy-deployment reviews helps get the enterprise thinking about making the work fundamentally better every month, as opposed to the maintenance focus of most monthly review meetings.

Strategy deployment is a very powerful process and a key part of what a leader does to ensure progress in the Lean transformation. But it is also a learn-by-doing approach that can be clunky in the first year, tends to improve a lot in the second year, and becomes a standard practice in the third year.

A3

Another tool that is used to develop business strategy, but is also used for everyday problem solving, is the *A3*. A3 is the name for an international paper size. Toyota developed an approach to problem solving that is designed to fit onto one A3 sheet. In typical (humble) Toyota fashion, the company did not come up with a fancy name, but just referred to it by the paper size. There are some slight variations in format, but a typical A3 would be similar to the nine-box A3 shown in Figure A.3.

A3 offers a format that forces you to cover all the key steps in considering a problem or an action. If you follow the nine boxes of information, you will have done a great job of understanding the problem, determining alternative solutions, and learning from the process.

A3 is also designed to use graphic data and sketches to outline concepts. It takes some work to come up with a sketch that will convey a key idea. (I am not good at it personally, but it is remarkably powerful.) Some people cannot really understand easily through words, and these team members will grab onto the idea of the sketch much more easily. And for everyone, the "words + sketch" make the idea much clearer and much more memorable.

At first, an A3 seems like a lot of work. But then you begin to realize that it prevents a huge amount of rework that results from implementing ideas that have not been thoroughly thought through. You also begin to see that after the organization is familiar with the format, A3 is incredibly efficient as a communication tool. The combination of words and sketches

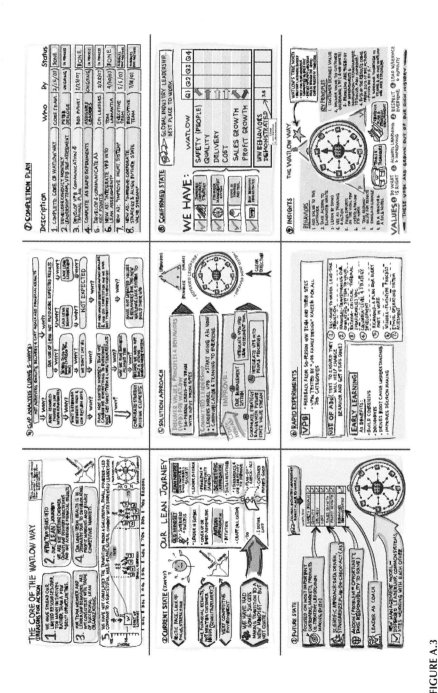

FIGURE A.3

Watlow TPOC (transformation plan of care).

makes it deeply effective. The focus on covering all key aspects of an issue (the nine boxes) also makes it deeply effective: Getting all the information summarized on one sheet of paper makes it very efficient.

TOOLS FOCUSED PRIMARILY ON QUALITY

The quality tool kit is an interesting mix. About half of this tool kit is what you would learn in a Total Quality Management (TQM) or Six Sigma effort. And then there is another half that is made up of some unique Toyota contributions.

Five Whys

One tool that is from both sides—originally a TQM tool but taken to a higher impact at Toyota by an order of magnitude—is the basic tool of asking why five times. The basic concept is that if you ask why five times, you are about 95 percent assured that the problem you fix is actually a root cause and not just a surface symptom. From personal experience, I suggest that about 90 percent of all quality problems can be solved just by getting the work group together, at the exact time of the quality incident, and then asking why five times. (After the work team asks why five times, you will have found a root-cause solution for 90 percent of daily quality issues. The next 10 percent of quality problems get progressively harder to solve.)

As simple and powerful as this is, most people almost never do it. I have spent much of my career trying to get organizations to use this practice on a daily basis, but by my estimates, the closest I ever got was about 15 percent compliance. This makes for an interesting cultural dilemma: We have, by far, the most efficient quality problem-solving tool and the easiest to learn, but it is very difficult to get people to practice it. This characteristic of the implementation of Five Whys is typical of many aspects of Lean. It is easy to understand the Five Whys (and similar Lean tools), but quite difficult to build them into daily behavior.

TQM's Seven Basic Tools

The next step is typically to apply what is known in TQM as the *seven basic tools*. These are the following seven simple quality tools:

1. Cause-and-effect diagrams (fishbone diagrams)
2. Flow charts (process flow diagrams)
3. Pareto charts
4. Run charts
5. Histograms
6. Scatter diagrams
7. Control charts

These tools may get you to the next 6, 7, or 8 percent of quality problems after asking the Five Whys. One lesson I've learned is to use the simplest tool to solve a given problem and escalate to a more complex tool only if the simpler tool is insufficient. As the problem gets more difficult, you find that these tools run out of juice, however, and for the last percent or two of quality problems, you will find that you actually need very advanced tools like Taguchi design of experiments (DOE) to address a problem with many potential causes that are operating simultaneously.

The good news is that if you use efficient tools first, you will solve most of your everyday problems at a root-cause level, so you will never see them again, and this gives you and your team the opportunity to work only on the few really hard quality issues. I use the word *hard* with a specific thought. I don't mean "expensive." You could, hypothetically, reduce costs by solving big quality problems with big cost impacts—in fact, many early Six Sigma efforts focused only on solving problems with a cost impact of over $250,000. That is a good way to reduce costs, but given that 99-plus percent of quality problems have a cost impact far under that threshold, most of your quality problems remain unresolved. To become Toyota-like, you can't leave any problems behind, even if you think they don't have a big cost impact. You need to organize to solve these as well.

Poka-Yoke

Toyota also includes a number of quality tools that are unique to its approach. One of these is *poka-yoke,* or mistake proofing. This is an approach to redesigning individual process steps so that no step can be done incorrectly. Poka-yoke actually designs out even the *possibility* of making a mistake, taking that possibility completely out of a process. A simple poka-yoke example may be found on your car, where the fuel fill opening is intentionally designed to allow only the smaller unleaded fuel nozzle to fit into it. This prevents making the mistake of putting the larger diesel nozzle into it, thus the defect will never occur. Figure A.4 demonstrates a few more examples of this concept. Poka-yoke needs to be part of your total transformation, but it is not often where you start on quality gains.

Note that if you've done some poka-yoke in your facility, there may be more you can still do. At HON/HNI, we had been working on and meeting a 20 percent annual quality improvement goal. For about four years, the simple stuff worked. But then our gains started to flatten. At that point, we used the motivation of missing our quality improvement goal to drive us to dig into the Toyota tool kit and evaluate how we were using the tools. It turned out that we had introduced many poka-yoke devices—every site could show one or two. So everyone talked about it as if they really understood it, and everyone thought that we had "done the poka-yoke thing." But when we looked at the number of processes that had experienced a quality error in the past year, we found that 99 percent had *not* been poka-yoked. That gave us a focus for that year. Just expanding the use of this tool across the organization (sometimes referred to as *horizontal spread*) got us that year's quality gain. The leadership lesson is that when folks start talking Lean talk, it is good to look closely at how widespread the particular practice is—often what you have is just a sample of use, not a broad application.

The ultimate poka-yoke is a product design poka-yoke. If you can get your engineers to design individual parts and components so that they *cannot* be manufactured or assembled incorrectly at the outset, you will not need to determine later (at higher cost) how to design the process poka-yokes.

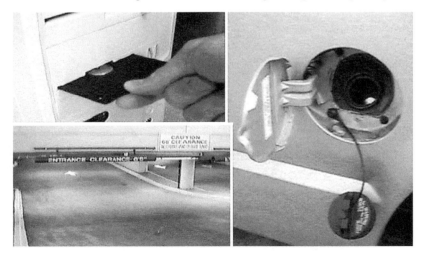

FIGURE A.4
Poka-yoke examples.

Andons

Another Toyota practice is the use of andons. In Japanese, an *andon* is a lantern or light. The idea is to trigger a signal when there is a potential quality issue. In a Toyota work area, you find andon cords that any team member is allowed to pull. Pulling the cord sets off a light that is visible throughout the work area. In most cases, the andons use a yellow light to signal, "I think I am running into a problem" and a red light to signal, "I have a problem for sure, and I have to stop the work because I am not to pass on a bad piece of work." Typically, the andon light also has a musical accompaniment that makes it easy for team leaders to notice that there is a problem.

There is a dynamic tension in this practice—the team member has an absolute requirement to pull the cord if there is an issue. At the same time, the team leader has an absolute requirement to initiate a root-cause problem-solving effort to ensure that the cord is never pulled again for that specific problem. Thus, the andon is not only a way to prevent defective work, but also a way to drive problem solving.

Toyota's practice is to keep track of the number of andon pulls per shift. If team members solve enough problems that the number of pulls goes down, Toyota will typically speed up the line a bit, as a way of uncovering the next layer of waste. Like many Toyota practices that have several dimensions to them, one level of understanding of andons is that they are there to keep associates from forwarding defective work. But at another level, andons are a dynamic stress problem-solving tool, and at a third level, they are a way of making the next level of waste visible by allowing the line to speed up. Specific examples of andons, such as those found in Figure A.5, portray other methods used for various types of process abnormalities. These range from a simple five-tier light to more advanced electronic designs.

Quality Checks

In our sixth year of transformation at HNI/HON, we again began to run into difficulty driving our quality improvement goal at the 20 percent pace. At this time, we adopted a Toyota practice outlined by Shigeo Shingo that he referred to as *self checks* and *successive checks*. The idea with these two quality checks is to have each team member do checks on critical aspects of their own work before moving the product to the next team member, and also do a few critical checks of the work that comes to them from a prior team member. Figure A.6 shows an example of workstations

FIGURE A.5
Andon and electronic control boards.

FIGURE A.6
Workstations and visual quality check boards.

with specific quality-check requirements, clearly identified and very visible. This approach helps with the very human possibility that someone gets a bit lazy and does not follow their standard work (see the section "Standard Work: The Tool That Focuses on Cost and Productivity" later in this appendix).

In the next year of our journey at HNI/HON, we found that we really had to do design poka-yoke to take us to the next level. We concluded that the most mistake-proof of the mistake-proof mechanisms were those that were designed into the product. So we initiated a monthly quality review on every product line and then drove to make changes in product design that would not allow this mistake to be possible. The engineers were not excited about doing this, as they thought they were done with the designs. But we found that once we focused on design changes to achieve mistake-proofing, over 80 percent of our quality issues could be designed out, and this focus led to several more years of achieving our quality improvement goals.

TOOLS THAT FOCUS ON FLOW AND LEAD TIME

In most of the businesses that I have been involved with, I found that we underestimated the value of faster lead times to our customers. Most Lean implementations focus on flow as a way to take inventory values down, but the really big gains come from pushing your growth rate up two to four times through shortening your lead times by 75 percent on all customer-interfacing processes/products.

If you look back at the history of major changes in manufacturing, the Ford assembly line system was a really big one. Taiichi Ohno, who was most responsible for creating the Toyota Production System, often said that he learned most of what he needed to know to build the Toyota System from Ford. There was an element of modesty in this, but also an element of truth, because Ford had built a system that could build a car—from iron ore to dealer—in three days. That was good flow. Of course, we have all heard the story about its limits on variety: "Any color as long as it's black."

Set-Up Times

A core contribution of Toyota and Shigeo Shingo was the idea of reducing set-up time. Most machines (and many intellectual processes as well) have a set-up time—a time during which the work area is made ready for a different product or service. This set-up time is the primary cause of batches in production; in administration, departments function like physically separate silos that connect only through a mailroom, thus creating batches of information flow. An early discovery was that set-up times, which were thought to be fixed amounts of time for a given machine, were not fixed at all. They could actually be reduced.

Over time, Shigeo Shingo studied set-up times and found that they could be reduced on any type of equipment. He developed a standard practice (often referred to as SMED—for single-minute exchange of die, a die being a crucial part of presses that were common at Toyota) to reduce set-up times. When redesigning the HON/HNI office furniture business around shorter lead times, we used this approach to reduce set-up times enough to allow smaller batch sizes and, in turn, faster flow. We found that every time you study a setup, on average, you can reduce it by 50 percent or more. That's right. If you come back a month later, you will find new waste and new areas of improvement and be able, with study, to reduce it by 50 percent or more again. Using this knowledge, we established a program to reduce every machine setup by 50 percent each year for five years in a row. And at the end of each year, we cut our batch size or lead time in half. After five years of this, we had reduced set-up times by about 95 percent and had also reduced internal lead times by 95 percent (we moved from monthly buckets of product to daily ones). We started with a one-month cycle time, the next year it was two weeks, the next year it was one week, the next year it was two-and-a-half days, and the next year it was one day.

Kanban

Another flow tool is *kanban*. Most folks are generally familiar with the idea of using kanban cards to control movement. There are a few leadership issues to consider. Setting up a kanban will not directly increase productivity, and kanbans must be maintained—so don't set up a kanban system until you have looked to see whether you can just link the processes without cards. Figure A.7 shows an example of a pharmacy kanban (pull system) for medications that are depleted and need to be replaced before the next anticipated demand for that item occurs.

Kanbans usually are necessary when you have a monumental piece of equipment through which many product lines flow. You need to set up a kanban to control the flow through the monument. But always keep in mind that kanbans are a form of waste in themselves—they do not directly add value (some folks have set up all kinds of kanbans, and then wondered why they did not become more productive), and they are a continuing cost to maintain. In the long term, the goal is to begin to design and build, or purchase, small-scale pieces of equipment that can support individual

FIGURE A.7
Kanban cards used in a pharmacy.

product-line flows, rather than having these monumental pieces of equipment. Equipment builders have a very hard time with this basic idea—it is deeply ingrained in them that if a machine of X size is good, one of 2X capacity will be, say, only 50 percent more expensive, and is thus a bargain. Of course they miss the cost of all the work our organizations have to do every day to take flows of various products (different volumes) and shove them through one machine/system. You often find that you cannot get a machine builder to grasp the idea of small-sized machines, which is why, when you get down to the most basic and smallest machine you need, it is easier to design and build it in-house (see Figure A.8). When you get to this point, you may run into a less well-known Lean tool: 3P.

3P

3P (production preparation process) is a tool that helps you invent new processes or designs, and also helps you ensure that a machine design fits with Lean system characteristics. The guiding principle of 3P is that every mechanism already exists in nature. True 3P, with its emphasis on using examples from nature to find new processes and designs, is so different that most organizations need several years of Lean before they start the 3P process.

However, the leadership learnings about 3P are rather interesting. After a couple of years of Lean at HON/HNI, we started to use 3P to design

FIGURE A.8
3P: from idea to correct size.

small-scale machines that fit with Lean practices. We also used it to invent new process technologies. The 3P process works in product development as well, but we had much less experience with it there. We eventually ramped up to where we were running fifteen 3P machine design events every quarter, and had five machine design and build departments building those designs. The general rule of thumb for leadership is that with 3P, you can normally get a given increment of capacity at one-quarter the capital cost of traditional approaches, and you can normally achieve a fourfold productivity gain. Note that I am reluctant to point out the sorts of gains you can get with 3P, as it will probably encourage some to try to do this before they are far enough along the Lean journey to have the principles of 3P make sense to them. But for experienced Lean firms, 3P is like a second wave of Lean. The first wave for manufacturing is to improve the system that was designed around batch- or Ford-flow concepts. Then, when you have developed a deeper understanding of your flows and of Lean practices, you can begin to reinvent every piece of process equipment you have and create a Lean production process from the beginning. As you can imagine, this is a very long journey, as you will not redesign and rebuild your whole manufacturing base in a couple of years. But with the faster growth that comes with Lean, you will get to the point where you want to do this sooner than you may have thought. And if you go this route, you can build process technology advantages that your competitors cannot match.

2P

The concept of 2P (process preparation) is related to flow principles, but without utilizing the ideas taken from nature that are found in 3P. The concept of 2P is an easier one to grasp than 3P, and consequently can be used earlier in your Lean journey. 2P is often used to design flow into the layout of a value stream. For instance, the ThedaCare Hospital Group used 2P to design flow into their in-patient process, as shown in Figure A.9 and Figure A.10.

FIGURE A.9
2P: ThedaCare collaborative care work area.

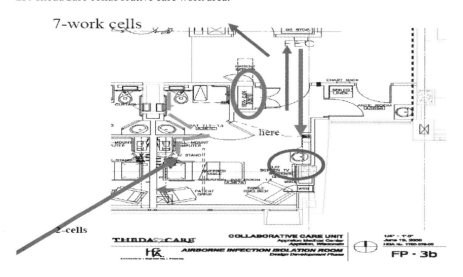

FIGURE A.10
2P: ThedaCare collaborative care layout.

STANDARD WORK: THE TOOL THAT FOCUSES ON COST AND PRODUCTIVITY

As you would guess, tools that improve quality and flow also tend to improve productivity and cost. But there is a key tool that is the primary source of productivity gains—both for administrative and production processes. In some ways it is the most powerful and widespread tool in the Lean tool kit: It is called standard work (not to be confused with work standards). *Standard work* incorporates a Toyota view of the industrial engineering of work with a Toyota view of flow. It also puts a strong focus on the value-adding steps at the work-process level. With standard work, you start with the *takt time,* the rhythm of output of the work process: how often you need a product to come out of the process to meet customer demand, or how often you need an output of information to meet customer demand. The concept of takt time is the truly unique one, as it redesigns the process around customer needs—whether it is a manufacturing, service, or administrative process.

Then you list every step in the process and take a quick time estimate of the human work content to achieve that step. While engaging in this process, there is a constant cycle of asking yourself:

- Is this truly a value-adding step?
- Do I really need this step?
- If a customer saw me doing this work step, would he or she be willing to pay me to do it?
- How do I ensure quality and safety in this step?

Answering these four questions for every small process step will improve the process. After the work in the process is both improved and documented, the manpower is applied to the process. Starting at the end of the process, you assign each person in the process a full day's work, based on the takt time and the work content.

One of the unique aspects of Toyota's way of looking at work is that you do not want to *balance work* (see Figure A.11). Balancing hides waste and makes it harder to remove. You want to assign each person a full day's work, and leave the last person with partial work (see Figure A.12). One aspect of this is that you are fully utilizing all the human resources in the process, except this last person. And a second aspect is that this person has spare time in his or

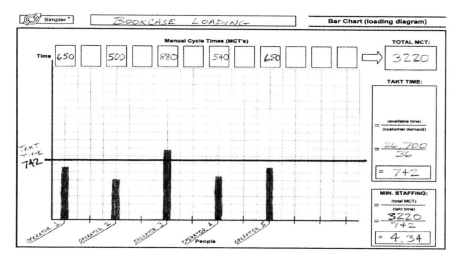

FIGURE A.11
Bar chart showing poor daily workload per operator.

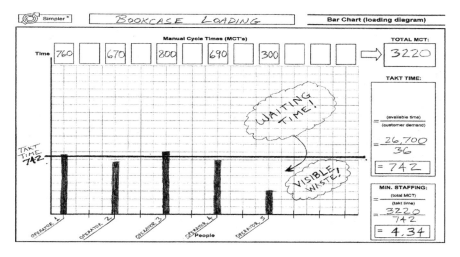

FIGURE A.12
Bar chart showing good daily workload per operator.

her day—the goal is then not to fill this time but to improve the work process further so that you can free up this person completely. This partial work concept is another way that Toyota helps to make the waste visible. Figure A.13 shows the improvement impact after a kaizen event has been done.

The outcome of the review is a revised work practice documented in standard work combination sheets. These are posted at the actual place where the

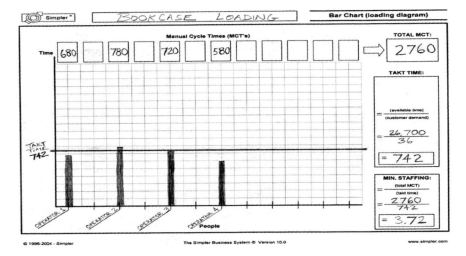

FIGURE A.13

Bar chart showing daily workload per operator after kaizen.

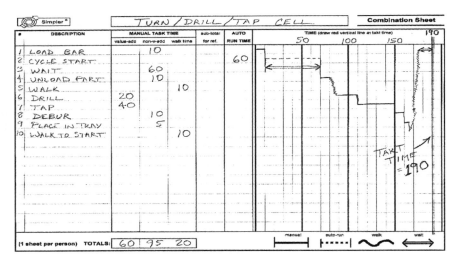

FIGURE A.14

Standard work combination sheet.

work is done. Figure A.14 illustrates exactly how much time it should take for each operational step or task in the process. These sheets are another tool for seeing waste quickly by observing normal versus abnormal conditions.

When Toyota senior leaders do site visits, one thing that is always reviewed is the standard work practice. Senior leaders look to see whether the standard work combination sheets are posted at each workstation.

They then sample a few workstations to observe whether the member is following the standard work exactly as detailed. If the work is being followed exactly, senior leaders then check the dates on the standard work combination sheets. If the sheet has not been changed in a long time, there is cause for a discussion about improvement in the work area, because if there had been any improvement since that date, the team leader would have had to update the standard work combination sheet.

Standard work may seem like a simple and mundane tool, but it is *the* key tool to finding and removing waste in any process—administrative, service, or production. Many people who have applied Lean tools have never learned standard work, yet it is the foundation stone. Typically, a standard work analysis, often done during a Lean improvement event week, will result in a 40 percent productivity increase. There will also be improvements to quality and safety/work conditions. And what you typically find is that every time you restudy an area with standard work, it opens your eyes to the next level of waste, and you will find another 40 percent productivity improvement.

At HON/HNI, in our fourth year of Lean transformation, we checked the standard work events of the prior two years. In that time, we had run 491 standard work improvement events (the weeklong, focused variety), and found that, on average, we had achieved a 45 percent productivity gain each time we studied an area. Many of these standard work events were the second or third pass at the area, and each generated about the same average productivity gain. We also evaluated the administrative standard work events that we had conducted, and the average administrative standard work event resulted in an 80 percent productivity gain.

Typically, I expect that real productivity gains will pay for all Lean transformation costs within 90 to 120 days. (It should never take more than 120 days for a total return of your members' time, your *sensei*'s [mentor's] time, and your physical redesign costs. If your improvement events are not paying back this fast on productivity, you need to reevaluate the quality of your events and follow up.) Standard work is the primary driver of those productivity gains.

Once an organization has learned how powerful standard work can be, there is a tendency for managers to do only standard work events. When you do this, you get a large productivity surge, but after a while the surge starts to falter because you haven't improved your quality or your flow. These quality issues then start to disrupt your process, and material or information flow begins to disrupt your process, too. As a crude average, you want to run about one-third of your improvement events as standard work events, and about two-thirds as events focused on improving process quality, improving human development, and building flow (things like establishing kanban around a monument or conducting a set-up reduction event).

The importance of standard work was driven home to me in the mid-1990s by a visit to Toyota's Georgetown, Kentucky, operations. My principal sensei, Yoshiki Iwata, had also been an important sensei early on to Fujio Cho, who was then president of TMMC (Toyota Motor Manufacturing Corporation; now chairman of Toyota worldwide). Iwata invited me to visit Cho in Georgetown, which had been in operation for about fifteen years. By this time, I had been a casual student of Lean for about twenty years and a serious practitioner for about ten years. I had, by that time, learned many of the tools and concepts of Lean, but I was looking for the next breakthrough concept or tool that could take my organization to a higher level of Lean performance.

I decided to ask Cho what was going to be his focus of improvement for the next year in Toyota's operations. I was sure that, at Toyota's level of experience and sophistication, this focus would be something revolutionary to me. But when I asked Cho this question, his answer was simple: standard work. His point was that there was still much waste in all of their work and that a reemphasis on standard work would allow Toyota to identify and remove this waste.

TOOLS FOCUSED ON HUMAN DEVELOPMENT

Human development is the cornerstone of the Lean enterprise. The new knowledge you build into your team members becomes your largest off-balance-sheet asset. There is a lot of loose talk in most firms about how important people are, but in a Lean firm, this is really true. The key to success for a Lean transformation is the continuous restudy and redesign of processes in all kinds of work, and this work is done by your own team members. They will need a sensei to guide their learning for a long time, because there is a lot more to learn than most people could imagine, but the real work of Lean process improvement will be the work by your team members. And out of this work, they will not only improve your processes, but also build the knowledge of how to do it. This knowledge becomes your greatest resource as an organization.

Event Participation

Although it is more of a practice than a tool, the use of teams with cross-functional groups of members from your own organization is a key building block of human development. It is through this experience that your team members will learn how to work in a team fashion, but they will also learn the tools, practices, principles, and leadership habits that create a massive human resource asset.

5S (or 6S)

Normally, the first tool used in either an administration or production setting is a deceptively simple tool referred to as 5S or 6S (where the sixth S is for safety). It is deceptive because the S's in Japanese are the basic steps in good housekeeping. They are:

- *Seiri* (**sort**): Eliminating everything not required for the work being performed
- *Seiton* (**separate**): Efficiently placing and arranging equipment and material
- *Seison* (**shine**): Tidying and cleaning
- *Seiketsu* (**standardize**): Standardizing and continually improving the previous three (seiri, seiton, and seison)
- *Shitsuke* (**sustain**): Establishing discipline in sustaining workplace organization
- **Safety:** Creating a safe work environment

5S/6S seems too simple to most managers, but it turns out it is a foundation stone for Lean. The impact of a 5S/6S effort is obvious to all in the work area. It gets things arranged and organized. And being organized makes the workplace more productive. 5S/6S also makes the workplace cleaner, safer, and less frustrating. These benefits are visible to all and begin to create buy-in for the Lean journey to come. In addition, the daily practice of cleaning and organizing your work area takes discipline, and the benefits of this discipline are easy to see, so it is easier to buy into this new work practice, thus getting your Lean effort off on the right foot. Given that a Lean system is much, much, much more disciplined than either a batch- or Ford-flow system, establishing this new sense of discipline is one of the core building blocks of Lean. As a leader, you do not want to underestimate how hard it is to get team members who have been doing free-form work to follow a disciplined and standard process.

With Lean, you always follow the standard work. You also periodically do a kaizen and test a new way; if it works, you adopt it. You always run to each successive standard work practice. This concept is a completely new way of working for most team members. So even though it seems simple, 5S/6S should be your first step; it will earn its way in short-term productivity gains and build a foundation of buy-in and work discipline that will pay off for years to come.

After getting geared, we also found that we typically got a 15 percent average productivity gain from an area that had been 5S/6S-ed. Figure A.15 shows an area that has a high standard of 5S/6S practice in place. At a glance, you can quickly identify anything that is out of place or missing.

Ergonomic Kaizen

There is also a tool that helps you redesign the workplace to fit with ergonomic principles. Often called *ergo kaizen,* this is another tool that builds buy-in and at the same time generates enough productivity to pay its way. Typically, after an area has gone through a 5S/6S effort, an ergo kaizen study will yield another 15 percent productivity gain. And, of course, it will lower workers' compensation costs and improve morale. In fact, as we acquired firms, we made the start-up of a safety program and ergo kaizen the first

FIGURE A.15
5S/6S: everything in its place.

step of Lean integration. Once the newly acquired team members saw how serious we were about safety, everything else went much more smoothly.

Teian System

There is also a uniquely designed suggestion system that fits with Lean. The *Teian system* emphasizes developing buy-in to the idea of improvement and developing human problem-solving skills, rather than emphasizing cost savings. In fact, a Toyota operation would typically not put any focus on the savings from a suggestion system for at least three years. The first three years would be focused on building participation (with the idea that if you participate, you will develop a more positive attitude toward any kind of improvement and also develop problem-solving/improvement skills that will be of value). For the first two of those years, the focus is usually on getting a higher percent of the workforce to participate—95 percent being a good second-year target. Then the third year focuses more on increasing the number of implemented suggestions from the average team member. The world-class benchmark (the optimum from Toyota experience) is around 24 implemented suggestions per team member per year; they may focus on safety, quality, productivity, or flow.

Keep in mind that this is not a suggestion system but an implemented suggestion system. There is support for team members or small groups of team members to implement their own suggestions; at the same time there is no credit for entering suggestions—only for improvements that are actually implemented.

Involvement is the key. Involvement will lead to changes in attitude as well as the motivation to improve and to build new skills. Involvement is the goal of the Teian system.

TOOLS FOCUSED PRIMARILY ON NEW PRODUCT DEVELOPMENT

It turns out that the tools and concepts covered in the rest of this appendix can all be applied to aspects of product development. However, Lean product development also involves a whole additional set of concepts, tools, and practices. This section gives you a sampling of the most effective tools. There are other tools in the Lean product-development tool kit, such as modular design, variety reduction, product clinics, etc. See Appendix F for an overview of Simpler's New Product Design System.

Early Decisions

One key concept is that of making early decisions. Most companies organize product development projects in a sequential fashion, but then find that late in the project, the team has to start over, because members did not agree on key decisions early on. At Toyota, there are "toll gates" at which the project is not allowed to move ahead unless key decisions are made.

Forced Innovation (or Set-Based Concurrent Product Development)

Another concept is *forced innovation* in each development project; this is also called set-based concurrent product development. The idea is to ensure that innovation occurs, and at the same time ensure that the product goes to market on schedule. Normal product development often misses the target date to market because of rework loops in the process of development (part of what the toll gate process in the preceding section addresses), and also because of efforts to come up with an innovation that then throws the project behind schedule. The Toyota practice includes a defined time, very early in the development project, at which there is a resource allocation to push improvement to basic concepts in the design. Typically, three alternative designs will go through an intensive development and test effort in a constrained time frame.

The first alternative will typically be a basic design, with only some modest design improvements. This is a design that can be implemented, for sure, within current project constraints for time, cost, quality, and functionality. A second, more advanced design alternative with potentially more benefit will be pushed through a rapid period of experimentation at the same time. And a third, very advanced design alternative that is rather far out will also be pushed through a series of rapid hands-on experiments. If a very advanced design (the third alternative) makes rapid progress and can be turned into a proven concept in the short, constrained time period, it will become the alternative choice for this development project. More often than not, however, this will *not* be the case. If this very advanced design is a bust, it is documented (on an A3) for learning, and will then be dropped. If the advanced design (second alternative) shows significant promise but cannot be ready for introduction after this short period of innovation, it is put into a further development cycle and developed to the point where it is a proven design ready for production during the *next* development program. The result is significant innovation, but no delayed product introductions.

Voice of the Customer (VOC)/Quality Function Deployment (QFD)

Another tool used in product development is the voice of the customer (VOC) process. Usually this is organized into a quality function deployment (QFD) house of quality. (QFD is a systematic method for translating true customer needs into product and service requirements.) The emphasis on understanding the true voice of the customer is the foundation for a good product development effort. The use of QFD organizes VOC data so that it is deployed into design specifications, into process choices, and into after-sale service support.

For most firms, the use of a good VOC process and QFD can make a huge positive impact on development efforts. Most development efforts are run by engineers who know the technology but are usually not allowed to learn much about customers. So we end up with technology solutions to problems that customers don't have. For the typical firm, just getting product development targeted at true customer needs is a huge step ahead that usually involves getting key development engineers to personally visit customers, with an organized approach to assessing their real needs in products and service. When developing key vehicles like the Lexus cars or the Sienna minivan, key Toyota engineers traveled around the country to see how target customers used similar vehicles; they even moved in with target customer families to better understand how they thought about their cars. The point is that you need the folks who know what is technically possible to get into direct touch with the folks who have the needs.

At Jake Brake, back in the early days of my Lean journey, we would gather our VOC knowledge, then put together a very broad group of our best and brightest from sales, marketing, design, and production. We would lock them together for a minimum of a week—and sometimes more—and require that they take the VOC and do a paper exercise of deploying it through the whole QFD process. This broad group would be open to lots of alternatives about how to meet the VOC. And by requiring them to go through the whole QFD process before the start of the project, we were able to get most of the early decisions made. After this QFD effort, we would then do a more detailed effort by the assigned project team. But the first one was a real brainstorming effort.

The key is that most companies have huge inefficiencies in development programs, most often because of not targeting the true VOC. We have to force ourselves to spend the time up front, where we can have an impact on project results without much impact on project cost and time. Think of it this way: The management time spent reviewing development projects tends to escalate as it gets close to introduction (by then it is mostly creating more non-value-added work), but at the beginning of the project, when significant impact on decisions at low cost in time and dollars is available, there is almost no management time spent.

Kano Analysis

Lean always works best as a growth strategy, and one of the best ways to foster growth is to apply a *kano* analysis to your product development efforts. The kano analysis tool looks at the typical product strategy of meeting VOC product-based definitions, and compares it with a product development growth strategy of delighting customers by fulfilling unspoken needs or wants (see Figure A.16). Given that Lean typically creates some productivity and margin improvements, it is normally appropriate

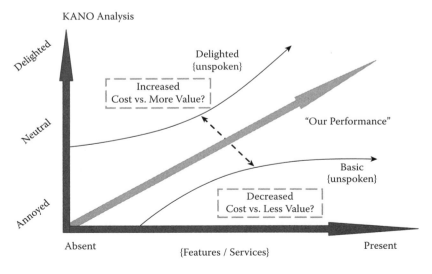

FIGURE A.16
Kano analysis.

to begin to refocus product development efforts toward delighting customers (that is, meeting those unspoken needs/wants). And successful VOC efforts are often able to identify these unspoken needs/wants.

Obeya

One other key tool is *obeya*. This is another typical low-tech Toyota practice. The word *obeya* stands for "big room," and the practice involves the key cross-functional team members all working in the same large room while on a project. (Toyota has found that computer interfaces are not a good substitute for this person-to-person interface.) The value is face-to-face communication throughout the development process, especially among functions that often do not talk to one another.

My experience is that communication decreases at the square of the distance that two people are apart (the science behind this was not great, but conceptually it is correct), and in product development, you want to encourage high levels of communication. I've gone so far as to arrange the folks who had the most interfunctional communication difficulty—product engineers and process engineers—with their desks facing each other. Simple but powerful. This concept is known as the *obeya* or the *big room* (see Figure A.17).

Your biggest impacts will come from truly understanding the needs (spoken or unspoken) of customers, connecting the knowledge of what is

FIGURE A.17
Obeya room: face-to-face communication.

technically possible with those needs, and then deploying this knowledge into design specifications, process specifications, and service design—at the very front end of the process of development. This is where senior leadership should spend its time.

SUMMARY

I have not covered all the tools and concepts in the Lean tool kit, and the ones I do cover I have not explained enough for you to actually be able to apply them. But you should now have a better idea of the range of Lean tools and some useful rules about the application of these tools.

Appendix B: Building a Sustainable Lean Culture— The Watlow Way

Peter Desloge
CEO and grandson of the founder of the Watlow Company

The more I know the less I understand.

Lao Tse

When George Koenigsaecker contacted me and requested that I write an appendix for his book, I was initially hesitant. Although I am pleased with the results of our five-and-a-half-year-old Lean transformation, I realize our journey is still in its infancy. It felt presumptuous to believe that our experience would be of interest to anyone but ourselves. Yet, in an effort to give back to the community of Lean practitioners who supported our journey (and after further arm-twisting by George), I agreed.

What follows is a brief account of our Lean journey, with particular emphasis on our work to build a sustainable Lean culture. My definition of a sustainable culture is one that will survive when I step down as CEO.

Although our Lean journey started formally five and a half years ago, the seeds for the journey were planted by my father and uncle, George and Louis Desloge Jr. They both instilled in Watlow a spirit of humility and an unquenchable desire to be the best. These values, which are still strong at Watlow 20 years after their retirement, are the fuel that drives our journey.

BACKGROUND

Watlow is a privately held, family-owned business with headquarters in St. Louis, Missouri. We were founded in 1922 by my grandfather, Louis

Desloge. Today, Watlow has over 120 shareholders from the second, third, and fourth generations.

Our company designs and manufactures thermal products and systems in ten global locations. Additionally, we have 43 sales offices in 14 countries, which provide a network of sales engineers, account managers, and technical support specialists around the world.

Our products include electric heaters, sensors, and temperature controls. We are known for our ability to create innovative system solutions to solve thermal problems. Figure B.1 will give you a sense of the product mix offered by Watlow.

Although the company is privately held, family shareholders have endorsed a board of directors that includes family members as well as outside directors. The outside directors have been CEOs at major businesses and have considerable executive leadership experience. They bring the expectations and discipline required of public-sector businesses as a balance to the family shareholders' desire to preserve the legacy and "uniqueness" of Watlow as a family-owned company. The insight and guidance of the board has been clear and consistent to the executive leadership team responsible for charting a course for the future of the business.

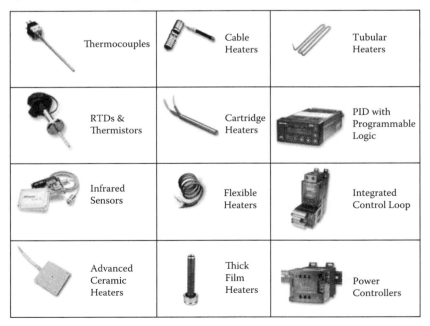

FIGURE B.1
Array of Watlow products.

STARTING OUR LEAN TRANSFORMATION

Throughout the last 40 years we have implemented several different continuous-improvement programs at Watlow, including total quality management systems (TQMS), quality circles, and Six Sigma. Each of these provided some benefit, but none of them stuck. After many years of attempting to implement the latest trend in improvement initiatives, our culture had a fairly distinct "Book of the Month Club" flavor to it and, frankly, employees were skeptical that we would commit to a long-term course of action and make it stick.

In mid-2004, after our second TQMS initiative faltered, the senior leadership team spent time reflecting on previous improvement initiatives, as well as time visiting companies with successful improvement programs. The learning from this, and George Koenigsaecker's encouragement, led us to the decision to begin a Toyota-like Lean transformation.

In early 2005, Watlow launched a rapid Lean rollout across seven plants with an aggressive year-end goal of conducting 150 weeklong kaizen events and assigning 60 people company-wide to full-time Lean improvement. This blitz approach, which emphasized getting as many leaders into as many events as quickly as possible, differed from previous initiatives and provided important learning. It generated a lot of excitement, and we produced significant improvements in safety, quality, and delivery early on in the process.

Watlow Insight

It's easier to act yourself into a new way of thinking than to think yourself into a new way of acting.

George Koenigsaecker

After several ineffective attempts to change culture through training and new system development, we found much greater success by quickly engaging people in Rapid Improvement Events. These events were light on classroom training and heavy on "learning by doing." The participants in these events quickly saw the power of Lean and became believers and advocates.

By 2006, the excitement had begun to fade, along with results. Upon deeper reflection, we realized that just conducting kaizen events was not enough. On the surface, Watlow had begun to speak the Lean language,

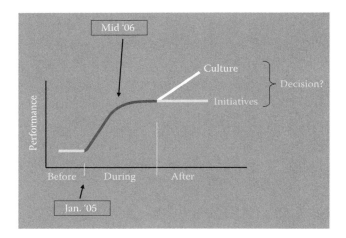

FIGURE B.2
Watlow decision—change culture or improvement stalls.

yet inside we were stuck in our old mind-set and behaviors. It was evident that we needed to describe and embrace this new culture more broadly or this initiative would stall, proving the "Book of the Month Club" members right (see Figure B.2).

In the past, senior management had tried to define Watlow's culture by creating value, vision, and mission statements that looked good on the wall, yet never took hold in the organization. We knew that to be successful this time, a completely new approach was needed. This new approach needed to create broad buy-in from our global population, as well as to define the critical values, principles, and behaviors required to ensure Watlow's continued Lean development.

With the help of Ed Constantine, the founder of Simpler Consulting, we developed an approach to bring together a cross-section of fifty Watlow team members from varying positions, backgrounds, and geographic regions as a representative sample of our population. The team would meet two days each month for as many months as necessary. Their charter was threefold:

1. To study and reflect on our past, in order to understand who we were and learn from previous efforts to change culture
2. To develop a cultural future state
3. To create a plan to begin to build this culture

Although my executive team was supportive, there was significant concern. The whole project felt pretty loose without a clear time frame, process, or tangible deliverable. Even more concerning was the feeling that we were letting go of the steering wheel and handing it over to this group of fifty. As CEO, I maintained ultimate authorship of the outcome, yet I knew that if I wielded too heavy a pen, I risked shutting down the process. For me, this was one of those times that occur in every leader's life, when you know you need to go forward without looking back regardless of your internal doubt. We pressed forward.

The team of fifty met monthly for six months. Between sessions, the participants shared the learnings from the previous session with their coworkers and gathered input for the following meeting. Somewhat by accident, we also took advantage of the most robust communication tool that existed in our organization, which was the rumor mill. As the meetings progressed, enthusiasm grew as everyone realized Watlow's commitment to the process and understood their ability to influence outcomes.

Although I led the process, I had Ed Constantine's help as a facilitator. The primary tool we used to organize our work was the A3, which is a problem-solving and communication tool commonly used by other Lean organizations. The A3 was new to us at the time. Today, the A3 is deeply integrated into the fabric of our emerging culture, and it is much more than a tool—it is a way of thinking, leading, and working together.

Near the end of the six-month project, as enthusiasm for our work peaked, the organizational pull for the completed A3 became powerful. The core team was so eager to share their work that I had a hard time ensuring that the documents being spread were the most current revisions. At that point, I could see our work going viral. I also realized that my original fear of turning our future-state definition over to a somewhat randomly selected group of fifty was unfounded. In fact, the outcome was far greater than I could have created with my small team of "expert" senior leaders. I gained a key insight from this experience regarding the role of a Lean leader.

Watlow Insight: The Power of the Team

I used to believe that, as CEO, I needed to control all major decisions. I realized through this process that a team of reasonable people with the right information, time, and resources will almost always develop a better solution than an individual will. And, when it is time to implement, the team with buy-in will move much faster. I began to see my role as CEO shifting.

THE WATLOW WAY

The outcome of the six-month project was the A3 shown in Figure B.3, which has come to be known as the Watlow Way. Given the quantity of content in this A3, I will not try to review all of it with you. Instead, I will note a few highlights.

In Box 1, Reasons for Action (Figure B.4), we knew that we were not getting the results we expected and our behaviors did not reflect those of a Lean organization.

Box 2, Current State (Figure B.5), created a very clear picture for all of us describing where we were as an organization when we held the event. Team members felt stressed because our Lean activity added emergent work to everyone's plate and, at the same time, it was not clear where this Lean work was going. We all felt like we were trying to cross a chasm, going from an old mind-set to a Lean mind-set, and yet it was not very clear how to get there. These descriptions of old behaviors and Lean behaviors still resonate with all of us today.

Box 3, our Future State (Figure B.6), was defined by five concepts that we wanted to integrate into our organization:

1. Better market focus and alignment
2. Broad use of a scientific approach to identify and solve problems
3. Widespread use of the "andon" concept (see Appendix A) to identify opportunities
4. Ensuring that the primary role of a leader is to coach and support
5. Implementing an improved, dispersed management system, which today is known as the Watlow Business System

We felt that if we were successful in implementing these concepts and changing behaviors, they would help us achieve our key breakthrough safety, quality, delivery, and cost goals.

Throughout our six-month project, we had several different discussions and debates about what was good Lean behavior at Watlow. We pulled all of these discussions together and put them in Box 9, Insights (Figure B.7). For us, this starts with our purpose, or Watlow's True North (see Chapter 3). To achieve this, we have four foundational values and five key principles. We believed that the acceptance and practice of these values and principles would result in these behaviors.

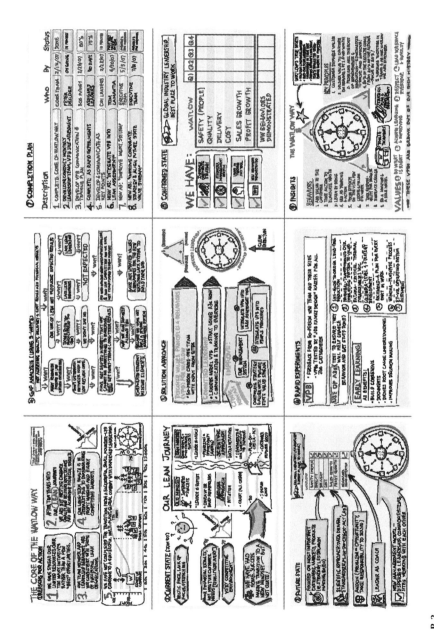

FIGURE B.3
The Watlow Way.

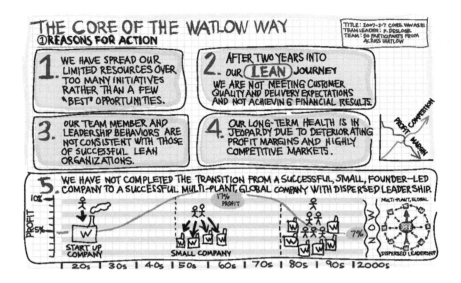

FIGURE B.4
Box 1: Reasons for action.

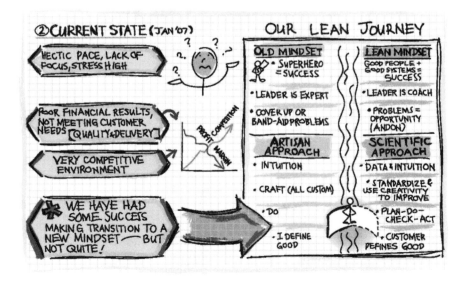

FIGURE B.5
Box 2: Current state.

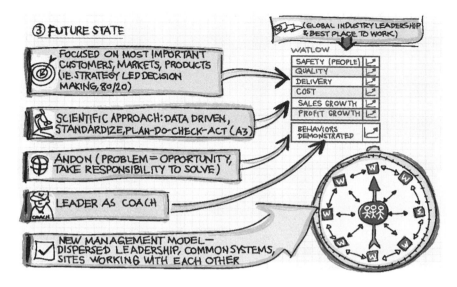

FIGURE B.6
Box 3: Future state.

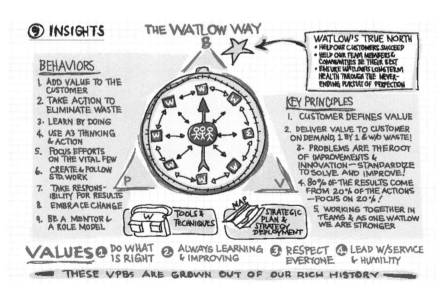

FIGURE B.7
Box 9: Insights.

These values, principles, and behaviors, along with our Lean tools and strategic plan, all act as a compass to help guide us toward our True North.

IMPLEMENTING THE WATLOW WAY: BUILDING BEHAVIORS

Watlow Way Launch

As our six-month A3 project came to a close, we discussed how we would roll out the Watlow Way. Our initial thought was to do what we had always done with a large new initiative. That would include printing posters, littering e-mail inboxes, creating pocket-sized laminated cards, etc. If you think in terms of the corporate version of a ticker-tape parade, you are directionally correct.

Upon further reflection, it occurred to us that the best approach would be to begin to model the behaviors we would soon be expecting of others. Instead of a top-down communication process, we gave site leaders the responsibility to develop their own roll-out process. My team's role would be to support the local team as they rolled out the Watlow Way.

In an effort to get my team personally engaged in the support effort, we all agreed to try something different. Instead of the normal PowerPoint presentation, I asked the members of my team to think deeply about Box 9, understand what the implications were for us as a team and as individuals, and then share those insights with others in the form of personal stories. We then divided up into teams of two and attended each site's roll-out day with our stories.

The stories were a big hit. Once the initial awkwardness wore off, the leaders started to have fun with it, and their passion and enthusiasm began to show to the local team members. The meetings began to have the feel of a college pep rally. At the end of the first round of meetings, the leaders in each location were asked to develop their own stories and cascade the messages to their teams.

By mid-2007, the Watlow Way values, principles, and behaviors began to show up in laminated cards, posters, and the signature box of people's e-mails. It was pretty clear that people were talking about the A3 and working through in their own minds what the implications were for them.

Watlow Insight: Timing and Pull

Several times, we tried to force change on the organization when the organization was not ready. These top-down initiatives either failed or achieved only marginal results. We have had much greater success exposing new ideas to smaller, cross-organizational teams and letting them develop and test the concepts. As these teams and concepts begin to take root, their peers see what is happening and are eager to get involved. Pull is created, and these new initiatives rapidly spread.

Practicing the Behaviors (Leadership Walking the Talk)

At Watlow, we believe strongly that leaders must model the behavior they expect in others. To promote this concept, I scheduled time at each of my executive team's monthly meetings to discuss how effectively we were living the Watlow Way (WW) and to rate how well we were practicing these values, principles, and behaviors on a scale of 1 to 10 scale (with 10 meaning "always demonstrates"). We posted the results of our quarterly self-assessment company-wide (see Figure B.8).

In 2007, as my team better understood what these behaviors really meant, our quarterly scores fell. The desired outcome of the discussion and assessment was to learn from one another, drive accountability, and communicate to the organization that the WW was important and leaders were holding themselves accountable to practice them. The organization took notice.

Along with our monthly assessment, each team member had a monthly WW communication goal, which was reviewed in their performance appraisal.

Integrating the Watlow Way into Our People Processes

As we launched the WW, it became immediately clear to us that most of the people-related processes in our organization did not fit well with the Watlow Way culture. Our recruitment and selection process, compensation system, performance management process, and other human-resources (HR) processes were based upon a different set of beliefs.

WW BEHAVIORS DEMONSTRATED	3.8	3.1	2.9	3.1

FIGURE B.8
2007 results of senior leadership's self-assessment (on a scale of 1 to 10).

It also became clear that, although we all believed we conceptually understood what the Watlow Way Behaviors meant, they were not granular enough to convey a common expectation of what "good" looked like. The effort to flesh out these behaviors into much finer detail and to build all of the people systems from scratch appeared daunting.

Just prior to the WW launch, in an effort to improve our hiring process, the HR team had been experimenting with a behavioral-based, targeted selection tool provided by Development Dimensions International (DDI). DDI has a robust set of off-the-shelf tools to support all HR processes, which are backed up with years of research in a variety of companies globally.

The HR team, fresh off a positive experience with DDI Targeted Selection, decided to use DDI as the platform for our HR processes. The challenge was how to link the WW values, principles, and behaviors to the right set of standard DDI dimensions. We held a Rapid Improvement Event (kaizen) that included our VP Business Operations, CFO, and VP of Human Resources, as well as a representative sample of leaders from various levels of the organization, to select these dimensions.

The outcome was the selection of ten DDI dimensions (the equivalent of behaviors) that mapped to our Watlow Way behaviors. We also identified six job families and showed which of the ten dimensions applied to each job family.

We next began to rebuild many of our people processes so they were congruent with the Watlow Way.

> **Communication**: We revised our intranet Web site to promote the Watlow Way, and every other week we asked a team leader to write a brief personal article about one of the values, principles, or behaviors. Also, to encourage members to view the site, we began some simple WW contests. Our monthly newsletter, the *Watlow World News*, was refreshed to reflect the WW.
>
> **Recognition**: We began a monthly recognition program where any member could submit another member's name to be recognized for demonstrating a WW behavior. From this pool, members were selected monthly for company-wide recognition.
>
> **Hiring**: We piloted DDI Targeted Selection methodology and created standardized interview questions and preferred answers for leadership roles. The process is behavior-based, which means that you look at a candidate's past behavior in order to predict future behavior. This process was later embraced company-wide.

Member development: We included WW training into our "development roadmap" and into our kaizen event standard work. We also recommitted to annual goals for member participation in kaizen events.

Leadership development: We established a formal leadership development program using some of the standard DDI tools and dimensions that we had previously mapped back to the WW behaviors. The development program lasted six months and used a "plan-do-check-act" closed-loop process, which included a 360° assessment, development plans, training, workshops, and ongoing feedback.

Performance management: We simplified our performance review process to include three WW questions (in addition to performance toward goals and personal development):

1. How did you exhibit the WW Behaviors?
2. How did you understand and use the WW Key Principles?
3. How did you live the WW Values?

Succession management: We established a process to develop and review succession plans for all level 1–3 positions company-wide. This process included an assessment of results and of WW behaviors.

WW site transformation plans: We established a process for all sites to develop and semi-annually refresh a WW site transformation plan designed to strengthen the WW culture at each site.

Mission control: We established a monthly visual "Mission Control" process for all value streams, sites, and the enterprise as a whole. At each Mission Control, the site transformation plan was reviewed and corrective actions were developed, if needed.

Use of A3s: The A3 tool was implemented broadly in order to promote plan-do-check-act thinking. Examples of its use included strategy deployment, personal development plans, problem solving, and weeklong kaizen events.

Watlow Insight: Power of A3 Thinking

We have now been using A3s with Plan-Do-Check-Act (PDCA) cycles in them for several years and have noticed a significant improvement in our decision making. We have developed a standard nine-question format and tools to help members develop A3s and to help leaders coach members developing A3s.

Three important A3 lessons for Watlow are:

1. Scope A3s so they can be completed in less than six months, to stress rapid learning cycles.
2. Encourage team-based A3s in order to encourage open collaboration.
3. A3s are a great tool to help people learn and develop, so how you coach the development of A3s is important.

ENGAGING THE HANDS, HEARTS, AND HEADS OF OUR MEMBERS

Our people processes were developed and used throughout 2007 and 2008. As it is with many new initiatives, when the Watlow Way was launched and the new processes were implemented, there was a lot of enthusiasm and acceptance. Unfortunately, by the end of 2008, with mediocre performance on goals, inconsistent cell performance, and a looming global recession, we decided to conduct a weeklong event to discover the root causes of our spotty success.

The event revealed that cell improvements were not being sustained, in part because we had insufficient levels of Lean expertise in cells, insufficient cell support resources, and cell members who were feeling that improvements were "imposed on" them versus being done "by" them.

During the event, the team used a fishbone analysis and compiled the following list of critical elements a flow-cell needed to be able to sustain and drive daily improvements:

1. Standard work must be used along with visual management so that waste can be identified.
2. Team members must have the tools and training needed to perform team-based, root-cause problem-solving.
3. The team members in the cell must have the time and support resources needed to make real-time improvements.
4. The team members must be involved, committed, and responsible for carrying out their assigned tasks and must be held accountable for process discipline and results.
5. An operating system must be in place through which the team posts the metrics of actual performance against the standards or targets expected.
6. Leadership must provide recognition and support.

The general sense by the team was that during the first four years of our transformation, our event- and tool-driven improvement approach had engaged the *hands* of our members. If we could successfully establish these features in all of our flow-cells, we could also engage the *heads* and the *hearts* of our team members.

As we reflected on the outcome of this event, we began to understand that our model of what good leadership looked like had been turned upside down.

> **Watlow Insight: Leadership**
>
> Traditionally, the people who became leaders at Watlow were the heroes or experts who had the answers to problems and who got work done by whatever means. In this event, we were reminded that customer value is created in front-line cells (production and nonproduction) and that a large part of leadership's role is to support and develop the people and processes in these cells. As CEO, when I asked myself how much time I was spending supporting and developing the members who were creating value for our customers, I came up short.

In early 2009 we launched model cells with these attributes at all of our US facilities. We called this addition to our Watlow Way, "Managing for Daily Improvement."

PEOPLE DEVELOPMENT AND LEADERSHIP

The addition of Managing for Daily Improvement (MDI) and our new Watlow leadership insights forced us to get serious about people development. We now clearly understood that we could not successfully sustain nor drive ongoing improvements without continuously improving the skills of our 2,000 team members and the leaders who would support them. Pockets of skilled enthusiastic heroes would not be sufficient.

In 2009, as part of MDI, Watlow began to focus more specifically on training and development for the frontline members and their immediate supervisors. We began with one "model cell" in each of our North American facilities. There were two primary sources of training. The first was called "Back to Basics," which was classroom-style training delivered by very experienced product engineers to all of the model-cell team members, regardless of tenure. It was, as you would expect, basic in nature. Topics covered included basic thermal transfer principles and product design. The training was then put into effect by designing standard work documents for all cell manufacturing processes. As additional knowledge was gained, the standard work documents were refined and improved. Supervisors received additional training in practical problem solving and were encouraged to begin problem solving in real time as issues emerged within the model cells.

Secondly, we introduced "Training within Industry" (TWI) methodology as a tool for quickly training new team members. TWI dates back to World War II and is utilized with some enhancements at Toyota. Watlow began by creating a training cell in our St. Louis, Missouri, facility. First- and second-level supervisors were trained in the methodology, and then this was implemented in the training cell. Our early results suggest that we have reduced the training time required by over 50 percent, and our retention rate for new employees has improved by over 70 percent in the first year of employment.

Team member response to this training has been enthusiastic and encouraging. In addition, quality and on-time delivery metrics have improved by over 25 percent within one year. The focus on developing the knowledge and skills of our personnel on the front lines of the organization has improved both performance and team member morale. As we project into the future, we believe that this work will be foundational to Watlow's ongoing Lean journey.

For several years we have had much of the normal leadership development processes in place, such as succession planning, performance management, and personal development planning. Although helpful, these development processes have been perfunctory. Our new leadership model, which was more servant-leader oriented and required all leaders to actively support, coach, and mentor frontline improvement activity, required a more aggressive development approach.

In 2010, Watlow created a certification program for both leadership and our support staff. With the support of Simpler Consulting, we established training at the bronze, silver, and gold levels, indicating increasing levels of Lean knowledge and skill development. These programs were complementary to our MDI initiative and were intended to provide leaders with the skills and abilities necessary to support development at all levels of the company. Watlow uses participation in weeklong kaizen events as a proxy for Lean knowledge acquisition. In 2010, we changed our leading indicator away from counting the number of people who had been in events to the number of people who had been in three or more events. Our hypothesis is that as people move into their third and fourth events, their knowledge of Lean principles and some of the tools improves their confidence that they can add value in the event.

We also created a leadership development rotational program in 2009, in order to bring in young talent. We successfully recruited a number of new graduate engineering students and started them in a series of rotational assignments to expose them to multiple products, customers, and locations in their first two years of employment. More important, they are learning the Watlow Way as they progress through each rotation. We repeated this in 2010.

As our culture has become stronger and more unique to Watlow, we have found it more difficult to hire leaders from the outside. Our data shows that candidates for leadership positions who were promoted internally are four times more likely to be successful in their next role than someone hired from the outside. Therefore, we have found it is very important to have a robust selection and inculcation process for external candidates and place considerable effort in people development.

Over the past two years, our selection process has improved considerably. Besides improving our skills at using a behavior-based selection process, today we have a much better understanding of the type of people who will be successful at Watlow. Additionally, part of our hiring process for all mid- through senior-level leaders is to undergo an external assessment. This is now a standard step in our selection process.

Selecting the right people is only the first step in making sure external hires are successful. The next step for Watlow is to immerse them in our culture and develop the needed WW skills to make them successful. Immersion plans vary, depending on the level in the organization. For senior leaders, a custom immersion plan is developed, which includes a focused orientation intended to quickly acquaint new employees. The process is broken up into four primary areas. First, there are a series of books and articles assigned as prereading. Ideally, this is accomplished prior to the first day of employment and is designed to give a high-level understanding of Lean and Toyota Production System principles. Second, the new member is given in-depth training in the Watlow Business System. This is intended to orient the individual into the processes and tools we use to run the business. Third, the individual visits Watlow's various site locations to meet the leadership teams and become acquainted with both products and customers. Finally, a series of meetings is held with functional leaders in the organization so that the integration and relationships between the functions and the business system can be understood. In all, this process takes roughly two months of dedicated effort on the part of both the individual and the company.

RESULTS

Over the last five years we have achieved the following Watlow-wide results:

Safety: 75 percent reduction in injury rate

Member development: More than 75 percent member participation in one kaizen event and more than 50 percent participation in two or more events

Quality: 60 percent reduction in quality escapes

Delivery: Significantly shortened product delivery times (We have changed our delivery metric several times in order to get a meaningful and objective measure. Although we have not been able to measure them precisely, our average product delivery times have gotten significantly shorter.)

Cost: 34 percent improvement in labor productivity

Shareholder value: 70 percent improvement in profitability and 20 percent improvement in asset utilization

THE SUSTAINABILITY CHALLENGE

Now almost six years into our transformation, the culture at Watlow has changed in very meaningful ways (see Figure B.9). Our team members today do not feel that Lean or the WW is just a passing fad. The WW is understood by most of our members from the front line to the executive team. We are also getting more and more members engaged in driving and sustaining improvements.

Even though we are pleased with where we are at, we still realize that our transformation is fragile. If we do not remain diligent, the progress we have made over the last six years could evaporate in six months.

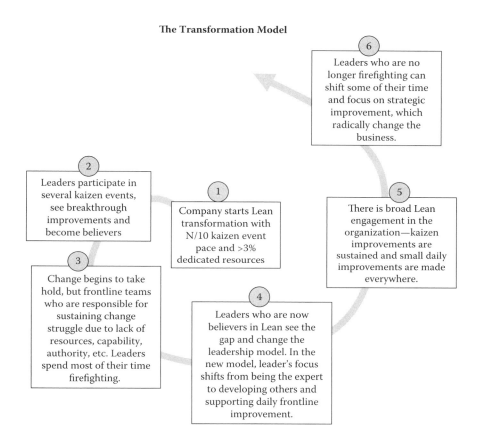

FIGURE B.9
The transformation model.

Some of our team members have reached the point in their Lean development where they will never go back—they are true believers. Our challenge, therefore, is to build more and more believers so that Watlow's Lean progress never stops. This is no easy task, since our workforce and the Watlow Way are always changing. Also, since we are striving for double-digit growth, we will be adding new people annually. For Watlow, this only means that the process of learning and people development needs to accelerate.

Appendix C: Watlow's Enterprise Visual Management System—Mission Control

Tom LaMantia
President of the Watlow Company

To understand our Enterprise Visual Management System, which we call Mission Control, you must first understand what we call the Watlow Business System (WBS). This system is all-encompassing and is the way we run the business. It has taken us many years to develop a deeper understanding of what a business system really is, and we continue to learn more every day. The simple illustration in Figure C.1 reflects the WBS, which is ultimately a Plan-Do-Check-Act (PDCA) process at the highest level. The system is built to develop and deploy strategy (Plan), execute actions to deliver the strategy (Do), monitor the effectiveness of our actions (Check), and provide countermeasures when the actions are not delivering as intended (Act).

We use the Mission Control process to help us in four areas. They are:

- Strategy development and alignment (Plan)
- Execution of our actions to deliver strategy (Do)
- Performance to our goals (Check)
- Improvement/countermeasures (Act)

We have also found that our visual management system has allowed us to better communicate our strategy and our ability to deliver it.

The Enterprise Mission Control Process is centered around the Check and Act parts of the PDCA cycle, but it can and does have a dramatic impact on the Plan and Do portions of the process as well. In essence, Mission Control is in place to ensure that the strategy, execution of the

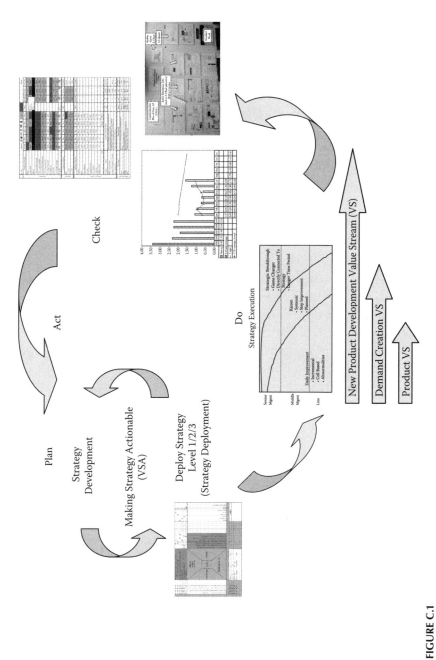

FIGURE C.1

The Watlow Business System is a Plan-Do-Check-Act cycle at the highest level.

strategy, feedback systems, and countermeasure processes are in place and functioning effectively. We have learned (the hard way, in some cases) that this is a system and must work as a system. When one of the components of the system fails, the system fails, and we must be able to detect this as close to the failure point as possible in order to ensure continued alignment and achievement of the goals.

WATLOW MISSION CONTROL PROCESS

Watlow implemented our Mission Control process in 2007, and we continue to change and refine it as we mature in our Lean journey. We knew that the intent of the WBS was to ensure that everything we did either helped to develop strategy or to align our actions to our strategic direction. We didn't know how the WBS really worked, but we did know that change was something we could count on and that our plans, as good as they might be, would need corrective action on a regular basis. In order to be effective in managing the change, we would need to understand what changed and why. As we deepened our understanding, it became clear over time that the Check part of the cycle was not as robust as we required. We were not always sure what data was important; our ability to access it was sometimes difficult; and we were not always sure what the data was telling us. As a result, our ability to understand whether our business system was working as intended was inconsistent.

"Mission Control," a term that brings a strong visual example to mind, became our phrase for visual management of the business system. Most of you have probably seen old World War II movies where executive officers of the army or navy were gathered around a mock-up of the battlefield. They moved troops and equipment around the board with a large stick as they discussed how the plan was proceeding or what countermeasures they needed to put in place as the battle moved and changed. Conceptually, this is the same thing that we were trying to do with our business. Our Mission Control was all about executing our plan, ensuring that what we expected to happen was happening, and quickly determining what actions we would take to get us back on track when things were not going as expected. We were also capturing learnings so that the next plan we developed would be more effective. I would like to say that we clearly understood this in great detail as we began implementation, but that was just not the case. Clearly, "learning by doing" was at work here.

Initially, our focus was on making the performance of our manufacturing operations visible, from a financial perspective as well as from the perspective of Safety(S), Quality(Q), Delivery(D), and Cost (C). We also decided to review the performance of our operations tactically on a weekly basis and strategically on a monthly basis. We felt it was important to establish a weekly and monthly takt time in order to ensure a focus on short-term results while meeting our longer-term strategic intent. As we have matured, the timing and intent have remained the same, but we have attempted to balance the review to better understand the interrelationships between our demand-creation and new-product-development processes in addition to our manufacturing processes. As we continue to learn, we have found that we are much more responsive to changing business conditions and are improving in our ability to forecast those changes.

WEEKLY MISSION CONTROL

The leadership team meets weekly (virtually, to allow global participation) for ninety minutes to review a standard set of metrics displayed on our Key Performance Indicator (KPI) board. These metrics flow down from our True North metrics (see Chapter 3), which align to our strategy. This is a stand-up meeting. The metric updates, which include key financial metrics, are loaded on the system the night before our review. However, we do not use the computer except for those who are calling in from the field. We have found that a stand-up meeting helps keep us focused and moving. Each business leader has six minutes to provide an update and to highlight variations to the plan, both good and bad. Our objective is not to help solve individual site issues in this meeting. Instead, we are interested in what the sites have learned and how they are approaching countermeasures. We work to maintain this cadence so that we remain focused on the few key things that matter in each business unit. The weekly board is shown in Figure C.2.

We use "box scores," graphs, and tables, all of which highlight the variation to the plan. We use colors to help us quickly identify variation. We started out with red, green, and yellow but quickly moved to red and green

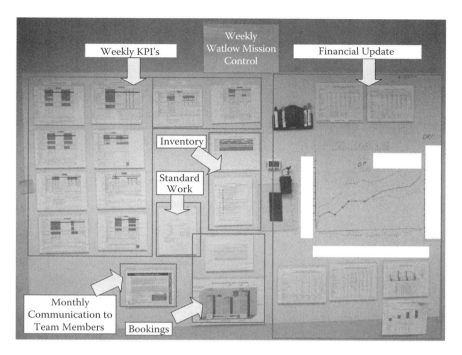

FIGURE C.2
Weekly Mission Control meeting board.

only. We found that, despite trying to define it several times, it was difficult to determine what yellow really meant. We do not place value judgments on red versus green. That is, green and red do not mean good and bad, respectively. Green means that we are meeting plan; red means that we have an abnormality, which is an opportunity for improvement and, maybe more important, an opportunity to learn. Green also provides an opportunity to learn what we are doing right.

As seen in Figure C.3, the weekly Mission Control KPI box score incorporates S (Safety), Q (Quality), D (Delivery), and C (Cost) metrics and goals, as well as a look at movement in the sales funnel, and finally a view of customer-demand-stimulation activity for the week. It also includes countermeasures for the metrics that are not progressing as expected. The concept of a box score is analogous to a baseball game box score. It attempts to give a complete picture of the business versus a single part of it, so that we can look at the business more strategically. In the past, we had looked at SQDC separately from the demand-creation data. We have learned that this is a complete system and that looking at them independently drives

St. Louis	Indicators	● ● ➡ ⬆ ➡ ⬇	X	X				Month:

Site → SQDC → (Operations)

Performance Measure	Prior Mo	Wk 1	Wk 2	Wk 3	Wk 4	Wk 5	Qtr (Fcst)	Yr (Fcst)	Yr (AOP)
Safety							2.5	1.8	1.8
Quality (PPM)	2,634	3,444	5,461	1,398	3,737	scorecard: RMA 38517 Goodrich / CAT 43 Pieces Units Not Baked Out		3,000	2,182
Delivery:									
OTR - Key & Advocate (%)	78.9%	75.7%	77.5%	79.0%	76.4%		85.0%	92.0%	92.0%
OTP - Core & General (%)	90.1%	87.2%	89.5%	90.3%	80.3%		94.0%	95.0%	95.0%
OTR Modified Std Quotes (%)	97.0%	100.0%	100.0%	100.0%	100.0%		95.0%	95.0%	95.0%
OTR Custom Quotes (%)	100.0%	N/A	N/A	N/A	100.0%		95.0%	95.0%	95.0%
New Designs General (%)	11.6%	0.0%	0.0%	17%	15%				
Productivity ($)	$108	$123	$94	$108	$106		104	107	109
Past Due ($)	$544	$289	$243	$283	$251		<$150K	$100K	$100K
Inventory Days of Supply	68.0	64.5	66.4	65.6	66.9		66.1	61.5	67.8
LT Trend	➡	➡	➡	➡	➡	➡	➡	➡	➡

Weekly Financial Forecast → (Financial)

Performance Measure	YTD	Wk 1	Wk 2	Wk 3	Wk 4	Wk 5	Qtr (Fcst)	Yr (Fcst)	Yr (AOP)
Sales	$23,567	$3,066	$3,066	$3,066	$3,048		$9,315	$38,316	$33,526
Lean OP $	$4,827	$530	$530	$530	$530		$1,435	$6,998	$5,705
Lean OP %	20.5%	17.3%	17.3%	17.3%	17.4%		15.4%	18.3%	17.0%

Sales Funnel → (Demand Creation)

Performance Measure	Prior Mo	Wk 1	Wk 2	Wk 3	Wk 4	Wk 5	Qtr (Fcst)	Yr (Fcst)	Yr (AOP)
Concept	$8,540	$8,540	$8,540	$8,596	$8,616				
Quote	$7,390	$7,390	$5,050	$4,991	$4,991				
Quote Evaluation	$7,390	$7,400	$7,380	$7,583	$7,596				
Prototype	$11,720	$11,730	$11,730	$11,702	$11,702				
Prototype Evaluation	$2,540	$2,560	$2,050	$2,052	$2,052				
Pre-Production	$5,090	$5,040	$5,660	$5,393	$5,363				
Production	$240	$239	$239	$240	$239				
Ranking Average	3.3	3.3	3.3	3.3	3.3				
Total				$48,816	$48,793				

Weekly Growth Activity

Customer	Phase	Growth Activity This Week	Terr Rank	PI Rank	12 mth Revenue	Close Date
AMAT	(Disc & Concept)	Ultramic team is refining potential solution for a vacuum chuck for wafer annealing application for presentation to AMAT			$400K	
Automated Packaging Sys	(Pre-prod)	As customer continues to evaluate prototypes, team is evaluating practical solution for rounding the edges of the Ultramic heater	4	3	$504K	Oct-10
Ipeco	(Proto Eval)	Customer visit on 9/13 (Selvy/Schloemann)	5	4	$352k	Jan-11

Counter Measures → (Countermeasures)

Root Cause	Countermeasure	Owner	Start	End	JDI/Event/Project
Quality	Est. Countermeasures for Design (marking), and "missed operation" drivers.	E. Schellenberg	Jan-10	Sep-20	Project
Delivery	Execute divestment plan by end of 3Q.	M. Duke	Jul-10	Sep-10	Project
Delivery	Align goal with focus (deemphasize non-strategic products)	M. Duke	Jul-10	Jul-10	JDI
Safety	Designing new tooling for feed at cut-off saw	S. McKenzie	Jul-10	Jul-10	JDI

FIGURE C.3
Weekly Mission Control KPI box score.

the wrong behavior and the risk of losing alignment from one end of the business to the other.

The financial information posted on the weekly Mission Control board is also updated weekly (see Figure C.4). The baseline is established from a quarterly forecast we call our Frozen Forecast. Each week, we update our revenue and operating income numbers based on any new data or actions that have occurred during the week. In essence, we forecast any observed changes in our financial results on a weekly basis, using the quarterly forecast as the baseline. We are beginning to use our Sales and Operations Planning Process to support the quarterly forecast. As a result of these processes, we have had very few financial surprises, either weekly or quarterly.

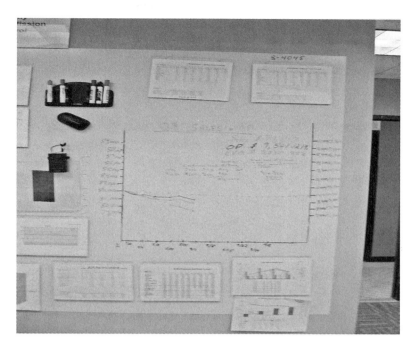

FIGURE C.4
Mission Control whiteboard.

MONTHLY ENTERPRISE MISSION CONTROL

The leadership team also meets monthly for a two-day comprehensive business review. This strategic meeting is attended in person by all US-based leaders, with telephone updates from international leaders in time frames that adjust for time zone differences. We do ask that the managing directors in Europe and Asia attend in person once per quarter.

The objective of the monthly Mission Control process is to understand and manage monthly the critical indicators affecting business performance while focusing on aligning the product lines of business (LOBs), demand creation, and functions with one another and with our enterprise strategy. We are striving to understand what is working in our current processes and what is not. Systemic and strategic issues are identified and countermeasures assigned. This is all in keeping with the Watlow Business System Plan-Do-Check-Act process.

Day 1: Enterprise Mission Control

On Day 1, we focus on the execution side of the business as it relates to our strategy (see Figure C.5). We review our True North metrics (Figure C.6), which are those long-term metrics we have determined to be critical to our success from both a customer and a business perspective. We delve deeper into individual metrics such as quality and supply chain (Figure C.7) when a specific business need arises. We also review strategy deployment in the form of an X-Box Matrix.

As we review the True North metrics, our real objective is to determine whether we are approaching the improvement process the right way so that (a) we will indeed see the improvement required and (b) we will be able to sustain it. Strategy deployment means, simply, determining what we are going to do to deliver on our strategy. More specifically, that translates to determining what changes we are going to make from a people and process perspective in the next six months in order to execute our growth strategy. We spend time talking about our Lean transformation as well, in the form of a Transformation Plan of Care (TPOC). What are the latest insights and learnings around our transformation? How are we progressing and what needs to happen next? This all goes back to the concept of "doing it the right way." We use A3s in the strategy deployment and TPOC

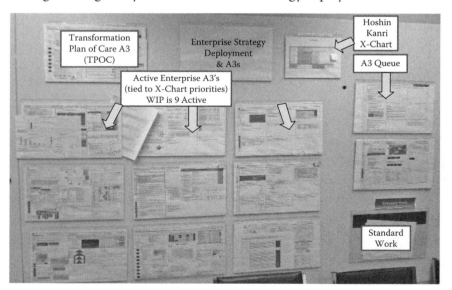

FIGURE C.5
Monthly meeting, day 1 agenda.

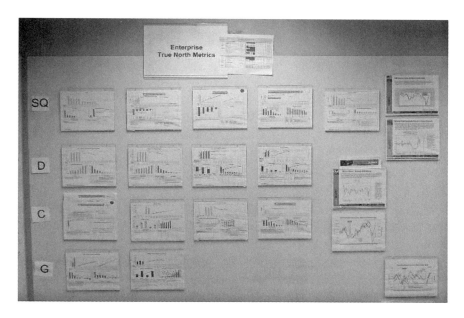

FIGURE C.6
True North metrics.

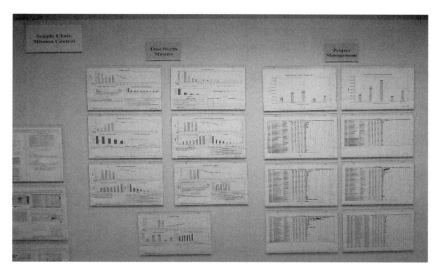

FIGURE C.7
Supply chain Mission Control board.

portion of the review to help us scope the issue, identify the current and future states, and develop a solution approach to get from the current state to the future state.

Throughout the two days, our intent is to identify processes or areas that need more work. When we find these, we add them to our Rolling Action Item List (RAIL) (see Figure C.8) and assign an owner. The owner will report on progress against the action item at the next Mission Control monthly meeting. The Day 1 Agenda is shown in Table C.1.

Day 2: Enterprise Mission Control

Day 2 is all about growth. We spend time reviewing demand-creation activities in North America, Europe, and Asia (Figure C.9). Marketing and sales both report on progress made on their Strategy Deployment activities (A3s) as well as customer activity. Marketing discusses our progress in identifying attractive markets. Sales discusses sales funnel growth, wins and losses and why they occurred, customer trends, etc. In this session, we also spend a couple of hours discussing and debating a growth topic, for example, what good business looks like, a strategic plan submitted by one of the businesses, or trends in the market. The discussion requires

FIGURE C.8
Rolling Action Item List (RAIL).

TABLE C.1

Enterprise Mission Control: Day 1 Agenda

Weekly financial update and general review	7:30–8:00	Steve
Supply chain	8:00–9:00	Paul
Break	9:00–9:15	
Large Account Mgmt. (LAMP)	9:15–11:00	Chad
HPS		
TK		
Executive Corrective Action Board (ECAB)	11:00–12:00	Paul
Lunch	12:00–1:00	
Rolling Action Item List (RAIL)	1:00–1:30	Tom
True North metrics	1:30–2:30	Metric Owners
TPOC	2:30–3:00	Steve
Break	3:00–3:15	
Enterprise A3s	3:15–5:00	A3 Owner

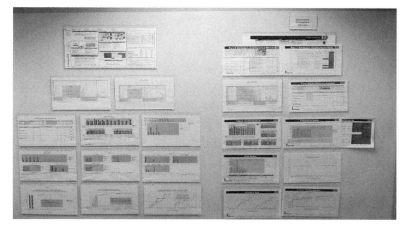

FIGURE C.9
Demand-creation review.

engagement by all, and we hope to leave with a better understanding of the topic and a plan going forward.

We also review Lean product development processes and activity. Our objective is to manage demand and capacity as it relates to new product development and our strategy. We also discuss our progress around Lean product development tools and techniques, a process that is still in its infancy; we will continue to learn what works for us as we move forward. Finally, we spend time each month discussing leadership and critical job-succession planning. Each year, based on our strategic initiatives,

TABLE C.2

Enterprise Mission Control: Day 2 Agenda

Europe update	7:30–8:00	Agnes
Demand creation	8:00–10:00	Chad
Break	10:00–10:15	All
Marketing review	10:15–11:45	Ray
Update on space research		
Update on deep learning		
Update on declared spaces		
Lunch	11:45–12:30	
New product development (NPD)	12:30–1:30	Lou
Capacity/capability		
Project status		
Model cell update		
Growth topic (includes break)	1:30–3:15	Ray D
Succession planning	3:15–4:15	Bob
TL notes update	4:15–4:30	Tom
Asia update	4:30–5:00	Chris

we identify specific positions that we want to upgrade, improve, or add bench strength to. We develop a plan and review it monthly. Again, the intent is always to check our progress against our plan and to ensure that the right countermeasures are in place, when required, to get us back on track—doing it the right way. Our Day 2 agenda is shown in Table C.2.

ENTERPRISE MISSION CONTROL HISTORY

When first implemented, our review process was rudimentary, and our visual tools took up only about 100 square feet of space. We were in our second year of using a Hoshin Kanri/X-Box Matrix system with limited success, and had only begun experimenting with using A3s as problem-solving tools. Our operating system involved headquarters leaders making multiple visits to site locations for reviews; our enterprise Mission Control review was scheduled for one day.

As we progressed, two major flaws in this approach became apparent. First, visits to facilities by headquarters stimulated a lot of preparation work for the site teams. Much of this work was a waste. Second, a single day for the Mission Control meeting was not enough. We found ourselves tactically focused, spending little time looking for systemic variation and cause-and-effect relationships. Time spent in strategic discussion as a group was limited, and the strategic discussions that took place during site reviews were necessarily focused on only one business unit.

We also came to understand that although we had applied Lean principles to our manufacturing operations, we had done little to extend the thinking upstream to demand creation. We needed to broaden our view to look at customer-to-customer value streams at the enterprise level. As our internal operations improved, we also discovered that we lacked a systemic view of our supply chain. During the economic chaos of 2009, inventory levels and materials costs were important drivers of our financial performance.

As we learned our way through these issues, we applied the concept of visual management through the use of our Mission Control room. As of the time of this writing, our visual tools cover about 500 percent more wall space. Still, in one medium-sized conference room, we are increasingly able to tie out our strategy deployment to demand-creation and fulfillment initiatives. We have become better at strategically forecasting our business and investing accordingly. As a point of comparison, in 2001, Watlow was significantly impacted by the economic recession. Our revenues fell off by roughly one-third, and the company struggled to remain profitable. It took about three and one-half years to rebuild the revenues and return the company to the predownturn level of profitability. The year 2009 was no kinder to us than most other companies. Again, our revenues fell off significantly. However, we responded much more quickly and managed a modest profit for the year. In 2010, our revenues grew quickly, and the company is doing well in terms of profitability.

A large amount of the credit due for our improved ability to respond to changing market conditions rests with the sage advice we got from our board of directors. However, we are convinced that the investment we made in creating a visual management system that better integrated the entire enterprise value stream was invaluable. The combination of making things visual and creating a regular cadence of review has improved our ability to forecast and to seize opportunities presented in the markets we serve.

As with most things related to Lean thinking, the Mission Control process is very straightforward conceptually. It seems like it should be easy to implement. In our case, it was very awkward initially but improved gradually as we used the tools. It became increasingly evident when a piece of the puzzle was missing, and we would then make the effort to put that piece in place. The visual system makes gaps apparent and forces the organization to learn what is necessary to fill them. Each time a gap is closed, the visual system improves and stimulates the next round of learning. Perhaps that is why it is called continuous improvement.

We have iterated the Mission Control process multiple times and will continue to do so. The more we learn, the more we want those learnings reflected in our Watlow Business System so that they can be sustained. We do not have all the answers, and I would not expect anyone reading this to do as we did. From our experience, you have to want to do this, believe it will make a difference, and then just do it and continue to improve.

Appendix D: The Origin of Simpler's Transformation Continuum^{SM}

Marc S. Hafer
CEO of Simpler

Organizations and their leaders pursue excellence through Lean transformation for a multitude of reasons and in a variety of ways. Whether or not their Lean journey begins with clarity of purpose and a clearly defined, systematic transformation methodology, most organizations come to realize that there may be a more efficient, effective path, and it would have been easier if only such an efficient path were documented. While enlightened and successful Lean leaders overcome awkward beginnings and find a method and a rhythm that work for their organizations, far too many leaders give up on their Lean journey because their launch, their early experiences, or both fail to meet expectations. The path forward is uncertain, and they find the challenges of managing expectations and painting a clear picture of "what's next" to be insurmountable.

In the early years of adopting the Toyota Production System (TPS), many of us were less strategic and more tactical in our transformations. If coached by former Toyota senseis or certain American disciples of Toyota, we were expected to keep our heads down and "learn by doing." Our senseis subscribed to the coaching method sometimes referred to as "guided discovery," which meant don't question … just do. As early adopters, we bought into TPS and didn't stop to wonder about the path we were traveling.

In today's environment, the novelty of TPS has worn off, and naïve devotion to adopting Lean on faith has given way to demands for answers not only to the "why" questions well in advance, but also to questions of how and where organizations will arrive at certain milestones in their Lean journey. This information is often required before leaders will commit to taking the plunge—not an unreasonable expectation.

Thus was born the idea for a roadmap documenting how to implement a systematic, proven transformation methodology, with key milestones and prescribed points for reflection (*hansei*) and course correction. A roadmap should serve as a guide to leaders and associates in a systematic, proven transformation methodology; help create efficiencies in the short run; and build organizations with enduring Lean cultures to leverage organizational excellence for industry-, game-changing performance. This road map is known as Simpler's Transformation Continuum[SM].

TRANSFORMATION CONTINUUM: THE BIG PICTURE

The construction of the Transformation Continuum (TC) was built on the premise that logical phases of learning exist in an organization's development of Lean capability and culture. In development, we paid close attention to the competence model, attributed to many authors, known as "Four Stages of Learning":

- Unconscious incompetence
- Conscious incompetence
- Conscious competence
- Unconscious competence

The relevance of this model for developing the TC was rooted in our collective experience in Lean transformations, as both practitioners and sensei. Countless times we have witnessed individual leaders and members begin to progress through these four stages of learning only to become stuck in one of the first three phases, and never achieve "unconscious competence" with Lean fully embedded in their culture, i.e., the enduring Lean culture that transcends individual leadership changes and overcomes inertia and resistance to change. A successful model was needed to help organizations bridge that gap.

As one examines the Transformation Continuum framework along the horizontal axis (see Figure D.1), note that there are three major phases that roughly parallel the four-phased learning model. In accordance with the way the TC model was constructed, the transition from "unconscious incompetence" to "conscious incompetence" should occur late in the first major TC phase, most likely as the first model cells are being built. The

Simpler®

			Committing to a new improvement system					Accelerating Capability and Performance				Leveraging your cultural transformation		
			Evaluation	Education	Start-Up	Build the Models	Reflection Point	Go Deeper	Go Wider	Go Beyond	Reflection Point	Intensify Human Development	Tipping Point	Redefine your Environment
Overview			A process of self-led learning and research to understand the gaps in performance and potential solutions.	Gathering knowledge and building coaching relationships to prepare to lead change	Setting the vision, choosing targets, and learning by hands on involvement	Developing the model flow cell and value stream in the first pass. Documenting own business system.		Making the second through fifth passes through the model value stream.	Expanding to all value streams (Demand, Delivery, Development and Support)	Deep linkage of the value chain from suppliers to customers		Accelerating the development of our people while protecting our investment.		Leveraging people, processes and improvement capabilities to redefine the enterprise.
Human Development	Developing Leaders	Education	Self-Led Learning (articles, books, referrers)	Senior Leaders establish relationship with Sensei	Deep learning from event participation; learn to see waste	Learn how to drive improvement in a value stream environment.		Understand how Strategy Deployment is used to drive improvement and break down organizational barriers	Understand how tools, techniques and principles apply to all areas of the business.	True immersion into VOE.		Understand the values, habits and behaviors necessary to develop irreversible continuous improvement		Learn how lean is applied to Business Acquisitions, Research and Development and other Organic opportunities.
Human Development	Developing Leaders	Roles & Responsibilities	Build consensus for change/improvement methodology	Preparing themselves and organization for change.	Team participant; model mentor and student behavior; define expectations	Develop a new management approach for model value stream		Make the necessary organizational and resource changes to achieve the next future state target.	Build leaders and infrastructure for all engaged value streams.	Become a truly customer centric organization; develop key supplier and customer relationships		Lead the HD process.		Redefine the organization's go-to- market strategy
Human Development	Developing Managers	Education	Assigned Learning (articles, websites, books, referrers, conferences)	Assessment on self and department. Prescriptive education of key books, articles.	Basic Lean education; learn to see waste; team facilitation; dealing with change	Learning how flow cells are linked to create value stream improvement.		Learn how to manage in value stream environment. Broadening their functional expertise.	All functional managers go through immersion in model value stream(s).	Learning to apply the tools, techniques and principles in other organizations.		Learn how to apply new values, habits and behaviors.		Being developed to increase leadership capacity.
Human Development	Developing Managers	Roles & Responsibilities	Run the business. Stay focused.	Run the business. Reinforce the message. Minimize distractions.	Managing change; learning lean problem-solving tools; committing to improvement	Ensuring hour-by-hour tracking with true root cause problem solving and corrective action.		Learn the standard work of all functions. Build interfunctional teamwork.	Manage value streams through execution of Strategy Deployment and Daily Management.	Stay focused internally while committing resources externally.		Live the new "Way"		Developing the leaders of the next businesses for which you will acquire
Human Development	Developing Members	Education	N/A	N/A	Awareness training; event training; team participant	Learning how basic problem solving is used to improve their daily work environment.		Learn their role as it relates to managing for daily improvement.	Develop tools experts.	Leading improvement teams in extended value stream.		Learn how to apply new values, habits and behaviors.		Learn how to apply new values, habits anc behaviors.
Human Development	Developing Members	Roles & Responsibilities	Stay focused on personal contribution	Stay focused on personal contribution	Contribute to problem solving and becoming open to change	Begin problem solving and waste elimination through daily management and team participation.		Offer suggestions via teian suggestion system; run the cell to takt time	Becoming sensei for various tools and techniques; team leaders on events	Run the value stream.		Live the new "Way"		Live the new "Way"
Align Structure / Culture		Infrastructure	Create an evaluation team	Transition from evaluation to governance (Steering Committee)	Steering committee; Full time improvement team with leader; Informal Leaders; Key Process Leaders; Mission control room; Budget for lean	Value Stream Improvement Team with 3% Dedicated Resources		Formalize succession planning process to include lean experience. Antibodies are assessed and addressed.	3% Dedicated Resources across enterprise; n/10 event pace of change; continuous improvement as a way of life	80% of all teams led by front line.		Define Standard Work for Human Development		Dedicated 3P Team, Business Acquisition Team
Align Structure / Culture		Beliefs	Status quo is not acceptable	Transformational learning requires deep personal involvement	Success requires deep personal learning from all levels in the organization.	Recognition that value streams are 95% non-value added.		The law of diminishing returns does not apply - there is more waste through each pass in the value stream	Lean works everywhere; strategy deployment drives breakthrough performance and breaks functional silos	Alignment, pull and flow of the value chain eliminates multiple layers of waste		From "Doing Lean" to "Being Lean"		We redefine the environment; we don't respond to it
Tools			Decision Matrix Benchmarking Assessments Strategic Planning Impact / Difficulty Matrix Recommended Reading List Sales Presentation Statement of Work Template RFP Template	A3 Thinking Guided Benchmarking & Education Business Case Letter Templates Leader PDP	TPOC Visioning Transformation Awareness Core Team Development Mission Control Room Value Stream Analysis Core Team PDP	Value Stream Management Managing for Daily Improvement Practical Problem Solving Being a Sensei SBS Architecture Sustainment Workshop OTI Building Leadership Personnel Basic Quality Tools Standard Work Tools		Strategy Deployment Middle Management Standard Work Value Stream Leader PDP Assessments Teian Systems Certification Toyota Change Model	Yokoten SDS Shingo Readiness	TVSA VOE Lean Accounting Supplier Development		Doing Lean vs. Becoming Lean Building a Cultural A3 360 Assessment Model Toyota Based Selection Model		Business Acquisition Model
Results			Understand your performance in Human Development, Quality, Delivery, Cost and Growth	Building expectations that double digit improvement is possible in all 5 dimensions	Ensure RIE, Value Stream and Enterprise Metrics are connected. Target double digit gains in model value stream(s) and minimum 4X ROI.	Target 75% reduction in lead time, 50% reduction in defects and 20% increase in productivity.		Annually: increased employee satisfaction; 50% reduction in defects; 50% reduction in lead times; 20% productivity gain; doubling inventory turns	True North measures translated to all levels, all value streams, all functions; 20-50% annual performance improvement in key driver measures	Cost reduced by lead time reduction, inventory reduction, and productivity increases passed through the value chain to end customers		Recruit the best talent without the highest cost		> 15x increase in market cap; 100x increas in quality; 5x increase in ROA
Outputs			Go / No-go Decision	Leaders prepared to lead early changes	Commit to model flow cell and model value stream.	1st pass through model value stream. Basic personal business system architecture.		A model value stream that pulls the rest of the organization toward the path of "What Good Looks Like"	A fully engaged organization all linked and aligned to the strategic objectives	On the path of a "true enterprise transformation"		End to end Human Development Process for the "new" organization		Perpetual growth engine

FIGURE D.1
Simpler's Transformation Continuum.

migration from "conscious incompetence" to "conscious competence" will occur mid-Phase 2, probably during the expansion of model value streams into multiple value streams—the "Go Wider" subphase. Finally, the holy grail of the Transformation Continuum model—gaining "unconscious competence"—occurs when the organization fully harnesses and deploys its human capital and leverages its Lean capabilities to redefine its industry and internal environment in Phase 3.

The vertical axis of the TC framework (see Figure D.1) demonstrates that multiple dimensions of a Lean transformation must be continuously developed and improved in a logical sequence along the pathway or phases of the Transformation Continuum. The highest, yet most often overlooked, priorities are the human-development components required to make the cultural and performance advances permanent in the organization. Leaders, managers, and members are the three basic tiers in an organization. A more granular dissection and definition of levels, roles, and responsibilities, however, is encouraged to ensure that all members of an organization understand and are achieving their full potential throughout the Transformation Continuum.

Noteworthy on the vertical dimensions of building capabilities and results is the position of tools in the hierarchy. Tools are enablers and essential capabilities to be mastered; however, they are a small fraction of the strategic considerations underpinning the construction of an enduring Lean culture. Tools are often introduced too early in a transformational journey, well before an organization and its members are "consciously competent" with the fundamentals.

The "big picture" of Simpler's Transformation Continuum is this: Organizations that want to undertake a Lean transformation in a systematic, efficient manner (i.e., the "way of least waste") will recognize that using this building-block approach will build a strong foundation of learning and capabilities within the organization to ensure an enduring culture of operational excellence.

PHASE 1: COMMITTING TO A NEW IMPROVEMENT SYSTEM

Phase 1 of the Transformation Continuum comprises four subphases. The fundamental decision resulting from the first subphase, "Evaluation," is "go/no go" regarding an enterprise transformation, or alternatively focusing more narrowly on making process improvements in targeted areas or training activities. In order to effectively evaluate the potential organizational impact, this phase becomes an intense period of self-led learning and research to understand performance gaps and optimal solutions.

Provided that the outcome of the evaluation subphase is to take action at some level, the "Education" subphase enables a deeper level of learning regarding the alternative methods that were explored during evaluation, such as Lean, Six Sigma, Theory of Constraints, and other improvement methods that promise similar outcomes yet have markedly different approaches, levels of involvement and, ultimately, results. It is during the education phase that outside resources are typically brought into play for the purpose of knowledge gathering and building potential relationships for coaching during the transformation.

In practice, both the evaluation and education subphases are often short-changed. In the eagerness of senior leaders to initiate change and demonstrate tangible results, deep learning and understanding of the journey are not allowed to fully develop. Steps necessary to prepare the organization and gain true commitment at all levels, particularly across the senior team and from key managers, are omitted and later translate into lack of traction and failure to move beyond "unconscious incompetence." While it is a tired cliché to insist on defining the "burning platform" for change, it is nonetheless vital. It is important to rigorously evaluate and educate the organization in order to create at least a solid, if not burning, platform based on a clear understanding of and commitment to the Lean journey.

Once the appropriate, systematic transformational approach is chosen, an organization should be well prepared (although probably still apprehensive) to get started. With an appropriate sensei (an experienced coach who has guided successful transformations), the organization is ready to enter the third subphase, "Start-Up." During this critical stage, the leadership team will set their vision, choose performance improvement targets (both True North and intermediate goals), and immerse themselves in learning through hands-on involvement. Early successes calm early jitters, and it is essential to choose targets of opportunity that meet critical success factors and avoid early failure modes, both of which an experienced sensei will help navigate.

As with the evaluation and education stages, at start-up the excitement of getting started can cloud the organization's judgment regarding proper goal setting, event preparation, and support infrastructure. Knowing where to begin means having the end in mind, not that a Lean journey has an end point (by definition, it most certainly does not). Rather, knowing the end means taking the time to strategically choose initial kaizen targets that will eliminate rework and pay long-term dividends. Key start-up activities include appointing a steering committee; identifying full-time improvement team members; establishing Mission Control for visual communications and charting progress; and conducting proper visioning and value stream analysis. Although start-up activities may seem like they postpone action and delay results, these preparatory steps are essential to achieving member support and buy-in. They enable the organization to achieve maximum return on investment for the effort and expense of improvement.

Proper start-ups flow naturally into the final stage of Phase 1, "Build the Models." The smallest building blocks of a truly Lean organization are its flow cells. Flow cells tightly connected together with pull form value streams, with "value" defined by the external customer. Failure to dive deeply into any given flow cell to create and demonstrate all the attributes of a model flow cell is one of the most common mistakes committed by neophyte Lean organizations. Also, jumping from "lily pad to lily pad" with improvement efforts will suboptimize performance and most likely result in the absence of true bottom-line, enterprise-wide results. Thus, the Transformation Continuum marks the end of Phase 1 by emphatically stating that an organization cannot move into Phase 2 unless or until both model flow cells and the first model value stream are accomplished. Completion includes proper documentation of the organization's business system, including principles and habits, which will enable the learnings from Phase 1 to be spread successfully throughout the enterprise.

When faced with the oft-asked question, "Where should we begin?" the answer is to focus on the visioning and value stream analysis at start-up, combined with a commitment to building models in Phase 1. Leaders should understand that every organization has (or should have) four categories of streams. The first three, which are entirely about providing value in the eyes of the external customer, include development (of products and services), demand generation and capture (marketing and sales); and delivery (including the operations that manufacture or provide services). The fourth set of streams, which we call "support streams," view value from both external and internal customer perspectives. They include the functional support areas of information technology (IT), accounting, human development, and other areas not in direct contact with external customers. When building models in Phase 1, the most commonly chosen value stream category is delivery, but it is also appropriate to consider initial possibilities in development, demand, and support.

Regardless of where an organization begins, start-up and the models must be first and foremost strategically selected; then, as part of "Committing to a New Improvement System," the organization must demonstrate the discipline to dive deeply into the chosen value stream, creating model cells and, ultimately, the initial model value stream.

Phase 1 ends with a deliberate pause for hansei—reflection on what has been accomplished in Phase 1 and identification of any gaps, either along the Transformation Continuum or vertically within each of the improvement dimensions. Root cause and corrective actions are appropriate at this time to address missteps and to ensure that a firm foundation has been established that will allow for acceleration of improvement in Phase 2. At this point, the organization should clearly be in the developmental or learning stage, "consciously incompetent," in which leaders, managers, and other associates are beginning to grasp the magnitude of what they don't know about Lean enterprise transformation.

PHASE 2: ACCELERATING CAPABILITY AND PERFORMANCE

Phase 2 of the Transformation Continuum has three subphases: "Go Deeper," "Go Wider," and "Go Beyond." In Phase 2, organizations begin to accelerate performance improvement, provided that they have systematically and diligently demonstrated the discipline prescribed by Phase 1.

Upon completing the first full pass through the model value stream, it is time to demonstrate through kaizen work performed in the go-deeper subphase that the law of diminishing returns does not apply in Lean organizations. Upwards of three to five additional, complete passes through the model flow cells and model value stream will yield ever-increasing returns on investment and expand the horizons of what is achievable in the Future State. During this subphase, the organization becomes properly prepared to accept strategy deployment and new and exciting ways to think of breakthrough, paradigm-changing levels of performance.

In the go-deeper subphase, organizations also encounter the interdependence of multiple value streams and support streams. The model value stream will highlight the dependencies and barriers that exist in functionally designed organizations and will pull for a new structure that gives additional autonomy to support all work elements required to deliver value to the customers. Leaders will be forced to devise ways to break up functional silos in support of restructured work flows along the value stream.

The organization will become anxious to spread Lean to other value streams. While this should be rigorously resisted in Phase 1, the next subphase in Phase 2, "Go Wider," is the appropriate time to expand the learning. At this point, the entire enterprise is potentially in scope. However, the cadre of internal experts must be commensurate with the leader's appetite to expand. To cover the entire enterprise, the recommended internal full-time Lean support is 3 percent of the total organization population; anything less than that will require the expansion to be scaled back to meet the level of dedicated human resources.

The pace of change, as defined by the number of weeklong improvement event teams, is $n/10$, as discussed in Chapter 5. At this point in the Transformation Continuum, before moving further, the learning curve should be reaching "consciously competent" in everything from real-time problem solving to strategy deployment to understanding all the basic tools of Lean. Additionally, some of the more sophisticated tools found in 3P (see Appendix A) and the Simpler Design System™ should now be introduced to accelerate performance through right-sized equipment and new product design. Successful use of these advanced tools and techniques is delayed until this stage to allow for the requisite mastery of fundamental Lean tools, which should be bordering on "unconsciously competent." Such mastery comes only from practice and experience, with dozens of repetitions required for them to become second nature. A common failure mode is to pursue advanced tools before the basic principles have been mastered and the habits engrained.

Having gone both "deeper" and "wider" in Phase 2, it is time in the Transformation Continuum to "go beyond." There are two ways to expand beyond the four walls of your enterprise: involving upstream suppliers and downstream customers in creating Extended Value Steams. This is where ultimate leverage resides. At this point, organizations recognize the inseparable nature of their supplier relationships and work to either "*change* their suppliers or change their *suppliers*." Internal experts now become external consultants, working with suppliers to improve connections and design products and flows that reduce waste for the ultimate customer.

Likewise, customers are integrated into the process of defining products and work flows that reduce waste for the ultimate end user. The "Voice of the Environment" is critical to truly understanding what defines value. Organizations at this phase of the Transformation Continuum seek knowledge beyond what they think they know about customers and their environment and become insatiably curious to redefine value that delights, not merely satisfies, the end customer. The goal morphs from simply improving internal value streams to identifying and driving out waste at every stage of the complete value chain.

PHASE 3: TRANSFORMATION CONTINUUM

Phase 3 of the Transformation Continuum has only two subphases: "Intensify Human Development" and "Redefine Your Environment." Mastering the human-development subphase enables the enterprise to solidify the gains of earlier transformation stages, transcend into the "unconsciously competent" learning stage, and more fully prepare to harness and leverage its capabilities to shift market paradigms and create the ultimate growth engine in one's industry.

While human development is a focus all along the Transformation Continuum, at this point it becomes apparent that transforming an organization's culture is wholly people dependent; as Toyota likes to say, "We build people before we build cars." The processes of member selection, evaluation, and development must tie directly to the shared values, habits, and behaviors of the high-performance culture being created. Standard work in these areas is essential for creating an enduring Lean-based culture and achieving game-changing performance. Members are now embracing change and, in fact, pulling change rather than waiting for it to be pushed by leaders. Hourly and daily problem solving and improvement are accelerating because all members are, first, trusted and empowered to eliminate waste; then, they are mentored and trained to create waste-free processes and solve problems robustly and in real time.

By this time in the Transformation Continuum, the enterprise should be reaping great benefits in all True North dimensions of performance: human development, quality, delivery, and cost/productivity. In the oft-overlooked fifth dimension of growth, the organization may or may not have harnessed developing capabilities to grow revenue and market share. Lean transformation and growth are inseparable concepts; however, the latter must be consciously and strategically developed, just as the former was consciously and strategically chosen as a differentiator. What an organization does with the competitive advantages of having achieved this advanced stage of the Transformation Continuum can forever change its market-sector paradigms.

An organization in the redefine-your-environment subphase will leverage its "unconscious competence" by redefining Lean transformation or expanding their served markets. By launching game-changing products and services with a dynamic, Lean-development value stream, organizations at this stage will separate themselves from the competition by being fast and first to market with concepts that delight their customers. By finding new routes to market and building brand excellence through Lean capabilities, organizations will shorten lead times in the demand-generation and -capture value stream. By working end-to-end in the delivery value chain with suppliers and customers to shorten lead times, drive toward zero defects, and produce and deliver at the lowest cost, organizations will shift the expectations in entire industries and create the new "normal." Additionally, "unconsciously competent" Lean organizations will often seek to expand by acquiring other organizations and taking them through the same journey. Their internal transformation capability enables the Lean organization to see waste and opportunity in other companies that can become targets of growth opportunity, not only for the company, but also for its members who are seeking personal growth.

At this stage in the Transformation Continuum, one might be tempted to ask, "Are we finished?" Naturally, the answer is, "We're never finished with this journey." Leaders often realize this when, at this stage of their personal Lean journey, they become incurably committed to pursuing perfection through Lean. There will always be new layers of waste to uncover and new challenges to overcome, as the journey along the Transformation Continuum has taught us.

DIMENSIONS OF CHANGE: HUMAN DEVELOPMENT

As previously stated, the development of human capital is a primary focus throughout the Transformation Continuum. Addressing different segments of the organization in human development by leaders, managers, and members highlights the important roles played by each level and acknowledges that each group affects and is affected by a Lean enterprise transformation in different ways. No one is exempt from the impact of change. Ultimately, as the new culture is being defined and constructed, everyone's role and responsibility will change, and some in very radical ways. Therefore, it is imperative that the human-development needs of the organization in transformation follow the same path of learning openly and systematically, from "unconscious incompetence" to "unconscious competence."

The most-often repeated failure mode along the Transformation Continuum is the impact of leaders and leadership. As George Koenigsaecker has written and spoken about countless times, Lean transformation is leadership-intensive. Leaders must learn new habits as their roles transform from command and control to a mentorship role in a servant-leadership style. Leaders often begin by delegating and being at arm's length from the detail work of the transformation, which is antithetical to the "learn by doing" nature of a Lean transformation. It is, after all, a learning environment that is being embedded in the new culture, and leaders must model mentoring and learning behaviors if the organization is to be successful in building an enduring Lean culture.

Managers in the middle are often caught in the crossfire of change. In many cases, their positions are rendered as waste and are eliminated. In other cases, managers cannot adapt and cede control to members of their team who become enthusiastically engaged in routine daily problem solving. Ultimately, the development of managers is one key to deploying new learnings throughout the organization and holding gains while supporting team members and driving performance to achieve targets hour by hour. Recognizing the impact on managers and developing a proactive strategy and processes for their development and buy-in is a critical success factor along the Transformation Continuum.

Developing members through both didactic and practical learning opportunities is also fundamental to Lean transformations. Creating the successful Lean culture requires involvement and the development of all people in the organization. Reaching the inflection point between push and pull for change at the broad membership level of the organization is a key milestone along the Transformation Continuum. At first, involvement of membership is minimal. However, by the time the start-up subphase is ready to commence, it is vital that all members be made aware of the intent behind the change and "what's in it for me." As the Transformation Continuum unfolds, member input segues from event-based to hourly participation and problem solving. Employee suggestion systems that empower members to recommend and implement improvement can be highly motivating. Evaluation, compensation systems, rewards, and recognition systems should be introduced or modified, as well, to be consistent with the values, habits, and behaviors of a Lean organization.

To summarize, many organizations say that their people are the most important asset. In Lean organizations on the Transformation Continuum path, there is a conscious and obvious effort to achieve the true meaning of developing human talent and going beyond rhetoric to live that belief every day at all levels of the organization.

DIMENSIONS OF CHANGE: ALIGN STRUCTURE/CULTURE

Non-Lean-thinking organizations are typically hierarchical and functionally aligned. They are designed on the premise that specialization by levels of education, leadership, and job function achieves efficiency. The concept of building an organizational structure to deliver value in the eyes of the customer, in the least wasteful way, is not a fundamental premise of the typical traditional organization. Conversely, Lean organizations see waste as inherent in functional silos and the vertical, suboptimized thinking that occurs in those silos, and as leading to more waste that is eventually passed along to customers in many forms: poor quality, long lead times, no steady flow of new or improved products, and other similar dissatisfiers.

Along the Transformation Continuum, organizations learn a new way of thinking about how to organize to deliver value. The learning begins at the flow-cell level, when model flow cells are implemented in Phase 1 to organize the work in flow with (a) right-sized equipment and staffing to meet takt time and (b) pull based on actual customer demand, not forecasts. When flow cells are linked in value streams, additional hansei is triggered about the way organizational silos create barriers to flow: flow of information, ideas, and products/services. Upon deep reflection and learning, the notion of demand, development, and delivery value streams, with intersecting support streams, is revealed as the target state for future organizational structure and alignment (see Figure D.1—value stream chart).

By the time the organization reaches the "consciously incompetent" stage of learning about flow and value in the eyes of customers, it becomes apparent that radical change is required to align human resources and redesign management systems in order to deal with the waste inherent in silo structures. This, in turn, triggers new human-development needs to support a new way of thinking about organizational structure. Since leaders, managers, and members are accustomed to dealing with and working around silos, value stream structures set them all back to zero and require intense education and adaptation.

The "consciously competent" stage is achieved when all resources are aligned to provide value in the eyes of the customer along the value stream; internal improvement teams are staffed at optimal levels to sustain a rapid rate of improvement (3 percent to achieve n/10); and cross-functional teams replace functional teams for problem solving in real time.

DIMENSIONS OF CHANGE: TOOLS

To accept the notion of a Transformation Continuum is to accept the premise that Lean tools are merely one key dimension of improvement along the journey, and that tools mastery is built sequentially and purposefully. The key to Phase 3 "unconsciously competent" Lean organizations is making the investment and taking the time to gain mastery in Lean tools while building models and promoting deep organizational learning and acceptance of the principles that make Lean work in Phases 1 and 2.

As this is not a tools-oriented chapter or book, this subject will be summed up with this simple caveat: Beware of experts selling Lean tools as the principal focus of Lean transformation. The Transformation Continuum teaches and reinforces that the tools of Lean represent only one of many levels of learning and improvement to be harnessed to ensure an enduring Lean enterprise transformation.

DIMENSIONS OF CHANGE: RESULTS

Achieving results begins with understanding and clearly defining the key performance indicators leading to customer satisfaction or delight. Most traditional organizations measure an inordinate number of things, many of which are distractions that lead to a dilution of effort and results. Framing an organization's key measures along the five True North dimensions helps achieve balance, consistency, and focus.

Successful Lean transformations have taught us to focus on driving double-digit improvement year over year in just a handful of key performance indicators. Furthermore, we learn that linking target measures from end to end in the value stream, using policy deployment to create connectivity and unity of purpose, accelerates breakthrough performance. As with tools, this book highlights many such breakthrough results. However, it is noteworthy to reinforce that a systematic approach to implementing model flow cells, linked to form a model value stream, and multiple passes of kaizen through the value stream will drive unimagined results.

Learn to measure results that matter by reducing the "important many" to concentrate on the "critical few." Finally, do not hopscotch around in random fashion, but rather follow the course of Lean transformation carefully prescribed by the Transformation Continuum; it is the key to building pay-as-you-go, continuously improving results.

Appendix E: Red River Army Depot—Accelerating Lean through Leadership Immersion

BACKGROUND

The Red River Army Depot (RRAD) is a Department of Defense maintenance facility providing maintenance, repair, and overhaul for Department of Defense wheeled and tracked vehicles, rubber products, and various other pieces of equipment for the US Army. With more than $1 billion in annual operating revenues in 2008 (projected to be $800 million in 2011) and with more than 3,000 civilian employees located in Texarkana, Texas, and another 500 employees located throughout the United States and internationally, the RRAD is a critical supplier of equipment for the US Army, especially for the Iraq and Afghanistan war arenas. The organization is made up entirely of Department of Army civilians and contract laborers, except for a commander and sergeant major who provide oversight and leadership to RRAD during three-year tours.

The work of the RRAD covers a vast array of activities, ranging from inspection and repair, reset, and overhaul to the complete remanufacturing of Army tactical wheeled vehicles, combat vehicles, and their components (see Figure E.1). Major areas of focus include the High-Mobility Multipurpose Wheeled Vehicle (HMMWV); the Family of Medium Tactical Vehicles (FMTV), which are 2.5- and 5-ton trucks, and Mine-Resistant Ambush Protective Vehicles (MRAP).

FIGURE E.1
Examples of vehicles worked on at Red River Army Depot.

A POWERFUL MOTIVATOR: BRAC

The fear of extinction is a powerful motivator. Competition in every industry is a reality; companies work to stay alive through innovation, quality, and/or cost efficiency in delivery of their products and/or services. Military industrial facilities face similar competition from alternatives in civilian industry and from other military sites providing similar services. To military facilities, survival means, for the most part, staying off the federal Base Realignment and Closure (BRAC) list, which has historically targeted savings through closure or reuse of military locations on a ten-year cycle.

Like many military locations, RRAD has been subject to scrutiny and consideration for closure in the BRAC process in response to federal government budget pressures. Although it was included on the BRAC list in 1995 and again in 2005, RRAD survived both of these threats.

When it was put on the 2005 list, RRAD was three years into its Lean journey. RRAD had a history of working to stay competitive through training, using performance improvement techniques, and seeking the best practices through benchmarking site visits and sharing with other industry leaders. It had expanded these efforts through the introduction of Lean techniques, with the assistance of Lean consultants from Simpler.

Initial Lean efforts had shown early success. One of the first areas of focus was the HMMWV value stream. Through multiple events (two per week minimum), RRAD was able to improve its output and productivity dramatically in the remanufacturing and up-armoring process, going from an output of one vehicle every two days to 100 HMMWVs per day. This represented a threefold increase in productivity and a more than 200-fold improvement in output, as well as enhanced protection for US troops in Iraq.

RRAD had also conducted multiple passes in the Heavy Expanded Mobility Tactical Truck (HEMTT) value stream. The operations tempo (OPTEMPO) increase in Iraq required more HEMTTs in the field rather than at RRAD in process. To accomplish the challenge, a value stream analysis concentrating on reduction of repair lead time was conducted. Approximately four months later, what started as an attack on repair lead time resulted in not only a lead-time reduction from 120 to 30 days, but also reductions in work-in-process (WIP) level and cost. In addition, in-process rejects decreased and process output increased.

These early successes and the efforts to embrace Lean did not go unnoticed. The BRAC commissioner took RRAD off the 2005 list because of its perceived efforts to embrace Lean and achieve improvements, as well as the increased demand for services stemming from the wars in Afghanistan and Iraq. The result: survival—at least for the moment. However, knowing that continued improvements in cost, schedule, and quality were essential for future survival, RRAD leadership remained focused on the Lean journey.

Over the next three years, RRAD received eight Shingo awards and two Robert T. Mason awards (Best Depot awards for maintenance excellence from the Department of Defense). In fact, Red River became known as "the place to see" to learn how to organize and operate an industrial base depot.

NEW LEADERSHIP AND A NEW FOCUS

In July 2008, new military leadership arrived at Red River when Colonel Mitchell started a three-year stint as commander of the Red River Army Depot. Colonel Mitchell came to RRAD with a strong knowledge of and commitment to Lean techniques: "I knew coming in that Red River had a reputation for Lean manufacturing by reading articles, and I had heard about the multiple Shingo awards. My job was to move the depot to the next level, but at this point, I didn't know how."

In addition to extensive training, including a Depot Leadership course in Lean/Six Sigma management and many benchmarking trips, Colonel Mitchell had recently completed a Lean internship with Caterpillar. He recognized the opportunities for RRAD to enhance its productivity and remain competitive. Six years into the Lean journey, leadership initiated a Lean assessment to answer the questions: Where are we? Have we transformed how work gets done? Do we have a culture of continuous improvement? What opportunities still exist?

The assessment showed that RRAD had made progress and was using Lean techniques and tools across the organization, but backsliding had occurred. Lean was not yet integral to the culture. Red River was still at the tools level; a widespread commitment to standardization and continuous improvement was not consistently reflected in daily management or daily work. Leadership responded. Over the next several years, leadership implemented a variety of Lean operating systems, models, tools, and techniques to foster a culture of continuous improvement that they had learned from other leading organizations like Honeywell and Caterpillar as well as from Lean experts.

A major focus of these efforts was the implementation of an operating model that integrated and standardized the use of Lean techniques in daily operations. These techniques included command centers with visual management tools; daily tiered meetings focused on identifying and resolving work-flow issues; war rooms to track metrics; and training of management and employees to understand cell creation—all while utilizing Lean tools such as A3s, 5S, standard work, visual management, flow, pull, and the pursuit of perfection (see Appendix A).

Following a benchmarking visit to see the Honeywell Operating System, depot leaders believed a version of this system would work well at RRAD and formed a Tiger Team to implement something similar. The biggest successes with the system were the daily "tier" meetings, which were run to help in meeting standard work goals and to solve problems and communicate more effectively. The command centers in every cost center helped RRAD to see itself more clearly. Each of the cost centers could see how they were doing in the areas of health, environment, safety, cost, schedule, and quality, and the information flowed up the chain on a daily basis. However, something was missing.

Colonel Mitchell had learned from the Caterpillar internship that they had faced similar problems with their first deployment of the Caterpillar Production System, their version of the Toyota Production System. They also had issues with accountability and governance in their first deployment of their system; so, they redeployed with more rigorous audits, incentives, and standardization. After the Caterpillar internship, RRAD formed another Tiger Team focused on expanding resources in the Lean support function. The goal was to increase the pace of Rapid Improvement Events (RIEs) for breakthrough thinking, to increase standardization, and to support the implementation of Lean tools for cell creation by adding an audit and training capability in the Lean Office, writing a vision and guiding principles for the Red River Operating System (RROS), and codifying all of this in a Red River Regulation.

In addition, a two-hour block of training covering the basic tools of Lean was created and used to establish a foundation to launch the program. A Transformation Plan of Care (TPOC) was also developed with senior leaders, using A3 thinking and identifying True North metrics. True North metrics were created to align the depot, division, and shop-floor levels (see Figure E.2). Daily tier meetings and weekly meetings occurred to review metrics and solve problems. The Lean Office created an immersion process, which was required within the first year of employment, and Lean experience/involvement was incorporated into hiring and promotion practices. These renewed efforts energized the organization and led to many improvements.

Metric Descriptions	Target Goal
Quality:	
Defects per # Items	.5
Cost:	
Expense per Total Employee	−20%
Delivery:	
100% Complete and on Time (COT)	100%
Safety/Morale:	
Lost Time rate	−25%
Case Rate	−25%
Employee Morale	TBD
Brac:	
Military Value	+4.0

FIGURE E.2
True North metrics of RRAD.

FIGURE E.3
Standard work in Iraq.

Some innovations were transported overseas. For example, depot employees in Iraq helped create flow cells for rebuilding HMMWV trucks, writing the standard work in Arabic on the wall for workers and providing only the tools required for the station (see Figure E.3).

This led to dramatic improvements. Similarly, employees in Kuwait established a work flow rather than using a bay approach for repairing MRAP vehicles. The flow-line approach resulted in a fivefold improvement over the bay-area approach.

ACCELERATING LEAN FOR SURVIVAL

Despite these improvements, top leadership wasn't seeing the leadership engagement or pace needed to fully transform the Red River culture. Although RRAD had increased its resources devoted to Lean and the pace of events, something was missing. By mid-2010, the economy and budget deficits were painting a future for RRAD that included certain reductions in Department of Defense resources and commensurate reductions in funding for the very work of Red River. The potential of a 2015 Base Realignment and Closure (BRAC) process was (and is) looming. Leadership knew then and continues to believe that the best immunization against being on that list, as well as the best way to maintain its future workload, is to reduce costs and significantly improve depot productivity and quality performance.

With continuing competitive and budget pressures, RRAD has pursued greater productivity improvements, such as double-digit gains, from its Lean efforts. Colonel Mitchell invited George Koenigsaecker to help evaluate the situation and identify what was needed to accelerate its Lean journey. This led to the development of the following critical elements:

- Targeted focus on a "model" value stream, rather than a depot-wide, broad-brush approach
- Accelerated pace of events and supporting resources, using the $n/10$ event pace and 3 percent dedicated resources supporting and tracking improvement efforts
- Leadership immersion

In early October 2010, a Depot Lean Deployment Policy was issued, launching RRAD into a new era of Lean and a radical immersion of leadership, and simultaneously focusing on and accelerating Lean activities and resources. The major elements of the policy reflected the three critical elements identified here. The command directive that launched the restart program, which includes the executive immersion plan, is shown in Figure E.4.

FOCUS ON "MODEL" VALUE LINES AT AN ACCELERATED PACE

Although RRAD had focused on the HMMWV rebuilding process early in its Lean journey, activity in subsequent years had expanded across the entire depot. Shifting focus to "model" value streams represented an opportunity to achieve gains faster by focusing on high-visibility, high-volume value streams within RRAD. The pace of activity and level of resources would be heightened for these value streams, ramping up to an $n/5$ event pace.

TARR-C   30 SEP 2010

MEMORANDOM FOR SEE DISTRIBUTION

SUBJECT: Lean Deployment Policy

1. The Department of Defense (DoD) is facing budget cuts and a severe reduction in reset, recapitalization, and overhaul funding. Red River Army Depot (RRAD) is forecasting a commensurate reduction on workload (2011-2015). Historically, the best and only condition that will reverse this forecast is to reduce costs and significantly improve depot productivity performance and quality performance. Furthermore, lower costs to the customer and improvement in depot productivity performance are the best immunization against a possible 2015 Base Realignment and Closure (BRAC) adverse decision.

2. Leadership Immersion: Successful Lean conversions are always led from the top. The Leadership team, at every level of the organization, must be aligned around the purpose and importance of successful implementation of the change initiatives. This group includes Command & Staff, Division Chiefs, Branch Chiefs, Supervisors and first-line leadership, down to the shop and office floor level. The leadership team will support Lean Manufacturing initiatives by:

   a. The Lean Manufacturing Initiative will be reflected in performance reviews at the individual and team level. The change efforts will not be seen as something other than a professional responsibility.

   b. Successful participation in Value Stream Analysis (VSA) and Rapid Improvement Events (RIE) will be a graded criterion for promotions and other management selections to supervisory positions, to include leader positions. For wage grade positions, where all other technical skills are equal, successful Lean participation will be the tiebreaker. These criteria will be well documented and clearly communicated to the workforce in advance and repetitively reinforced.

   c. Select Command & Staff Directors and Office Chiefs are required to participate in eight Lean events prior to 31 May 11 (see Figure 1A below). This participation will consist of fully engaged participation with no blackberry or meeting distractions.

      (1) Of the eight events required by Command & Staff personnel, four will be in a model value stream area.

      (2) The following is a schedule depicting event weeks and Command & Staff personnel required to participate in the events scheduled for that week. OCI will populate the schedule with events. OCI will attempt to work through any schedule conflicts. POC for the schedule is Patti Chisum, ext 3516.

FIGURE E.4
Command directive.

TARR-C
SUBJECT: Lean Deployment Policy

Figure 1A

WEEK OF 9/13/10	WEEK OF 9/20/10	WEEK OF 9/27/10	WEEK OF 10/4/10
WEEK OF 10/12/2010	WEEK OF 10/18/2010	WEEK OF 10/25/2010	WEEK OF 11/1/2010
WEEK OF 11/8/2010	WEEK OF 11/15/2010	WEEK OF 1/3/2011	WEEK OF 11/29/2010
WEEK OF 12/6/2010	WEEK OF 12/13/2010	WEEK OF 1/31/2011	WEEK OF 1/10/2011
WEEK OF 1/18/2011	WEEK OF 1/24/2011	WEEK OF 2/28/2011	WEEK OF 2/7/2011
WEEK OF 2/14/2011	WEEK OF 2/22/2011	WEEK OF 3/28/2011	WEEK OF 3/7/2011
WEEK OF 3/14/2011	WEEK OF 3/21/2011	WEEK OF 4/25/2011	WEEK OF 4/4/2011
WEEK OF 4/11/2011	WEEK OF 4/18/2011	WEEK OF 5/9/2011	WEEK OF 5/2/2011
Personnel Required:	Personnel Required:	Personnel Required:	Personnel Required:
Chief of Staff	Business Mgmnt Office Chief	Deputy Commander	Commander
Director of Maint/Prod	Systems Mgmnt Office Chief	Safety Office Chief	Deputy Dir of Information Mngmnt
Director of Information Mngmnt	Director of Contracting	Director of Maint/Log	Deputy Dir of Maint/Prod 2
Director of Resource Mngmnt	Director of Emergency Services	Deputy Dir of Emergency Services	Deputy Dir of Public Works
Director of Quality	Director of Public Works	Deputy Dir of Quality	Deputy Dir of Maint/Log
Deputy Dir of Maint/Prod 1		OCI Chief	Sergeant Major

3. Model Value Streams: RRAD will implement model value streams that will reflect the highest levels of Lean implementation. We will push the bar on Lean implementation in these areas to reach new heights putting the model value stream far in front of all other value streams on the depot and in the Army. The model value stream is a strong change management tool, providing the whole organization with a constantly improving vision of its future.

a. The implementation of the model value streams will be the responsibility of the Chief, Office of Continuous Improvement (OCI), the Directors of Maintenance Logistics/Production, and the Value Stream Manager (VSM). The primary model value stream will be FMTV. The next priority is Secondary Items. However, MRAP will become primary if funded and supersede FMTV and Secondary Items.

(1) FMTV: The FMTV value stream is an ideal candidate for primary model value stream due to the number of assets in the Army (77,578) and potential workload for the depot. Starting immediately the FMTV value stream will complete a Value Stream Analysis (VSA) and conduct Lean events at an N/5 event pace. This pace means the value stream should be conducting approximately two events per week.

(2) MRAP: The MRAP value stream is a high visibility program, the DoD's highest priority acquisition program (19,000 purchased by the Army to date), and, thus a high priority program for the depot to excel in resetting or overhauling.

(3) Secondary: The Secondary Items value stream is the value stream with the most staying power and work load in out years and the workload that is most vulnerable to transferring to other activities. Starting immediately the Secondary value stream will initiate their 18 month plan at an accelerated event pace of N/5. This pace means the value stream should be conducting approximately two events per week.

FIGURE E.4 (continued)
Command directive.

TARR-C
SUBJECT: Lean Deployment Policy

b. Research has proven that approximately 50% of administrative processes are waste and less that 10% of administrative processes are error free. Starting immediately, administrative areas that directly affect production of the above model value streams (i.e. MMD, Quality) will complete a VSA and conduct all follow on Lean events at an accelerated pace. All other administrative areas will complete a VSA and all follow on Lean events at an N/20 pace.

c. Every time you restudy a process, Lean tools expose new levels of waste and improvement opportunities. Each model value stream will conduct a VSA and implement associated Lean events over a 6 to 10 month period. At this point, a new VSA will be conducted on the improved value stream. This process will be conducted three more times resulting in an implementation of five "passes" of improvement through every value stream. The goal of the five "passes" is a 90% reduction on throughput time and a 50% increase in productivity.

d. All other value streams will be required to conduct Lean events at an N/20 pace.

4. Concept for Execution:

a. Each Director, Office Chief, and VSM will be responsible for ensuring their organizations employ the Lean principles listed below.

(1) Standard Work - A simple written description of the safest, highest quality, and most efficient way known to perform a particular process or task. Standard work represents the only acceptable way to do the process it describes. Expect standard work to be continually improved and updated by supervisors.

(2) 5S - 5S refers to workplace organization and standardization. It is how we have our areas organized, free of clutter, efficient, safe, and pleasant to work in. It lays the groundwork and develops the discipline necessary to support the successful implementation of other Lean concepts throughout an organization. 5S stands for Sort, Straighten, Shine, Standardize, and Sustain. The 5S Training Module will be available on the intranet no later than 13 Sep 10.

(3) One Piece Flow - One Piece Flow refers to the concept of moving one workpiece at a time between operations within a workcell.

(4) Visual Management - Visual management is the application of any visual aid or device that promotes safer, more efficient, and less wasteful processes. Our goal is to implement a visual management system that enables you to see production metrics, whether we are ahead or behind schedule, with a fifteen second glance of the area. Visual management leads to identifying and solving problems "at-a-glance".

(5) Pull - The concept of pull in Lean production means to respond to the pull, or demand, of the customer.

FIGURE E.4 (continued)
Command directive.

TARR-C
SUBJECT: Lean Deployment Policy

b. Each organization will utilize the Lean events listed below to implement Lean principles in their work processes.

(1) Value Stream Analysis (VSA): A VSA is used to create a value stream map of the process and develop a detailed improvement plan for the next 6 to 12 months.

(2) Rapid Improvement Event (RIE): An RIE is a Lean event that focuses on eliminating waste, improving productivity, and achieving sustained continual improvement in targeted activities and processes of an organization.

(3) Problem Solving Corrective Action (PS/CA): A PS/CA concentrates on a specific defect/problem and creates a plan to eliminate the defect forever.

c. Team Design:

(1) Team Leaders will be the supervisor of the work area.

(2) The team make up will consist of an OCI Facilitator (if available), ½ employees from work area and ½ employees from "other" areas including support organizations, suppliers, customers, and management.

(3) VSM's will be team members and will be on teams to gain personal learning concerning identifying waste and determining the Lean skill level of the team leaders (work area supervisors). The VSM's participation must be full time with no interruptions or absences. If the event involves the VSM's value stream, then the VSM will be the sponsor and a team member.

d. Investment costs associated with improvements must be approved by the VSM. Investment costs will be kept to a minimum and not to exceed $1,500.00. Any cost that exceeds $1,500.00 must have Directorate approval or above if required.

5. POC is Mr. Kennith Brumley, ext 3455.

DANIEL G. MITCHELL
Colonel, LG
Commanding

DISTRIBUTION:
RRAD Command & Staff
RRAD Office Chiefs
RRAD Supervisors

FIGURE E.4 (continued)
Command directive.

The Lean Deployment Policy stated: "RRAD will implement model value streams that will reflect the highest level of Lean implementation. We will push the bar on Lean implementation in these areas to reach new heights, putting the model value stream far in front of all other value streams on the depot and in the Army. The model value stream is a strong change management tool, providing the whole organization with a constantly improving vision of its future."

Two value streams were selected to be "model" streams. The Family of Medium Tactical Vehicles (FMTV) value stream was selected as the primary one, because of the number of assets in the army (almost 78,000) and the potential workload for RRAD. Working at an $n/5$ event pace meant conducting approximately two RIEs per week. The second model value stream selected was the Secondary Item value stream. Secondary items, such as engines and transmissions, are items used in support of other value streams. This value stream provided the greatest workload and longevity for RRAD, and was considered most vulnerable to being transferred elsewhere. At an $n/5$ pace, this value stream would also be conducting approximately two events per week. The Mine Resistant Ambush Protective Vehicle (MRAP) value stream, representing the Department of Defense's highest priority acquisition program, was selected as a possible future model stream. This poised the value stream to be a significant opportunity for RRAD to excel at resetting and overhauling.

Because continuous improvement is just that—continuous—it is considered critical to restudy a process, thereby exposing new levels of waste and new opportunities for improvement. The Lean Deployment Policy directed that each model value stream conduct a value stream analysis (VSA) and implement events over a six- to ten-month period. At that point, a new VSA would be conducted on the improved value stream. The policy called for a goal of five "passes" through every model value stream, targeting a 90 percent reduction in throughput time and a 50 percent increase in productivity.

Although the primary focus of Lean efforts would be on the model value streams, RRAD intended to continue value stream analyses in other value streams, as well as in administrative areas. The policy directed that all administrative areas directly affecting production of the model value streams would also be scrutinized using Lean techniques. That required the Materiel Management Division (the depot's supply chain managers); Depot Contracting Office, Public Works (the depot's facility and equipment managers); and the Depot Quality Department to complete a VSA and conduct Lean events at the accelerated pace ($n/5$). Other administrative areas and value streams would be required to conduct VSA and events at an $n/20$ pace (see Figure E.5).

INVESTING FOR SUCCESS

Supporting the Lean Deployment Policy and acceleration of Lean passes in the model value streams and support organizations required increased resources and capabilities in the Lean Office. RRAD had beefed up the Lean Office resources with its push in 2009, targeting the 3 percent guideline recommended. However, additional resources were needed to support the accelerated pace and leadership immersion. The event cycle runs seven weeks, including time to prepare, support, and follow up on events. A formal process has been developed to provide training to facilitators and conduct data gathering for value stream analyses and events. Currently, RRAD employs 51 facilitators across the organization supporting these Lean events, augmenting the permanent Lean staff.

Additional focus on sustaining improvements was considered critical to the success of the Lean Deployment Policy objectives. The Lean Office has developed a method to track the sustainability of improvements and to support those efforts, as well as to determine how best to redeploy talent affected by Lean improvements within the organization. The Lean Office also tracks event pace and event ROI (return on investment). Surveys have been developed to help measure culture change by monitoring the morale of employees and leadership involved in Lean activities. Similar to study results by other industry partners using Lean manufacturing tools, leadership has found that, in most cases, employees' feelings about their jobs, coworkers, and management improve as Lean event experience increases.

LEADERSHIP IMMERSION

The success or failure of Lean conversions is frequently determined by the commitment and support of leadership. Effective and transformative Lean efforts are always led from the top. Colonel Mitchell saw that the leadership team, at every level of the organization, needed to align itself around

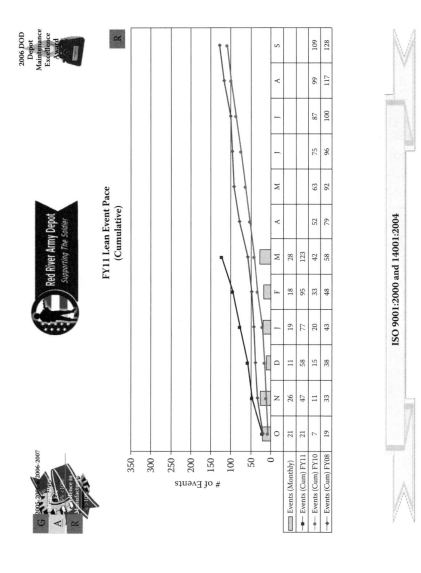

FIGURE E.5

Lean event pace for the 2011 fiscal year.

the purpose and importance of successfully implementing change initiatives. Lean transformation data reveals that participation in eight to ten events is required before an individual completely "buys-in" to the benefits of Lean and begins to change the way he or she thinks about eliminating waste. Therefore, senior leader participation in events is critical to success.

The Lean Deployment Policy directed specific expectations and involvement of leadership, including:

- Having all leaders fully participate in a Lean event every month. This included the top thirty-five individuals on the leadership team, including command and staff, division chiefs, branch chiefs, supervisors, and other first-line leaders, and required their full and active participation in a weeklong event every month. In the first eight months, half of those events needed to be in a model value stream area.
- Incorporating participation in performance reviews at the individual and team level.
- Making participation in value stream analysis (VSA) and Rapid Improvement Events (RIEs) part of the graded criteria for promotions and other management selections to supervisory positions. For other hiring, in cases where all other technical skills are equal, successful Lean participation will determine selection of candidates for wage-grade positions.

The Lean Office assigned and tracked participation in events by individual leaders. This represented a significant commitment of leadership time. Every month, participation is discussed and reviewed in command staff meetings. In addition, "war rooms" were established that included metrics for the depot, division, and shop-floor levels. Weekly meetings were held in the war room to review metrics, discuss progress, and solve problems (see Figure E.6).

Leader participation did not exclude Colonel Mitchell and the command group. Committed to the principle that it "starts at the top" and the philosophy of leading by example, Colonel Mitchell participates in monthly Lean events. In addition, he takes a two-hour gemba walk daily, where he reviews progress on change initiatives, asks questions, and talks to staff. He observes that this experience has been invaluable: "Having participated in an event, with the in-depth analysis and knowledge of an area that comes from that experience, I am able to ask much better questions as a leader during my gemba walks and debriefings."

FIGURE E.6
The "war room."

Similarly, leadership immersion has made a substantial impact on both results and culture. Participation by senior leaders in events alters their perception and often facilitates faster change. Colonel Mitchell notes the following impacts seen to date:

- Leaders take a personal interest in the work stream or area in which they were involved, even if they aren't the executive responsible for it.
- Involvement causes leaders to check back and ensure that improvements made as a result of the change process are sustained.
- When work process changes are recommended or resources are required, having a senior leader involved in the weeklong event and change typically results in making necessary resources available more quickly.
- The visibility of leadership in events and follow-up enhances the overall participation, engagement, and ongoing work changes by staff, who know that senior leaders are monitoring improvements.
- Leaders use A3 thinking and Lean tools as their standard problem-solving and planning methodology.

Anecdotally, the experience has been a positive one for leadership (see the quotations in Table E.1). Excitement, increased awareness, and

TABLE E.1

The Impact of Leadership Immersion at RRAD

Quotes from senior leaders who have participated in the leadership immersion

I am a firm believer in leadership by example. Experience has proven that if a leader is not willing to walk the walk, few will follow. This leadership immersion has demonstrated to members of the workforce that "getting back to the basics" of Lean is important enough that senior managers are willing to clear their calendars and commit the time to participate in a Lean Event. Participation has provided me and other leaders insight into daily problems that would have otherwise gone unnoticed. Sustaining the momentum in Lean is essential to our Continuous Process Improvement journey that will prepare Red River Army Depot to accept the challenges of today and posture the depot for tomorrow.

Dennis L. Lewis
RRAD director for business management

The Lean process has been invaluable for finding and eliminating waste. At face value, the production tasks that appear rather simple can bring the biggest challenge. It is often the undocumented work, the unknown parts or hardware issues, the location of parts, the rework or preparation, and the quality of the tools used that—when placed on paper, discussed with subject matter experts, and brainstormed—reveal the most waste. I was impressed with how the Lean process allows you to synchronize, streamline, and ensure that flow is efficient, Lean, and focused to support your end product. A revelation for me was that frequently you will find the waste and savings in the "simple" tasks.

Wallace Embrey
RRAD director of security

With each event I complete, I continue to be impressed with the depth of knowledge and good ideas that come from the employees who work on the various value streams. When employees are involved, empowered, and equipped with the Lean tools, they are quick to identify waste that can be eliminated. Employee involvement is a great way to facilitate "buy-in" and build organizational culture change, which is essential for sustaining transformation.

Theresa Weaver
RRAD chief of staff

Participating as a team member on a Lean RIE was an eye-opening experience and provided me with an excellent exposure to the Lean process. Working as a team, we were able to isolate waste and non-value-added steps in the Directorate for Maintenance FMTV inspection process and significantly reduce the time required of the inspection team. Each individual brought valuable insight and perspective to the RIE process and benefited the team and the overall FMTV value stream. There is no doubt in my mind that active participation and leadership immersion in events are an effective method for strengthening the Lean culture that we wish to see in each and every employee every day.

James P. Tidwell
RRAD deputy to the commander

personal observation of how quickly changes can be made—as well as enhanced understanding of work flows and the challenges facing staff— have been powerful cultural forces within the RRAD leadership.

Leadership participation is critical, but ensuring that the organization is employing Lean principles in daily work is essential as well. Part of the Lean Deployment Policy clearly outlines expectations for leaders to ensure that their divisions and areas are using the following Lean principles/tools. It states that "each Director, Office Chief, and Value Stream Manager (VSM) will be responsible for ensuring their organizations employ the Lean principles listed below." These include:

- **Standard work**, with a written description of the safest, highest quality, and most efficient way to perform any particular process or task (should be continually improved and updated by supervisors)
- **5S** for workplace organization and standardization
- **One-piece flow** when moving one work piece between operations within a work cell
- **Visual management** using visual aids or devices to see production metrics and status within a fifteen-second glance
- **Pull**, responding to the pull, or demand, of the customer

CHANGING CULTURE

Based on the philosophy that an organization's focus is largely driven by what you are focused on and that "you manage what you measure," RRAD leadership has invested substantial time and resources in tracking Lean metrics and activities and is continuing to implement and develop methodologies to track and support sustainability of improvements.

Training is provided to all staff, with a two-hour block of training covering the five areas outlined in the Lean Deployment Policy. Opportunities are also provided to staff to spend two years as a Lean facilitator, which is considered a high-profile position and supports promotion.

In addition, briefings on Lean are a major focus of all meetings and communications, with the intent for the Lean process to become the "way we do business." Lean is part of quarterly leadership training, and Lean activities, goals, and results are a major component of the content in communication mechanisms used within RRAD. Colonel Mitchell has a monthly closed-circuit TV communication with the workforce, during which he ensures that the Lean Deployment Policy and the importance of Lean work are a major focus. A monthly employee newsletter reinforces the messages, rationale, and progress on Lean. Most important, however, is the emphasis Colonel Mitchell puts on Lean in terms of leadership time and focus in daily and weekly meetings with organizational leaders.

The depot conducts daily team leader meetings to discuss the progress in and the resources needed to sustain ongoing Lean events. Two Lean event sessions are also held daily, with depot leaders and team members, to report on the results of VSAs, 2Ps (process preparation, see Appendix A), RIEs, and Problem Solving and Corrective Actions (PSCAs) and to celebrate team accomplishments.

Employees are empowered when their voice is heard and they can effect positive change in their work area. Under the Red River Operating System, employees are empowered in several ways. With an aggressive Lean event pace, $n/10$ ($n/5$ in model value streams), they improve their work processes as team members on Lean events. They also have Command Center continuous improvement boards, located in each cost center, for identifying ideas or issues. They can participate in the Army Suggestion Program, with the possibility of receiving financial rewards for good ideas. Probably most importantly, they provide their own ideas for improvement in daily problem-solving meetings with their supervisor at the beginning and end of each day. Empowerment is another strong force in changing the culture and improving workforce job satisfaction.

KEEPING THE MOMENTUM

Colonel Mitchell has seen results in culture, outcomes, and, even more important, in thinking. "Since we initiated this policy, I have observed more breakthrough thinking and a willingness to challenge what we do and how we do it," he says. Although RRAD faces a burning platform in terms of competition, federal funding, and the ever-present risk of the BRAC process, Colonel Mitchell also has a sense of urgency for a different reason. He faces the end of his three-year command over the RRAD in just a few months. Although they have recently updated the TPOC and laid out a strategy deployment for the next five years, his goal is to create an irreversible momentum in the Lean culture that will carry forward beyond his tenure and position RRAD for future survival and success.

Through the Lean Deployment Policy and the significant leadership immersion, along with the structure and tools in place, it is clear that the momentum is there and that the culture of Lean is deepening within RRAD and likely to persist into the future. If so, it is likely to be just the immunization needed to inoculate the organization from a possible future BRAC and ensure that the depot becomes a world-class organization.

Appendix F: A New Product Design System That Uses Lean Principles

Chris Cooper and Rob Westrick
Simpler

Lean can enhance the design of new products, and early decision making is key. Most who are on the Lean path are likely to apply first the principles that aim to unblock the new product development that should be flowing into your value stream. For those wishing to attack issues further upstream, we provide the following tips for the new product development process:

1. At the highest level, you must see the new product development process as nonrecurring flow that should not be treated as analogous to factory production processes.
2. Design work can be thought of as a flow and, generally speaking, the adoption of colocated, cross-functional teams helps the design work flow with much less waste.
3. The elimination of waste should be pursued along three key dimensions:
    a. Elimination of product waste (features that, either by inclusion or omission, do not add value to the customer)
    b. Elimination of knowledge waste (relearning things the organization has already learned and forgotten or learning what the organization failed to capture previously)
    c. Elimination of process waste (the same eight wastes found in any process; see Chapter 2)
4. Allow each project a degree of self-definition in its process by avoiding documentation of the new product development process at too low a level.

5. See two distinct macro-level phases in the overall design process:
   a. Exploration phase—in which learning takes place and concepts are generated
   b. Execution phase—in which decisions are made and the design concept is realized

Basically, your new product development (NPD) process must be so simple that everyone can understand it within fifteen minutes. The foundational principles need to be applied regularly and pragmatically so that they become group habits. For many in the field of NPD, pragmatism and simplicity are not viewed as defining characteristics of the world they inhabit on a daily basis. Technical work is often complex, by its nature, and easy to get lost in. When working with data, specifications, and evidence-based decisions, attention to detail is a highly prized characteristic. As a result, many of the people involved in NPD will struggle initially with the idea that "less is more."

WORSHIP THE TRADE-OFF CURVES

Once you clearly understand the needs of the customer, much of the work involved in NPD involves creating solutions that optimize many conflicting requirements. For example, modern cars have complex electromechanical suspension systems that can be optimized for different conditions. Each condition represents a different trade-off of ride comfort versus control of vehicle dynamics for optimum performance.

All NPD work is a balancing act between trade-offs. Knowledge and learning around this is the true "secret sauce" of any organization's NPD capability. It is critical for an organization to capture and present this knowledge for future team members. Without trade-off knowledge, each project becomes a start-from-scratch operation, and that is risky.

KEEP IT RUTHLESSLY SIMPLE

As mentioned previously, the NPD process flows through two distinct phases:

1. Exploration
2. Execution

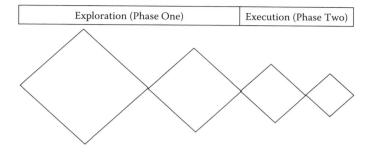

FIGURE F.1
The two distinct phases of new product development (NPD).

These phases are quite different from each other, and although they are often caused to overlap in practice, with the intention of working concurrently or in parallel to save time, we argue that they should always be considered separately, as shown in Figure F.1. Each macro-level phase breaks down into two subphases. These are shown as diamond shapes to reflect several key points:

- The overall NPD process needs to be understood as containing further levels of detail (subphases);
- The size of each diamond reflects the reduction in uncertainty as the project progresses;
- The work itself is all about mentally expansive thinking followed by contraction; and
- Each subphase is essentially a different mental challenge, so it is essential to preserve mental efficiency by not mixing them up.

The exploration phase (Figure F.2) involves the pursuit of the question: "What don't we know about this project?" and the generation of answers, followed by the creation of potential solutions and their evaluation against success criteria. The execution phase (Figure F.3), by contrast, is all about detailing the best solution and creating the tangible elements of the product or service.

At this point, a common question typically arises: "If all the wisdom about improving this process points to more up-front resources, why do leaders rarely sanction this?"

In the exploration phase, few things seem tangible. Most of the phase happens conversationally and, even using the best methods, the output will be contained in a few short documents, such as experiment outcomes,

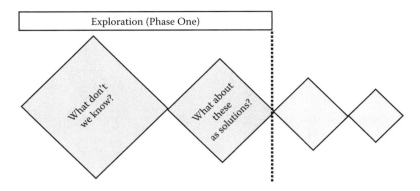

FIGURE F.2
Phase 1: Exploration phase.

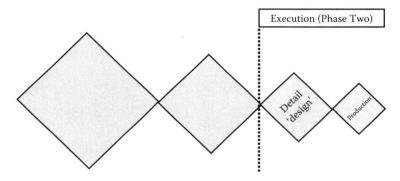

FIGURE F.3
Phase 2: Execution phase.

tables, and trade-off charts. It seems that leaders, as humans, need visible, tangible outputs to believe they are actually getting a return on the investments. The reality is that the best returns are a big list of "what we don't know," followed by a big list of findings and new knowledge gained from experiments. Only then can you be confident that the flow of knowledge and decisions has generated solutions that have been correctly explored and then refined into a chosen few.

This approach also ensures that the execution phase will focus exclusively on detailing the design of all the tangible outputs to be realized in the new product or service. That includes drawings, tooling, production facilities, service manuals, and many other concrete outcomes. These tangible outputs feel more like "progress" and can be seen. However, investing the time and resources in the exploration phase is critical to ensuring a productive execution phase.

THE IMPORTANCE OF THE PROMISE POINT

The "Promise Point," a critical concept for leaders to understand, is the point at which guarantees are given to people outside the project about outcomes. This can take a variety of forms, such as costs, time scales, capability, and availability. The earliest possible Promise Point can occur only when the "what don't we know" portion of the exploration phase has been completed. Even then, this would represent the rare case when the team has learned that the customer needs are familiar and have been seen before, and that the project goals can be met with existing solution combinations that have been used before.

For most projects, however, the reality is that gaps will exist even when there is a clear sense of "what we don't know" and "what we think the solutions should be." Most organizations get caught here, being pushed unwittingly into a Promise Point by others outside the project seeking any possible information during the "what about these solutions?" subphase. There is still a place for groundbreaking, visionary projects in the style of John F. Kennedy's "We choose to go to the moon in this decade," but turning each project into a "moonshot," as many leaders and marketing professionals do, is highly inadvisable!

The most sensible place for the Promise Point to occur is after completion of the exploration phase (see Figure F.4).

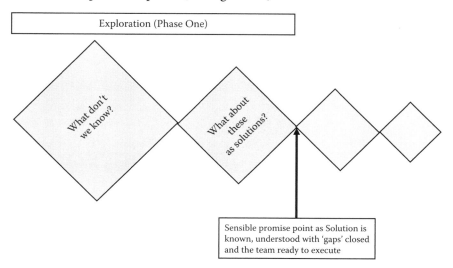

FIGURE F.4
The "promise point" in new product design should occur at the end of the exploration phase.

EXPLORATION SUBPHASES

What activities encompass the subphases in this process? Let's first look at what takes place during the first half of "What don't we know?" Essentially, the first part of the exploration subphase consists of a multidisciplinary conversation of the most experienced technical staff from each area. The aim of the conversation is to understand the needs (from the perspective of all stakeholders) and what is not yet known about these needs, thus identifying the current knowledge gap across all stakeholders (see Figure F.5).

Because this part of the process is conversational and multidimensional, a Lean approach of fast action, face-to-face communications in an *obeya* studio (see Appendix A) designed for such work should replace the typical, painfully slow, e-mail-based discussions across strong departmental boundaries. The selection of people is critical. You need people from all stakeholder groups who are smart enough to know what they don't know and comfortable enough to say so. By its nature, this will be an expansive discussion, and the leader must ensure that time is allowed to air all issues and unknowns. Ongoing, deliberate effort is required to avoid closing down the dialogue too early with quick decisions.

Conversely, in the second half of the "What don't we know?" diamond, the team will begin focusing their learning and knowledge generation. As needs are refined and become better understood, gaps in current knowledge and capabilities will become clearer (see Figure F.6).

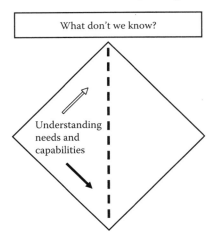

FIGURE F.5
Exploration subphase 1 starts with understanding needs and knowledge gaps.

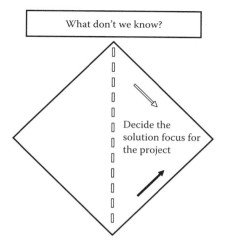

FIGURE F.6
Exploration subphase 1 ends with focusing the knowledge.

The multidisciplinary team that started the exploration subphase must finish it, and they must document three key aspects:

1. The rationale and content of their discussion
2. If the team has "layered" their challenge using systems thinking, then the layers they have defined and the rationale behind them
3. The organizational learning gained

An internal team-only review should be conducted halfway through the first subphase or diamond, followed by a wider stakeholder review before moving to the second diamond in the exploration phase.

The second diamond or subphase, "What about these solutions?" covers the simultaneous generation and study of multiple solutions. Solutions should be aimed at a combination of what best meets the needs of the project and the knowledge gap(s) discovered during the previous subphase (what don't we know?). The key in the first half of the solutions diamond is to avoid quickly narrowing down to one answer and instead keep the collective mind open to many solutions (see Figure F.7). Known as "set-based concurrent engineering," this approach is a difficult discipline for those used to being in organizations that value decisiveness and have "hurry-up" genes in all of their managers. As a leader, you have to believe that it really pays to "rush slowly" during the exploration phase.

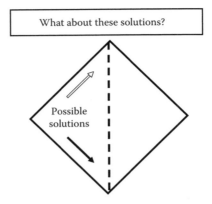

FIGURE F.7
Exploration subphase 2 starts with exploring many possibilities.

Persevering with many concepts simultaneously provides the dual rewards of enhanced organizational learning and a resulting *set* of knowledge that will be highly useful in the next subphase.

In working to identify the "best possible solution," during the second half of this subphase, the team will invariably narrow on a so-called "super concept," which often encompasses many attributes from the concepts explored in the first half of the subphase (see Figure F.8). This always results in much richer solutions and greater breakthroughs than the more typical "pick a winner and work it to conclusion" approach. At the end of

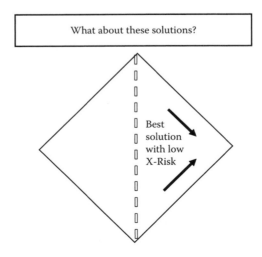

FIGURE F.8
Exploration subphase 2 ends with narrowing down to the best possible solution.

this second diamond, then, the team will have a hybrid solution representing a composite of the best elements from each possible solution evaluated previously. Narrowing down is pursued until the solution is fixed and all required knowledge gaps have been explored and resolved through breakthroughs, trade-offs, or conscious compromise.

Exploration-phase activities should always be kept in-house, away from the gaze of the public, with outside involvement limited to strategic partners who can respect your privacy. Breaching that strategic privacy in any way inevitably leads to declaring victory too early, and often to compromising the next steps. The aim is to move into the execution phase in such a way that the team can concentrate on exactly that—execution.

EXECUTION SUBPHASES

The execution phase breaks down (as shown previously in Figure F.3) into the subphases of "detail design," the third subphase in the NPD process and "production," the fourth and final subphase. The third diamond or subphase is labeled "detail development and definition." As the team begins the first half of this diamond, all the big questions have been resolved and the remaining focus is on detail design (see Figure F.9). In the old days,

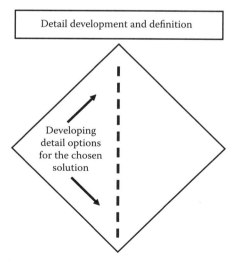

FIGURE F.9
Execution subphase 3 starts with a multidisciplinary approach to developing detail options.

this would mean creating detail drawings, while in the three-dimensional (3-D) world of computer-aided design (CAD), it means detailed modeling. However, in new product development using Lean principles, this detailing should remain a multidisciplinary activity and should be even more collaborative in nature. The idea is to simultaneously develop detail options for all stakeholders' aspects of the project. For example, while the designer is modeling detail options, the tooling expert can be defining tooling detail options, the logistics people can be detailing their solution options, as can the service support people and all other stakeholders.

Keeping the team in simultaneous working mode is paramount. After the exploration phase, resist the tendency to fall back into the "easier and safer" sequential working mode. Also, avoid fixating on single detail options without generating the simultaneous solutions required. The secret is to constantly challenge the team on "what they *can* be doing" to maximize the potential of working with constant cross-team dialogue. This encourages the expansion of detail options, just as the expansion of concept options was encouraged during the exploration phase. Similarly, an internal team review midway through the third diamond will help to ensure that the entire multidisciplinary team has a broad understanding of the whole project across all stakeholders.

Having completed the expansive work, the team can then narrow down the chosen details and physically complete their definition. The definition will be the agreed-upon detail solutions that constitute the best cross-disciplinary combination to achieve the project goals (see Figure F.10). Pressing on with simultaneous working will collapse the lead time to a minimum. All major decisions were made in the exploration phase, so the level of risk left in the project should be very low, and reworking should be minimal at this point.

The final diamond in our design system is that of production itself. Most NPD people mentally switch off at this stage, making it the part of the process in which the "throw it over the wall syndrome" is most often felt. Of course, if the recommended multidisciplinary involvement has been sustained throughout the project, this should not be the case.

The first part of the last subphase is ramping up production (see Figure F.11). During production, it is critical to maintain a multidisciplinary team to plan and execute the ramp-up and not slip back into sequential work or, worse still, "just leaving it to production." Resources should be scaled back by this stage, but the ramp-up plan will be much easier and less error-prone if the team remains multidisciplinary.

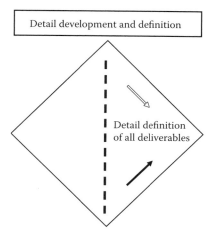

FIGURE F.10
Execution subphase 3 ends with completing the detail solutions for all deliverables.

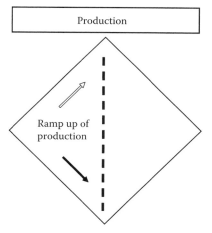

FIGURE F.11
Execution subphase 4 starts with ramping up production.

The second half of the final diamond is focused on "series (or mass) production and continuous improvement" (see Figure F.12). Again, a multidisciplinary team is recommended to help with continuous improvement, as many of the project goals will not be fully realized until the actual production and delivery of the new product takes place. In NPD terms, this phase is also where lessons learned can be fed back into the organization's knowledge base, to serve as input for future projects.

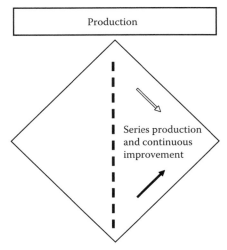

FIGURE F.12
Execution subphase 4 ends with series or mass production and continuous improvement.

TOOLS FOR NEW PRODUCT DESIGN USING LEAN PRINCIPLES

Many tools can be used in both the exploration and execution phases of the NPD system. Figure F.13 shows an array of tools along with the typical phase in which they may be used. Of course, as with all Lean tools, they will only be effective when used appropriately.

Finally, to wrap up this brief overview of the NPD system, here's a word about overlapping work across diamonds—*don't*. There will always be situations where the desire to go faster will result in the urge to begin working on more than one subphase at a time. But this is how projects get into all sorts of problems and effectively waste time and resources. If you do find yourself in a situation where it looks like time is running short, it is *always* better to seek improvement in the next subphase than to try to overlap activity of the diamonds.

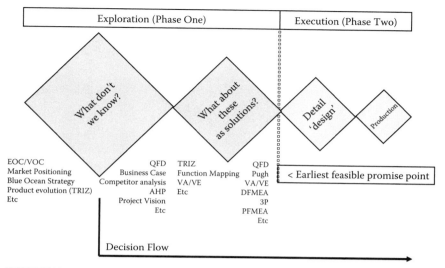

FIGURE F.13

The NPD system, with the tools that are likely to be used in different phases.

Appendix G: Autoliv—Empowered to Solve Problems

Kathy Whitehead and Scott Saxton

On any given day in northern Utah's Autoliv Ogden assembly plant, you can find teams gathered in their work cell concentrating their energy on something other than building the 21 million airbags this plant ships to Autoliv customers around the world each year. These teams—comprised of cell members from all shifts, along with a facilitator, a mentor, a maintenance technician, and any support roles needed—are focused on improvement (see Figure G.1).

Granted, there is nothing particularly unique about their team-based approach to positive change. In fact, these "focused workshops," as they are called in the Autoliv vernacular, may seem quite commonplace to a casual observer. Nonetheless, they have become the backbone of Autoliv's culture of continuous improvement. They are also considered to be a critical competitive advantage to the company as it strives to maintain its market leadership position in safety products for automobile occupants.

The reason for this may have much less to do with the company's processes than you might think, although the plant is a two-time winner of the Shingo Prize for Excellence in Manufacturing. Rather, management and teams alike credit much of their success to the atmosphere of empowerment that pervades these workshops, as each cell member takes an active role in getting to the root of the problem and implementing the corrective actions required to ensure a lasting solution.

Using tools from the Autoliv eight-step problem-solving method as a foundation, teams uncover and eliminate the root causes of performance roadblocks. And, because team members will ultimately be responsible for ensuring that correct countermeasures are taken and performance

FIGURE G.1
A problem-solving team at Autoliv's Ogden assembly plant.

improvements are standardized, they are also fully vested in making sure the root cause of any problem is identified correctly the first time.

THE EVOLUTION OF IMPROVEMENT

Needless to say, this kind of empowerment has not always been the norm. Like any company in the evolutionary stages of Lean, Autoliv has been at this for some time now. Its first foray into standardized problem solving took place in the mid-1990s, as operations management introduced the concept of constraint management. By focusing on the bottlenecks in its processes, Autoliv was able to increase overall product flow and become more efficient. However, much of the activity surrounding this approach was dictated by management, leaving front-line associates almost entirely out of the decision-making process and leaving many good ideas for improvement on the table.

In 1998, Mr. Takashi Harada of Toyota began mentoring Autoliv in the Toyota Production System. With his encouragement, Autoliv embarked on a formalized process for soliciting employee suggestions as part of the kaizen process. While this was a step in the right direction, it also plunged Autoliv into an administrative tailspin as managers tried to determine how best to promote the process, how to administer it, and how to reward employees. Early efforts to reward employee suggestions through payouts and prize drawings soon consumed huge amounts of resources as supervisors and managers tried to understand the real impact of each idea for the company. Additionally, the turnaround time just to review the suggestions climbed to a staggering thirty days!

Grasping for a way to make the process more efficient, Autoliv turned to computers, with the intent to make the process less burdensome for both employees and the management staff approving the kaizen suggestions. The results were mixed. While the more structured data helped to smooth and reduce review time, the computerized process took away the valuable one-on-one interaction between associates and management during the course of approval. Essentially, associates could take their kaizen suggestion from inception to completion without ever talking to another team member or supervisor.

Making improvements in a vacuum stands out as clearly counterproductive today, but at the time, because the suggestions kept on coming, management's attention remained focused on stabilizing the foundation of the Autoliv Production System (APS) house patterned after the Toyota model (see Figure G.2). It was a period of great change and rapid expansion for the company. Mexico was gaining strategic importance as a manufacturing hub, requiring personnel with expert knowledge of APS processes to successfully integrate Lean manufacturing principles across the North American region. Responding to this urgent need, Autoliv sent managers from its US plants, many of whom had been mentored personally by Mr. Harada, to coach their colleagues in other countries about the operational philosophies of APS and establish the firm foundation of teamwork and standardized work that is prevalent today.

WAKING THE SLEEPING GIANT

In the mid-2000s, with APS principles firmly established across its plants in Canada, Mexico, and the United States, North American management was finally in a position to turn its focus inward. With material costs rising, prices for occupant-safety products decreasing, and industry competition becoming brutal, management was ready to unleash the sleeping giant—the power of the people.

FIGURE G.2
The Autoliv Production System (APS) house.

Of course, merely drawing power without directing it accomplishes little and can waste and eventually exhaust a valuable resource. Similarly, targeting the power in too many directions creates a dilutive effect, preventing anything from functioning well. This is where Autoliv North America found itself. Working for several years from a top-down function-based strategic plan that contributed to departmental silos, the company was struggling to get its people all working toward the same goal. Each functional area had been working independently to solve problems and make improvements, but few had harnessed the full potential of cross-functional, cross-plant teams working on a common objective. Enter *hoshin kanri*, or policy deployment (see "Strategy Deployment" in Appendix A and Figure G.3).

Autoliv's North American leadership recognized the necessity of channeling all the energy and creativity of the thousands of employee suggestions away from the trivial toward accomplishing the group's vital overall objectives. This would be critical for the company to remain competitive in

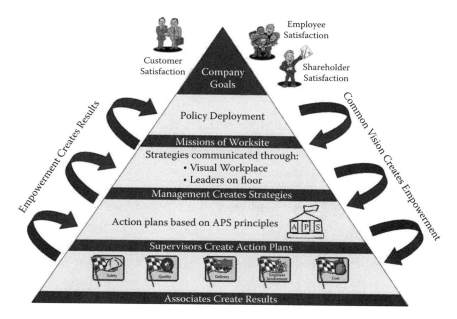

FIGURE G.3
Autoliv's vision and direction is communicated across the organization through policy deployment.

the new industry landscape. With just three top objectives established in the North American vision—customer satisfaction, employee satisfaction, and shareholder satisfaction—plant managers began to align strategies in a systematic way, reaching out to their associates to create desired results through focused problem-solving and improvement activities. Guided by the axiom, "It is better to tell people *what* the problem is rather than *how* to solve it," management was astonished by the ingenuity of the associates as they responded to this newfound sense of empowerment.

Because empowerment is meaningless without knowledge, all associates regularly attend training designed to reinforce the fundamentals of the company's APS processes. Hundreds of associates enroll each year in intensified training at the "APS University," where, through hands-on experience in their work cells, they learn to apply such principles as first-time quality, poka-yoke, and six sigma.

Putting this experience to work on the lines and in functional groups, plants like the company's airbag assembly plant in Ogden saw their kaizens skyrocket from roughly fifteen per associate to more than sixty per associate in just three years. And, with a more focused scope of achieving company objectives through policy deployment, nearly 100 percent of the kaizens submitted at the plant were being implemented by 2008.

SHIFTING THE PROBLEM PARADIGM

Today, associates in Autoliv plants across the world participate in a variety of proactive team exercises designed to drive continuous improvement through application of APS principles. One of the most successful of these approaches is the "focused workshop" used daily at the Ogden airbag assembly facility. These workshops are used to improve the kaizen process by involving associates to solve the specific issues of their work cell. Hands-on experience is utilized to educate and train the team as well as to improve their problem-solving skills. Because these workshops include day-, swing-, and night-shift team members in the same process, all associates on the line have a direct influence on the kaizens implemented and the improvements made to the process.

In the past, one of the biggest obstacles to creating an empowered problem-solving culture was simply deciding what constituted a "problem" in the first place. Because the company had, in effect, been using the "squeaky wheel" as a pseudo-process for identifying and elevating problems, it soon realized that by the time the wheel had begun to squeak, it was often too late for a simple solution. By then, management was usually forced to dedicate a substantial amount of time and resources to solve the issue.

But as the company began to put robust systems in place to measure performance to expectation, Autoliv saw its traditional definition of a "problem" give way to the idea that *any* unmet expectation, large or small, should be viewed as a problem. With this progressive new mind-set, managers could engage everyone to work the smaller daily issues at the same time they were subjecting the time-intensive issues to greater scrutiny. A higher level of mutual trust was created as management involved the workforce, solicited their feedback, and implemented their suggestions. In addition, problem-solving tools such as the Autoliv eight-step problem-solving method were added to the toolbox, giving teams an easy-to-follow template for finding improvement solutions.

Today, through the application of policy deployment at the work site, each plant has put in place specific strategies, or "missions" of the work site, to ensure a coordinated approach to problem solving. Safety, quality,

Missions of Worksite	Team Status
Safety	
Quality	
Delivery	
Employee Involvement	
Cost	

FIGURE G.4

Status boards provide visual guidance for team improvement activities. Red, yellow, or green colors indicate current performance to goals. In this example, the work cell could focus workshops toward improving cost and delivery.

delivery, and cost are examples of the work-site missions that guide employee improvement activities at Autoliv.

Each mission has corresponding APS systems in place to measure performance and highlight abnormal conditions, making problems visual. A visual workplace is especially powerful for creating an "equal opportunity" environment, where everyone can see the problems. A status board at each work cell reflects that team's current performance and provides guidance for improvement activities (see Figure G.4).

Using these boards as a guide, members on the work cell can readily identify problem areas, review the data, and organize a team to develop and implement solutions.

MANAGING FOR CHANGE

The objective of any problem-solving process is to give teams a systematic road map by which they can combine their knowledge and backgrounds to focus on finding the root cause of a problem and implement actions to eliminate it. It should be fairly obvious that such an endeavor is doomed to fail without total management support. Failing to set clear expectations, provide resources, set aside time, or follow up with teams are all common ways managers sabotage their teams' efforts. Conversely, managers skilled in empowering teams simply ensure that everything necessary for success is in place, and then they get out of the way as their teams achieve and, most often, exceed expectations.

Employing a four-step approach, managers and supervisors are expected to grasp and understand the problem, set expectations for improvement, and then provide timely follow-up. Consistency in this approach is key to driving success. However, the "when" is no less important than the "how to" in this equation. Clearly, a once-a-year rollout of problem-solving activities will not be sufficient to effect change, nor will it produce teams skilled at applying problem-solving tools for continuous improvement. True change through problem solving requires both regular management follow-through and constant employee engagement.

GETTING TO THE ROOT OF THE PROBLEM

Every day at Autoliv, team members are engaged in collecting, analyzing, and understanding the biggest opportunities for improvement in their work cell related to the five missions of the work site. Using a simple chart like the one shown in Figure G.5, teams can systematically plan for success as they follow Autoliv's step-by-step workshop method, based on Ford's eight-D process.

Because all Autoliv teams follow this same eight-step problem-solving process—whether the problems are related to first-time quality, safety, or any other mission-critical goal—these steps are elaborated here.

Step One: Form a Team

No individual team member has as much knowledge as the whole team of which they are a part. Therefore, the first step is to gather a group of people most affected by the problem to work together to find a solution. Generally, cross-functional teams combining different skill sets and levels of expertise will be most effective. Each team will have a designated facilitator and team leader or mentor who is well trained in the problem-solving process.

Step Two: Define the Problem

Although this may seem very simple and almost unnecessary, describing what the problem is can be one of the most crucial steps in finding the root cause. Without a clear and precise understanding of the problem, there

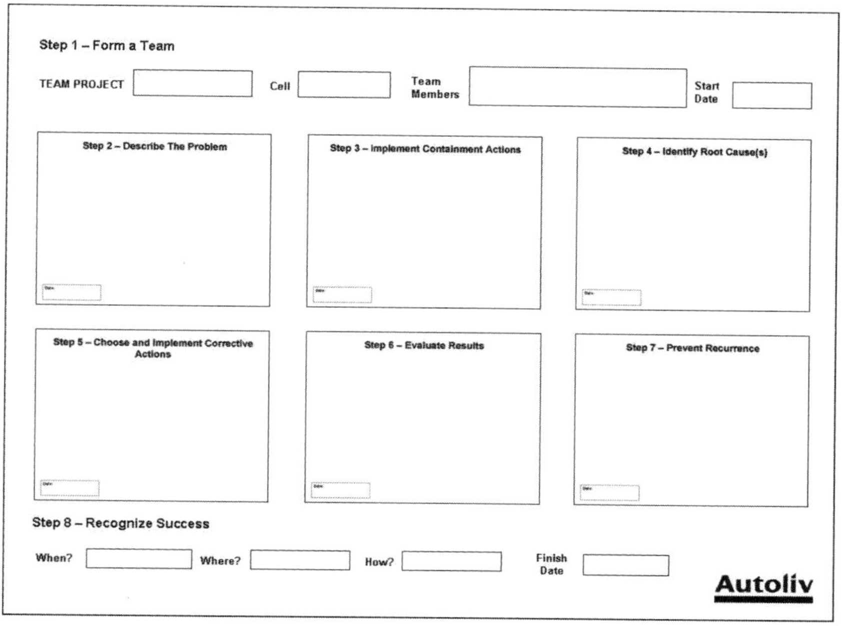
Step 1 – Form a Team

TEAM PROJECT | Cell | Team Members | Start Date

Step 2 – Describe The Problem

Step 3 – Implement Containment Actions

Step 4 – Identify Root Cause(s)

Step 5 – Choose and Implement Corrective Actions

Step 6 – Evaluate Results

Step 7 – Prevent Recurrence

Step 8 – Recognize Success

When? | Where? | How? | Finish Date

Autoliv

FIGURE G.5
Teams use a one-page form to capture the significant steps of the problem-solving process as they pursue solutions. The form summarizes the team's progress for customers, management, and other teams.

is very little chance that the team will be able to solve it. There are four primary questions the team should ask themselves at this point:

- What is the problem?
- How do we measure it?
- How is solving the problem defined?
- What is the current condition of the process/product?

As mentioned previously, the definition of a problem is any discrepancy between actual results and customer expectations. So, when answering the above questions, teams must also take into consideration background information, such as who the customer is, what the customer's expectations are, and how the process/product failed to meet those expectations.

Once the problem is well understood, the team is ready to describe what the solution looks like. This "future state" understanding is critical because it will ultimately drive the actions of the team. Teams must therefore avoid the urge to "think small." To help set a useful objective, Autoliv uses the SMART acronym.

- *Specific*: A clear and specific objective will keep the team focused and avoid potential deviations that don't solve the problem at hand.
- *Measurable*: Having a metric is critical for measuring success or failure.
- *Ambitious*: While teams must be cautious of setting an objective so difficult that success is unachievable, the objective should be ambitious enough to provide a true challenge.
- *Relevant*: The objective should directly relate to the customer's unmet expectations.
- *Time bound*: Without some kind of time limit, there is a large chance that the project can drag on until it dwindles and fades away without any benefits.

Finally, to sufficiently quantify the current condition, teams employ a variety of methods, including the following: a "go and see" approach to understand what is and is not currently working in the physical process, sketches and photographs to help the team visualize the problem, diagrams to display process flow, Pareto charts to identify inputs and/or outputs with the highest values or occurrences, and statistical analysis of process/product variation versus expectation.

By the end of step two, the team has established a clear problem statement, including who the customers are for this project. It should also have a SMART objective, which includes a metric by which we can measure success. Finally, the team should have the current situation sufficiently quantified.

Step Three: Implement Containment Actions

Whenever a problem occurs in a process, it is necessary to contain that problem to protect the company and its customers from further adverse effects. The actions necessary to contain the problem may take more resources and effort than the normal process, but must be kept in place until the team can demonstrate it has eliminated the root cause. These actions are like a temporary bandage on a wound until proper medical care is received.

An action register can be used to document and follow the containment actions and to record who is responsible for completing them, when they were implemented, and how they were verified.

Step Four: Identify Root Cause

The key to problem solving lies in establishing a workforce skilled at finding the root cause of the problem. This step is therefore the most important and intense in the eight-step process. Companies waste a tremendous amount of time and money on their problem-solving efforts, only to find solutions that do not effectively eliminate recurrence. When teams focus only on eliminating the visible symptoms of a problem, much like a weed, the roots will be allowed to re-create the problem over and over again. It is therefore imperative that the team uses its few resources to take actions that will eliminate the problem at its root.

Getting to root cause is not easy. Team members must be trained and mentored throughout this process. And, just as with anything else worthwhile, it takes steady practice to become skilled at eliminating root cause. As associates are trained and mentored in the problem-solving process, they become more effective month after month in applying long-term solutions that move the company's metrics in a positive direction (see Figure G.6).

Learning to ask the right questions is an essential part of this training. At Autoliv, team members quickly learn that asking these questions helps them avoid the pitfalls of going into the process with preconceived ideas about what the root cause or its solution might be.

Because this step is often the longest and most difficult for any team, it also has the most tools available for teams to employ. Fishbone diagrams,

FIGURE G.6
Team interaction at Autoliv.

Pareto charts, fault-tree analysis, Six Sigma, comparison tables, and timelines help teams gather and select potential root causes. Using the Five Whys technique (see Appendix A), teams peel away the symptoms of the problem to expose the roots. Once the team has reached a cause that, if controlled, could resolve the problem permanently, it has peeled sufficiently deep. Analytical graphs and other statistical tools then help the team verify the cause or causes.

Step Five: Choose and Implement Corrective Actions

Once the team has found and verified the root causes of the problem, it must choose and implement the corrective actions necessary to eliminate the causes, or at least reduce their influence on the process. Brainstorming solutions helps generate ideas that may not have been considered initially, but are perhaps more ideal. This type of activity also allows teams to challenge their own paradigms, such as "We don't have enough time," or "The customer wants it this way." As teams objectively review all ideas, weighing the benefits and risks associated with each, they work to select the best solution and then list the required actions (see Figure G.7).

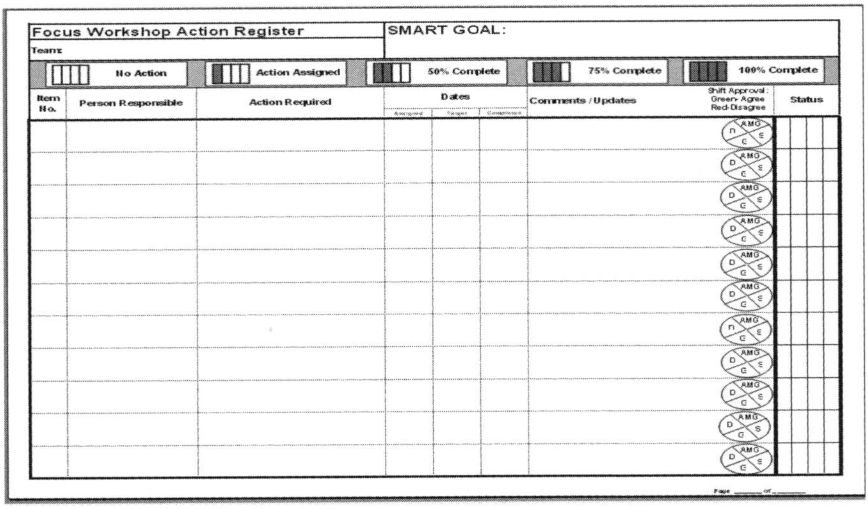

FIGURE G.7
Documenting corrective actions through the use of an action register allows both the team and management to keep track of what the actions are, who is doing them, where support and/or follow-up is needed, and when the actions will be complete.

Step Six: Evaluate Results

If the root causes have been identified correctly and the corrective actions implemented have sufficiently eliminated the causes, then the metric established in Step Two should demonstrate this improvement. Teams evaluate the metric to see if a significant, positive change has occurred and if their improvements have helped them meet or exceed the team's goal.

Step Seven: Prevent Recurrence

Preventing recurrence involves understanding why the root cause happened and what the team can do to stop it from happening again. This is the time for questioning and changing procedures and standardizing performance improvements to ensure that the solution is sustained over time and across the company. By documenting the changes made through Design and Process Failure Mode Effects Analysis (DFMEA and PFMEA), drawings, work instructions, poka-yokes, control plans, and other resources shared across the organization, the team prevents other areas with similar processes from experiencing the same issues.

Step Eight: Recognize Success

Recognition feeds the human need to achieve and focuses attention on individual and team efforts. It also serves as a proven method for boosting morale and encouraging future participation in problem-solving activities. Too often, companies associate recognition solely with monetary reward. Though this can be an effective means of expressing appreciation, it should not take the place of meaningful acknowledgment and praise from management and peers. Allowing teams to present their successful improvements to management is one of the most effective forms of recognition at Autoliv. This sends a clear signal that the company values its culture of continuous improvement and is committed to promoting problem-solving behavior.

SIMPLE MATH

The first principle of good design is to "keep it simple." This same maxim applies to Autoliv's approach to continuous improvement and problem solving. By eliminating the expert systems and standards that relatively few could interface with, the company opened the floodgates of employee involvement. With problem-solving channels in place to capture ideas, and with clear goals and objectives to direct enthusiasm, the steady stream of continuous improvement has allowed this occupant-safety company to maintain its leadership position in a fiercely competitive industry.

In most companies, the majority of the workforce works closest to the problems. Yet, most companies fail to fully engage this abundant and formidable resource, and, in so doing, fail to realize its awesome power. The key to success really comes down to simple math. A company with only one problem solver is doomed to get better only one problem at a time. Imagine the possibilities for improvement when *everyone* is engaged in solving problems. At Autoliv, employees are imagining and fulfilling those possibilities every day.

AUTHOR'S NOTE

At the end of the book (at the end of Chapter 7), I discuss my recently firmed up views on the key behaviors that have been fundamental to true Lean transformation success stories. The third of the three basic behaviors is "a DRIVE for disciplined execution." The reason for capitalizing *DRIVE* is that the whole behavior is at a level of commitment, or DRIVE, that is, roughly, 10× or ten times the level that you might normally experience.

It is hard to get this idea across, but one example here might help. You have just read about the overall effort at Autoliv to incorporate problem solving into their day-to-day culture and include everyone in this process. I have visited Autoliv on a number of occasions, and one of the things that impressed me was the discipline around their efforts to achieve their policy-deployment goals and their focus on solving problems, lots and lots of problems, every day. One example is the way they have set up standard work for problem escalation in each work cell. The basic approach is that, as soon as any problem is detected, the first-level team goes to work to find a root-cause solution, while the problem is logged in, in real time, into a software system.

As I recall the details, the first-level team member has two individuals designated to help if needed—a technical resource (typically the area maintenance person) and a system resource (typically the water strider for the area). And they have fifteen minutes in which to determine a root-cause solution and corrective action. If they are successful, this is logged into the system while being implemented in the area. If they are unsuccessful, the problem is automatically escalated to the next level, and the area supervisor leads a new problem-solving cycle, using a designated technical resource (area maintenance person) and system resource (area materials support person), if needed. A half hour after this, if no root-cause solution is determined, the problem is escalated to the next level, the manager of production, and the same type of problem-solving cycle repeats. An hour after this, any problem that has not been resolved by the preceding steps is escalated to the plant manager—twenty-four hours per day.

So think about the discipline to have a problem-solving system where any problem will get to the personal attention of the plant manager if not resolved within three hours and forty-five minutes—night or day. Keep in mind that this is a result of over fifteen years of serious Lean work at Autoliv, and that this particular part of their system has been in place, and continually refined, for five years or so. But the key point is that it takes this kind of discipline about your Lean execution to achieve the true world-class performance that is possible—a DRIVE for disciplined execution.

Index